Meet the

BROKEN ARROW CENTENNIALS

100 Legacy Makers from 1902-2002

"If I have seen further than others, it is by standing upon the shoulders of giants."
– Isaac Newton

COVER PHOTOS (L-R)

FRONT COVER
Top: Onis Franklin, Al Graham, Phenie Lou, Roy Pauli
Bottom: Newt Williams, Mildred Childers, Ivan Brown, Ben Haikey

BACK COVER
Top: Gladys Walton Tomlinson, Lester Randall, Dora Sullivan Esslinger, and F. S. Fears
Bottom: BA Main Street, James McHenry, F.S. Hurd, Ivan Brown/ TM Hunsecker

Meet the BROKEN ARROW CENTENNIALS

100 Legacy Makers from 1902-2002

Written by Jan Collins
Including writings by the late Roberta Parker

A BOLD TRUTH Publication
Christian Literature & Artwork

Meet the BROKEN ARROW CENTENNIALS
Copyright © 2020 Jan Collins
ISBN 13: 978-1-949993-62-2

FIRST EDITION

BOLD TRUTH PUBLISHING
(Christian Literature & Artwork)
606 West 41st, Ste. 4
Sand Springs, Oklahoma 74063
www.BoldTruthPublishing.com

Available from *Amazon.com* and other retail outlets. Orders by U.S. trade bookstores and wholesalers. Email: *boldtruthbooks@yahoo.com*

Quantity sales special discounts are available on purchases by corporations, associations, and others. For details, contact the publisher at the address above.

Artwork, formatting and overall design by Aaron Jones.

Cover photograph used by permission.

All rights reserved under International Copyright Law. All contents and/or cover art and design may not be reproduced in whole or in part in any form without the express written consent of the Author.

Printed in the USA.
10 20   10 9 8 7 6 5 4 3 2 1

Permissions

Permission was given to use Roberta Parker's writings, personal notes and unpublished material when her family donated her files to *The Museum Broken Arrow* after her death.

"Permission to use copyrighted information and material, such as biographies, articles and quotes has been approved by *Broken Arrow Ledger*, aka *Tulsa World*, and *BH Media Group* and *Tulsa World Media Company*. The author is appreciative to have a good working relationship with this company."

Permission has been granted to use pictures and documents from *The Museum Broken Arrow*.

Permission has been given by *Broken Arrow Genealogical Society* (BAGS) to use articles written about Broken Arrow *Hall of Fame* recipients by members of BAGS.

Permission has been given by *Broken Arrow Alumni Association* to use articles written and published by them for the *Broken Arrow Great Graduates* programs.

Permission has been granted by descendants of James McHenry, Mildred McIntosh Childers and C. Benjamin Haikey to use family stories and historical information.

Dedication

This historical book of Broken Arrow's 100 most influential citizens is dedicated to the memory of two people who loved the history of Broken Arrow immensely. They both diligently researched and wrote about Broken Arrow's beginnings to share with all who had common interests in our hometown.

Roberta Parker

The late Mrs. Roberta Parker was a faithful and steadfast reporter for *Broken Arrow Ledger,* our hometown newspaper. From her favorite *Cornerstones* column to the articles written during Broken Arrow's centennial celebration, her fervent work was a labor of love and is forever etched in our hearts.

Mrs. Parker credited much of her work to the labor begun by the late H. Cecil Rhoades as he laid the foundation almost 70 years ago for what we read about our hometown today.

Dedication

Mr. Rhoades began the journey discovering Broken Arrow's founding and heritage long before 1953, when he submitted the thesis for his educational degree. Rhoades' research and writings have been the most frequently used references of documentation in publications and books about Broken Arrow than any other.

H. Cecil Rhoades

More about both of them are in the Appendix at the end of this book.

Our desire is to bridge the gap from young to old, as you read the history of our Legacy Makers and the hope for our hometown's future.

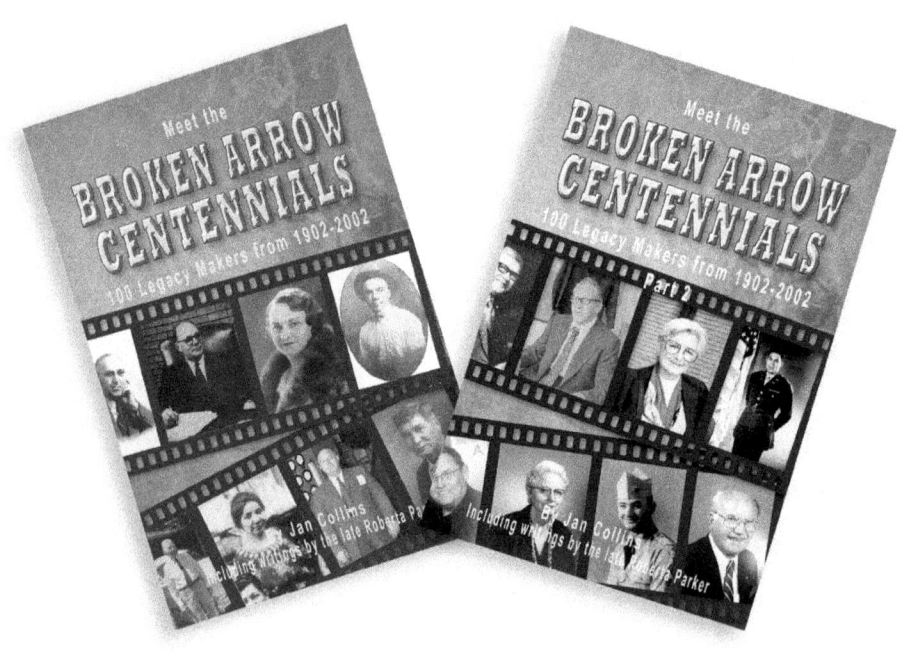

This is only the beginning. Watch for Part 2, more inspiring biographies of our Broken Arrow's pioneers.

These books available at The Museum Broken Arrow and select local retailers.

Contents

Preface .... *i*

Acknowledgments .... *iii*

Introduction 1

Chapter 1
Oklahoma... 'Where the Wind Comes Sweeping Down the Plain' 5

Chapter 2
Muscogee Creek Inhabitants 9

Chapter 3
M K & T Railroad 35

Chapter 4
From Elam to Main Street 43

Chapter 5
The First Ladies of Broken Arrow
'City of Roses and Sparkling Water' 65

Chapter 6
Territorial Days 79

Chapter 7
Foundation of a Strong Community
Churches and Schools 111

Chapter 8
Politics on the Prairie 135

Chapter 9
Early Statehood 153

Contents

Chapter 10
From the Cotton Fields to the Battlefields
"The War to End All Wars" 191

Chapter 11
Roaring Twenties: A Time of Peace 223

Chapter 12
Dust Bowl, Depression and Dredging
The Challenging 30s 237

Afterword 289

About the Author 291

Appendix 292

Bibliography 294

Index 300

Preface

Various books and publications have been written about Broken Arrow, Oklahoma. The diversity of these stories and historical knowledge have established the success and versatility of this community. *Rooster Days* Festivities, national award-winning high school band, the *Rose District*, and an excellent community safety record all contributed to a 2018 U. S. Conference of Mayors' vote for B. A. as the most livable small city in America.

This book was a dream for several years by the ones who compiled information about its history. It became a goal for Dr. Clarence G. Oliver, Jr., former Superintendent of Broken Arrow Public Schools. It began with H. Cecil Rhoades' inspiration to write *Establishment and Development of Broken Arrow, Oklahoma.* From Oklahoma history records, national archives and other resources, it was written as a partial requirement for Mr. Rhoades' master's degree in education. Although written in 1953, it became a personal project of Dr. Oliver's as he assisted in its publication in 1976.

At 91 years of age, Dr. Oliver, a favorite son of Broken Arrow, is a prominent figure in Oklahoma. His desire is to see this project go forward to describe much more than typical geographical and historical information. It includes even more personal and inspiring stories about the people who settled in and worked diligently developing Broken Arrow.

Preface

Younger generations frequently wonder about the value and importance of knowing their heritage, while the earlier generations have an eagerness and desire to share memories and history about the development of their community. They had grandparents who shared their stories and experiences. The same descriptive process is true with the development of the *Rose District* in downtown Broken Arrow. Sharing the humble history of this town and region bridges the generational gap between the younger and older residents and informs the visitors of Broken Arrow.

Our elite *Legacy Makers* group, which includes Dr. Oliver, goes far beyond Broken Arrow's history. Whether descendants of the settlers and pioneers or other contributors to this book, we all join in an effort to inform, share, and hopefully delight the reader in the following pages.

— Jan Simmons Collins

Acknowledgments

First, I would like to recognize all the descendants of our *100 Legacy Makers*. To the life-long friends and the new friends I have met in the completion of this project, I appreciate and thank you.

I would like to acknowledge the family of the late Roberta Parker, who donated her files to *The Museum Broken Arrow*. She was a talented and gifted reporter for the former *Broken Arrow Ledger*. Without her writings, this book would not have been written. She shared articles which helped in the writing of my dad's biography. It was because of her diligence and integrity that she persevered to publish many of our *Legacy Maker* stories in our hometown newspaper.

A majority of credit, appreciation and a huge "Thank You" is extended to *BH Media Group* and *Tulsa World Media Company* for allowing us to reprint Mrs. Parker's biographies in this book.

Kenny Collins, my husband, has always been an ardent supporter of me in working on this project. He has spent a great amount of time assisting me in all areas, including reading and editing. He wanted to see the completion of this project maybe more than I did.

I appreciate Aaron Jones, the publisher of my previous four books, and admire his God-given talent of art, imagination and graphic design. I am amazed at his abil-

Acknowledgments

ity to perceive what I wanted in a book cover and layout. He goes beyond my expectations in visual creativity.

Without Jae Jaeger, who has backed up my research and writing, this book would not have been expedited as much as it was. She is a fact-checker like none other. Her expertise in the bibliography and index was beyond my expectations. Jae was supportive and motivating.

I am very thankful to have "an extra set of eyes" from the perspective of a friend and almost-native of Broken Arrow. Sandy Deonier Montgomery knew many of these 100 as Kenny and I did. I appreciated our conversations, reminiscing and knowing "being from Broken Arrow, we have a comradery" just as many of our readers do.

I acknowledge *The Museum Broken Arrow*, which provided resources, materials, space and allowed me time to do research in their area. "I depended on a great deal of assistance from Julie Brown, Executive Director, for her knowledge and abilities in research, who also was a tremendous help with her editing. Allie Cloud, Museum Associate, was a valuable asset in researching for information, especially pictures in the archives, as well as former Executive Directors Betty Gerber and Lori Lewis.

I am grateful to *The Museum Broken Arrow's* Board of Directors for their approval and support of this project which has been a desire and goal of Dr. Oliver and myself.

Acknowledgments

I need to once again mention how precious and invaluable my association and friendship with Dr. Clarence G. Oliver, Jr. as my own former Assistant Superintendent years ago, and now a colleague as a fellow author. His advice and encouragement through the years has been priceless.

I thank Marmie Apsley and other members of *Broken Arrow Genealogical Society* who assisted me in using their resources, including a room in which to research.

Janet McDougal Collier, Sharon Summers, Thelma Moran Wilkerson were irreplaceable and helped this project along, assisting with biographies, phone calls and emails to locate descendants and local family members of the Legacy Makers. As fellow Broken Arrow graduates, it was easy to connect with stories and the people we knew.

Introduction

In today's world, people are encouraged to have dreams, visions, to make plans and set goals. Nowadays it is not uncommon for people to gather together and create Vision Boards. Most people in 1902 probably didn't think beyond protecting and supporting their families. A vision board was unimaginable at that time.

People traveling from surrounding states and further, came with ideas outside the conventional thinking of the time. With large imaginations, their dreams were bigger than life itself.

The people in this book chose an area within a vast territory of prairie land. Those who came to Broken Arrow in the early days were not ordinary. They are thought to be one-of-a-kind and were very few. Even those who did not initially relocate on their own volition made the best of their new lives and prospered in leadership and courage.

Our community has had phenomenal growth at different phases of its first 100 years, from 1902-2002, and continues to thrive at an exponential rate. Growth began in the mid-1940s and again in the early 1970s. Contributing factors have been the welcome for new commerce balanced with the desire to "Keep Broken Arrow History Alive." The construction and operation of *The Museum Broken Arrow,* built right in the heart of the Rose District, connects people from all generations.

Introduction

For many decades, especially during the 1940s, Broken Arrow was known as a *City of Roses and Sparkling Spring Water* due to the natural springs in the southern part of this area and because of the beautiful roses grown here by the ladies' rose and garden societies. It was natural that from this history the *Rose District* would evolve. The contributions of the women's *Self Culture Club* made many developments possible. Broken Arrow's schools advanced and churches were able to show benevolence due to this group's organization and contributions during the town's early days. In their tradition, Broken Arrow continues to be a philanthropic-minded community.

It is not unusual to meet and visit with our older citizens only to discover that they actually knew or were related to many of the ones who pioneered this area. Even those of us who grew up in Broken Arrow during the 1950s and 60s, may not have known some of our heritage. Younger people may have known there were small farming and coal mining communities surrounding Broken Arrow long before our town was incorporated. But, they may not be aware of the beginning of the railroad and how early residents moved their homes to meet the demands of progress.

The annual *Pioneer Dinner* was started by these "Legacy Makers" who established Broken Arrow, as a way to connect, reminisce and discuss their achievements. They continued making plans for success as they envisioned progress of a new and modern city. The get-togethers evolved

Introduction

into an opportunity for Broken Arrow graduates to enjoy reuniting with classmates. The *Pioneer Dinner* became a weekend when the graduates chose to have their official class reunions because it coincided with *Rooster Days*.

At one time Broken Arrow celebrated *Cotton Jubilee,* held at the height of the cotton harvesting season. This jubilee was replaced by *Rooster Day* when it became a necessity during the Depression Era for farmers to gather in town to exchange their roosters. Once a one-day event, *Rooster Days* has continued to grow into one of Oklahoma's largest and longest-running annual festivals.

During the 2002 centennial year, Broken Arrow selected 100 of their most influential citizens. These remarkable 'movers and shakers' spanning through Broken Arrow's first hundred-year history, are who we thank for our historical heritage. We appreciate and respect the leadership of those who pioneered the way. We must never forget the hardships they endured to make a better life for those who have traveled the sod in this area that was once just a prairie.

We want to give them the honor they deserve. Some are still living today, but most live on only in our hearts. Now, eighteen years past that centennial mark, we believe they would be proud to see the continual progress of the remarkable city they birthed.

Their biographies and stories, many written by their own

Introduction

family members, and *Broken Arrow Genealogical Society* members, and others written by Roberta Parker, a dedicated reporter for *Broken Arrow Ledger,* are inspiring and memorable. Many of their descendants still live in this area and can attest to their ancestors' bravery and fortitude.

Meet the Broken Arrow Centennials—true *Legacy Makers*. WE ARE BROKEN ARROW PROUD!

– *Jan Simmons Collins*

Chapter 1

Oklahoma
'Where the Wind Comes Sweeping Down the Plain'

When the word "Oklahoma" is mentioned, one may think of the Land Run of 1889, the Trail of Tears, cattlemen, cowboys and the open prairies, the drilling of oil wells or even the Depression times and dust bowl scenes from *The Grapes of Wrath*. When our hometown of Broken Arrow is voiced to local citizens, even more visual memories are conjured up.

The history of Broken Arrow, Oklahoma is rich in cultures of both our Native American Indian citizens and settlers. Census records and even birth certificates reflect either O.T. or I.T. for *Oklahoma Territory* or *Indian Territory* pre-statehood. Because of this shared community with both cultures and heritages, we honor both Broken Arrow's first citizens and the pioneers.

From its origin in 1902 to our centennial celebration in 2002, we take a chronological journey to describe each era separately. Connecting with national and world events is a way to allow a greater understanding of how and why they chose to develop this area.

Many folks who lived in Broken Arrow between the 1940s and 1960s remember these first two groups: American Indians and pioneer settlers. They were our community leaders. One such leader was H. Cecil Rhoades, who is remembered as the principal at Southside Elementary on Houston Street between Elm and Main Streets. He was respected as a Broken Arrow educator who left this life much too early. As mentioned, Mr. Rhoades' book *Establishment and Development of Broken Arrow, Oklahoma* discussed the origin of the name of our beloved community. No matter the source of that name, in the foreword of his book, Dr. Clarence G. Oliver, Jr. said it best: "…it is a name rooted deeply in Indian culture and the name is applied to a city with only the vastness of the sky as a limiting element."[1]

As our story begins, the emphasis is on how the first citizens of this nation came to our state. *The Five Civilized Tribes* were drastically affected between colonial times to the *Indian Removal Act of 1830* signed by President Andrew Jackson. This act began the Trail of Tears from their homelands, lasting 1836-1839. But the stage was set for them long before 1830. Some tribal inhabitants were first brought to *Indian Territory* as early as 1826.

---

1. Rhoades, H. Cecil. *Establishment and Development of Broken Arrow, Oklahoma*, Moongate Enterprises, 1976. iii.

Oklahoma

Our primary focus is on the Muscogee Creek Nation. Before becoming a nation when the first thirteen colonies were developing, as many as 20,000 citizens of the Muscogee Creek Confederacy, occupied a large portion of Georgia and Alabama. The names *Muscogee Creek Confederacy* and *Creek Nation* are used interchangeably. They profited from their association with the Europeans who began moving in and trading goods.[2]

The Creeks thrived well and had strong economic and social lives with a central local government. All the Creek towns joined together to form the great Creek Confederacy and were divided into the Upper and Lower towns. The Upper Towns were along the Coosa and Tallapoosa Rivers and the Lower Creek towns were located close to the Flint and Chattahoochee Rivers. One of the greatest and oldest of these towns was Coweta Town (Koweta) near the Chattahoochee. A daughter town of Coweta was Thlikachka (Broken Arrow), a hub where many Creek councils were held. Each had its own councils, but the two divisions joined together when important decisions were needed. Extensive documentation from both Georgia and Oklahoma can be found from interviews and recorded Creek history.[3]

In the records researched, Georgia is the first time and

---

2. Rhoades, 8.
3. Childers, Mildred McIntosh. *Private Letters and Papers,* Broken Arrow, Oklahoma.

Meet the BROKEN ARROW CENTENNIALS

place the name "Broken Arrow Town" was mentioned.[4] It often happens, when groups of people migrate to other states, names of towns and areas are often duplicated. Efforts are made herein to distinguish the difference between original towns and rivers and current towns and regions in Oklahoma.

The first five citizens recognized as our Broken Arrow's Centennials, whose families settled in this latter area, are James McHenry, C. Benjamin Haikey, David McKellop Hodge, Mildred McIntosh Childers and Harry Alexander Sells. These five individuals are members of the Muscogee Creek Tribe and represent a strong heritage of descendants.

---

4. Wise, Donald. *Broken Arrow Vignettes: Brief Local Histories* (Broken Arrow, Oklahoma. Re Tvkv'ce Press) 1989, 38.

Chapter 2

Muscogee Creek Inhabitants

During and after the removal from their homelands in Georgia and Alabama, there was a concern for the welfare of the Indian people and wanting to introduce them to Christianity. The Baptist, Methodist and Presbyterian Churches sent Missionaries to this area. Among those who came to Broken Arrow were a Baptist Missionary, Rev. R.H. Buckner; Presbyterian Missionary, Dr. Robert McGill Loughridge, and Methodist Missionary, Rev. James McHenry.

Unlike James McHenry, C. Benjamin Haikey and David McKellop Hodge were born in the Broken Arrow area. McHenry and Hodge were followers of Dr. Loughridge and received Christian instruction and training from him. C. Benjamin Haikey followed his calling into the ministry also. As will be shared in their biographies, they were all dedicated to their tribe as their life's mission.

JAMES McHENRY
(1818 – 1883)

James McHenry, once known as Jim Henry, was born

on January 1, 1818 near Flint River, Georgia. There seemed to be some question who his parents were but most information states that his father was a Scotch trader and his mother was a Hitchiti Indian woman from Chehaya Town on the Flint River.[5] On occasion, European traders had more than one wife, often an Indian woman. One family report is Henry's father, Scotch trader, James McHenry, had two sons who bore his name. It is speculated the one in our story is the second son whose name is slightly different.[6] Jim Henry's early years are obscure, but it is known that his early education was obtained at the *Asbury Manual Training School* in Alabama which was operated by the Methodist Church. After schooling, he was employed as a clerk in a mercantile firm in Columbus, Georgia.[7]

REVEREND JAMES MCHENRY

Jim Henry's educational training and work ethic later became an important part of his destiny. America was in a

---

5. "Janes McHenry," *Broken Arrow Hall of Fame:* 1990, Broken Arrow Genealogy Society (BAGS). 7.
6. Interview, Charles (Chuck) McHenry, family history. August, 2019.
7. McHenry. *Hall of Fame:* 1990, 8.

Muscogee Creek Inhabitants

great deal of turbulence during the mid-1830s, especially in the southern states. It started with the beginning of *the Indian Removal Act in 1830* and was followed by the Civil War.

The removal of the Creeks to Indian Territory began between 1835 and 1836. Angered by the atrocities on his people, Jim Henry retaliated against the government in two armed conflicts. Jim Henry, Eneah Micco, Eneah Emarthla, along with about 300 Creek Indians attacked and killed settlers, waylaying stagecoaches near Columbus, Georgia, virtually forcing all survivors to flee.[8] It was followed by an attack in May, 1836, when desperate and starving Creeks fought back against a Roanoke settlement in Georgia. It resulted in killing fifteen inhabitants, burning the town, and became known as the *Creek War of 1836*. Federal troops under the command of Major General Winfield Scott, with assistance from loyal Indian warriors, gathered thirteen thousand troops and armed forces to put down the Creek uprising.[9] Most of the Creek Indians involved in the uprising were captured, put in chains and sent west to Indian Territory. Jim Henry was one of seven men who were sentenced to be hanged.

Some thought of Jim Henry as the hero of the Creek War of 1836 and considered those destined to be hanged "as

---

8. Debo, Angie, *The Road to Disappearance: A History of the Creek Indians.* Norman: University of Oklahoma Press 1941, 101.
9. Wright. James Leitch. *Creeks and Seminoles,* Lincoln: University of Nebraska Press) 1986, 268.

the government's reward for their efforts." In an interview with the author, Henry's great-grandson, Charles McHenry shared this about the captors: of the three who initiated the conflict (Henry, Micco and Emarthla) his great-grandfather was "the last one to surrender."[10] Because Henry was from Georgia where the crimes were committed, he had the forethought to escape to Alabama before being captured, even though he was wounded in the shoulder. The two states quarreled over jurisdiction.[11] Henry was separated from the others and transferred to the Russell County, Alabama jail. The public's interest centered on the six Indians who were captured early in the uprising and were hanged on November 25, 1836.[12]

Because Henry's father was a prominent trader, many believed he used his influence to release his son. Other records indicate that Henry was sincere in his piety.[12] For eighteen months, Jim Henry had been ill. Georgia and Alabama continued the "tug of war" to vie for the honor of hanging him. After much deliberation, sometime between April, 1837 and January, 1838, there was a turn of events. Because of some "defects" in the proceedings in Jim Henry's case, and "no grand jury in attendance…" he was acquitted in Alabama and extradited to stand trial in Columbus, Georgia. According to the Columbus Enquirer, the basis for the disposition of Henry's case in

---
10. Charles McHenry Interview, 2019.
11. Coss, Richard H. "Jim Henry," *Muscogiana* 3 (Fall, 1992) 55-63.
12. Horton, Chad. "James McHenry," *ArtEFacts*. Graphic Arts Department. Broken Arrow Public Schools, 1990, 5.

Muscogee Creek Inhabitants

Alabama have never been located There is a record for Jim Henry's acquittal early in 1838. But, as in Alabama, no court records of his court appearance in Georgia have been located or accounts of the details in newspapers.[13]

Once this former fugitive was acquitted, Georgia authorities took precautions to protect Jim Henry. Captain John Page escorted Henry and another man from Fort Mitchell, Alabama to Fort Gibson, Indian Territory, arriving on March 31, 1838. He changed his name to James McHenry, and perhaps it helped put the past behind him to start a new life with a new name. It appears he traded his weapons on the battlefield for spiritual weapons of his faith.[14] In an interview with James McHenry's grand-son, Walter McHenry quoted, "a lion has become a lamb"[15] from an 1855 writing of Bishop George Pierce, during the Indian Mission Conference (IMC). Pierce emphasized the power of Christ in McHenry instead of his stance on Creeks' rights as he presided over McHenry's admission into the IMC.

"The lion has become a lamb - the brave, a preacher. The war-hoop is hushed: the midnight foray is with the past: the Bible and Hymn Book fill the hands that once grasped the torch and tomahawk... the bold valiant savage, who spread consternation among

---

13. "Peddy's Creek War 1835-1837," *Columbus Enquirer*. Columbus, Georgia, April 23, 1837.
14. Parker, Roberta. "The People Who Made the History, Who Are the History of Weer." *Broken Arrow Scout*.
15. Walter McHenry Interview, McHenry Family History, 2019.

the peaceful settlements on either side of the Chattahoochee now travels a circuit, preaching peace on earth, goodwill to men."[16]

James McHenry played an important role in shaping the area in and around Broken Arrow. His family received an allotment and settled in the area that would become known as Weer. McHenry's legacy went well past the battlefields that made him well-known. He was converted to the Methodist faith and became an ardent advocate for his faith. He became a Pastor and joined the Asbury Mission, riding a traveling circuit and preaching the Gospel, assisting in the establishment of four Methodist churches in multiple counties.

Early in the Civil War he joined the 1st Regiment *Creek Mounted Volunteers,* Confederate Army, as a Private on August 19, 1861. Jim McHenry's talents were soon recognized so he was commissioned as a Captain then later promoted to the rank of Major.

After the war, James McHenry resumed his profession as a Methodist Minister and active missionary in Indian Territory. He established the Methodist Church in Okmulgee in 1869 and later the Broken Arrow Indian Methodist Church in 1874. McHenry was elected to the Creek Nation Council in 1866 and served as President of the House

---

16. Smith, Tash. *Capture These Indians for the Lord.* University of Arizona Press: The Arizona Board of Regents. 2014, 61.

of Kings for four years. During this time, he chaired the Committee to draft the *Creek Nation Constitution* along with developing civil and criminal laws for the Creek Nation. He served on the Creek Council House Building Committee to oversee the construction of a new Capitol of the Creek Nation at Okmulgee which was completed in 1878. After that time, he served as a District Judge for the Coweta District, Creek Nation.[17]

James McHenry and Rachel Smith were married circa 1865. They had two children, Lewis McHenry (1866-1916) and Henrietta (McHenry) Berryhill Sarty (1874-1940s). Lewis and Henrietta's children were Lewis, Jr., David J., Jess, Onis F., Aud Harris and Abbie B. Moore Dodson.

James McHenry passed away at the age of 65 on May 2, 1883. His wife, Rachel, had died at the age of 45, on September 15, 1874. Both are interred in the McHenry Family Private Cemetery in Broken Arrow, located in the Jasper Estates Addition off 185th Street between Tucson and Jasper Streets. In 2002, *Trail of Tears* recognition was given to McHenry's journey on the Trail of Tears by marking his grave.[18, 19]

(BAGS gave permission for this partial reprint of McHenry's biography.)

---

17. "McHenry," BAGS. *Hall of Fame:* 1990, 8.
18. Interview, Charles (Chuck) McHenry, August, 2019.
19. Lori Lewis. "Looking Back at James McHenry," *Broken Arrow Ledger*; news@baledger.com; June 30, 2016.

Meet the BROKEN ARROW CENTENNIALS

JAMES MCHENRY'S TOMBSTONE MARKER

The Legacy Lives On

James McHenry's son Lewis also became a prominent Indian Methodist preacher, obviously influenced by his father's life and testimony. Following in their footsteps, Lewis' son, David J. McHenry, was a Minister at the *Broken Arrow Indian Methodist Church*. When David J. passed away in 1964, it ended 90 years of ministry by the same family. David J. has a son living in Broken Arrow by the name of David J. McHenry, Jr., known by friends as Junior. He graduated from *Broken Arrow High School* in 1944 and is now 95 years old. His daughter is Glenda Allred ('81).

Another son of Lewis, Walter McHenry, became a certified lay speaker in the *United Methodist Church*.

He was a member of the Senior Methodist of Northeast District and a member of the *Broken Arrow Indian United Methodist Church*. Walter graduated from *Broken Arrow High School* in 1932. He played football under Coach R. D. Patterson.

Walter and his wife, Josephine (Dolly) Alexander McHenry's four children graduated from *Broken Arrow High School*. Ronald ('55); Janis McHenry Imotichey ('56); Charles or Chuck ('58); and Tina Alexander Boyce ('66). Ronald and Chuck both played football under Coach Joe Robinson.

Walter's widow, Dolly, living at the beginning of this writing, passed away less than two months before reaching the age of 104. She was still living in the Weer community close to their son Chuck's family on the original land allotted to Walter's mother's. Walter's brother, Onis F. was delivered by early Broken Arrow doctor, Dr. Onis Franklin and given his name. Onis' son, Onis F. McHenry, Jr., wrote extensive family history as partial fulfillment for his Master of Education Degree in 1981. Descendants of James McHenry's granddaughter, Abbie B. Moore Dodson, also live in Broken Arrow. They include Donna Williamson ('64); Ralph, Jr. ('66); Abby Epperson ('70); Cheri Stanley ('73); Anita Smith and Dorothy Moore-Staggs ('80).

Walter's grandson and Ronald's son is Eli McHenry, Pastor of the *Broken Arrow Indian United Methodist*

Church. There are many more descendants of James McHenry's and other early Creek Indian families in this area who attend this church.

C. BENJAMIN HAIKEY
(1868 – 1940)

C. Benjamin Haikey

The Haikey name is well-known by area residents. The nucleus of Haikey Creek Park is 160 acres of land allotted by the Creek Nation to our honoree's father. C. Benjamin Haikey, a Muscogee (Creek) Indian was born near Broken Arrow, Indian Territory on December 24, 1868. His parents, Maisie Grayson and B. Benjamin Haikey, were full-blood Creek Indians.[20] They lived on a farm near Haikey Creek west of the present site of Broken Arrow. Young C. Benjamin Haikey had eight younger brothers and sisters.

Mrs. Walter "Dolly" Alexander McHenry's grandmother was Kizzie Alexander, B. Benjamin's sister. Dolly recalled she and others affectionately referred to B. Benjamin as "old

---

20. https://www.findagrave.com/memorial/156991491/maisie-haikey

man Ben" to distinguish between father and son.[21] Ben was educated at *Wealaka Mission, a Creek National School,* and in Tulsa public schools. He was elected Permit Collector by the *Creek National Council* on November 10, 1894.

On June 12, 1899, Ben Haikey was married by the Reverend George Mowbray to Louisa Chisholm Sunny (1876-1939) also a Creek Indian. Ben and Louisa had seven children: Maymie and Birdie Haikey; Bertha Haikey who married Douglas Bemore, Clarence W. Haikey who married Freida Young; Alpha Haikey; Herbert C. Haikey who married Hope Evans; and Naomi Haikey who married Joe Cleveland Eades.

A farmer from 1901 until 1907, Ben operated mercantile businesses in Broken Arrow in 1907, in Fry community in 1908 and again in Broken Arrow from 1924-1930. He joined the *A.F. & A.M. Masonic Lodge 243* in Broken Arrow and *Akdar Temple* in Tulsa. He was a Republican.

Haikey was converted and baptized a Methodist by the Reverend William Jimboy, a famous Creek minister.[22] A Sunday School teacher, Haikey was licensed to preach in 1907. He was ordained a Deacon by Bishop Warren Candler in 1912 and as an Elder by Bishop Edwin D. Mouzon on November 13, 1921. He served a number of charges including 15 years as Minister at *Haikey Cha-*

---

21. McHenry, Josephine "Dolly" Alexander. *McHenry Family History.* July, 2019.
22. Halbert, Henry Sale and T.H. Ball. *The Creek War of 1813 and 1814.* Chicago: Donahue and Henneberry Printers and Binders, 1895, p. 301.

pel on 101st Street between Memorial and Mingo Streets. Haikey was appointed Presiding Elder of the Creek District in 1935 and served in that position until his death on March 11, 1940 death at the age of 71. His wife preceded him in death on August 12, 1939. They are buried in the Bixby City Cemetery.[23]

Haikey Chapel still stands today on 101st Street between Memorial and Mingo Streets. Many memories were made inside those hallowed walls as C. Benjamin Haikey's paternal granddaughter recollects:

"Walk with me. Let me share with you this particular memory of my childhood. It is so vivid as I recall it now and it is especially dear to me because it was a time spent with my beloved grandparents. As the bell pealed the call to services, its sound echoed through the fall acorn laden oak trees that surrounded the church grounds… The white, wooden frame structure with its squeaky floors and long, narrow windows stands today as a reminder of its founder – my paternal great-grandfather. I still recall the odor of stale prayer and song books and the strains of 'The Old Rugged Cross' coming from the piano (not always properly tuned), … this warm, humid climate. As the ladies cooled themselves with their decorative paper fans to gain some relief from the still air, the long hard straight back benches began to feel like

---
23. C. Ben Haikey. www.findagrave.com/memorial/22671452

roughened concrete. One peculiarity of the service was the practice of the men sitting on the left side of the church and the women sitting on the right side. Perhaps it was a custom of the times …. You may ask… did I grow… did I learn?... To a young child, growing spiritually is also accomplished by observing others and remembering."

Betty Jean Haikey Tobias
September 19, 1982

(Courtesy of The Museum Broken Arrow, Haikey file)

An elementary school that stood on the southwest corner of 101st Street and Yale Avenue was named for C. Ben Haikey. Presently, Jenks Southeast Elementary stands at that location. The Haikey family played a prominent part in the history of the Broken Arrow area. C. Benjamin Haikey was nominated by daughter Naomi Haikey Eades and honored by the *Broken Arrow Genealogy Society Hall of Fame* in 1991.

(Permission to reprint by Broken Arrow Genealogy Society.)

DAVID McKELLOP HODGE
(1841 – 1920)

David McKellop Hodge was from a very different background than McHenry or Haikey who had studied under Dr. Robert McGill Loughridge, then had become Ministers of the Gospel. Hodge made his mark as a translator, orator and leader of the Creek Tribe. Unlike Jim McHenry, Haikey and Hodge learned of the *Trail of Tears* vicariously through their parents and family, but all three knew purpose in promoting their Creek heritage.

David McKellop Hodge was born at Choska, Indian Territory, in April, 1841, to Nancy Ann McKellop, a Creek Indian, and Nathaniel Hodge, a native New Yorker.

Hodge attended the *Coweta Manual Training School* and also studied under Dr. Robert McGill Loughridge, a prominent Presbyterian missionary and educator.[24]

DAVID MCKELLOP HODGE

Many of the Creek citizens who advocated for the South joined different divisions of the Confederacy. David Hodge joined Company H, 1st Regiment *Creek Mounted Volunteers*, Confederate Army, as a Private on August 17, 1862, at Choska, Creek Nation.

In 1864 David Hodge married Susan (Sukie) Yargee, a Creek Indian. He became involved with the Creek Nation politics, was a translator of Creek and English, an orator and leader in the *Creek Nation Council House* at Okmulgee. He was licensed to practice law in the Creek Nation; trans-

Muscogee Creek Inhabitants

lated the *Creek Nation Laws of 1880-81*; was a Trustee of the *Tullahassee Mission*, 1876-82; a member of the *House of Kings, Creek Nation* to serve on the committee to negotiate with the *Dawes Commission* for Creek Rights; represented the Creek Nation on numerous occasions in Washington, D.C. before Congressional committees and the Courts.[24] Over the years, an attempt was made by the *Five Tribes* to make each of the two territories a separate state.

At the time, Broken Arrow's destiny was abruptly changed when these "twin territories" became one state instead of two.[25] "The concept of the Twin Territories was highlighted by the publication of *Twin Territories: The Indian Magazine*. It designated itself as 'the only publication of its class in the Indian Territory, and named in honor of both the Indian Territory and Oklahoma.' This publication highlighted the commonalities and differences of these two territories from the American Indian's point of view."[26]

Finally came the *Sequoyah Convention of 1905*. Hodge was appointed as a delegate from District 7 of the Indian Territory, to represent Broken Arrow at this convention held in Muskogee in 1905. At the Convention, David Hodge was on a *Committee of Three*, which included Charles N. Haskell and Robert L. Owen, to aid the Chairman, Pleasant Porter, to appoint subcommittees.

24. "David McKellop Hodge," *Broken Arrow Hall of Fame: 1990*. BAGS. 5.
25. Rhoades, iii.
26. *The Twin Territories: The Indian Magazine*; https://www.okhistory.org/publications/enc/entry.php?entry=TW002

Meet the BROKEN ARROW CENTENNIALS

On December 3, 1905, David Hodge was in a group of prominent Creek Indian leaders going to Washington, D.C., to lobby for the proposed *State of Sequoyah*. They met with members of Congress and with President Theodore Roosevelt. While at the White House, Hodge heard the President tell the delegation that it was not expedient to form the new state. He became disgusted and walked out of the White House with Roosevelt calling him to come back and to talk things over. *That day* in history, *Indian Territory* and *Oklahoma Territory's* destiny was changed forever. Oklahoma's State history was about to begin. Hodge caught the next train west for *Indian Territory* and changed that day from a life-long Republican to an active Democrat.[27]

Susan (Yargee) Hodge and David M. Hodge were each granted their 160-acre allotments from the Creek Nation. These tracts of land were located in the present City of Broken Arrow fence line. Their general legal description would be in Sections 5 and 6 of Township 17 N, Range 14 East, which lies west of Olive Street, adjacent to Jasper Street near the historic *White Church and Cemetery.*

David Hodge is credited with translating some parts of the Bible into the Creek Language. He collaborated with Dr. Robert McGill Loughridge to complete and publish the *English and Muscogee Dictionary* published in St. Louis in 1890. Hodge was involved in establishing and donating

---
27. "Hodge," *Hall of Fame: 1990.* 6.

one acre of land for the *Loughridge Memorial Presbyterian Church* (now known as *White Church*). He also encouraged a subscription school which operated out of the church building during the period of 1870-1900.

David and Susan Hodge had no children. Susan Hodge died on February 14, 1918, and is buried in the *Park Grove Cemetery* in Broken Arrow. David M. Hodge died in Muskogee, Oklahoma, on December 13, 1920. His brothers and sisters decided that he would be interred in the Hodge Family Plot in *Oaklawn Cemetery* in Tulsa.

(Permission to reprint by Broken Arrow Genealogy Society.)

MILDRED McINTOSH CHILDERS
(1869 – 1944)

Mildred M. Childers

Mildred McIntosh, a Creek Indian, came from hardy stock. She was the daughter of Bessie (Vann) and Roley McIntosh III. Her family carefully recorded their heritage. She was a descendant of Chief William McIntosh of a Creek tribe in Georgia. The McIntosh family belonged to the Lower Creek towns near the Chattahoochee River. Records show when the family came to Oklahoma, they first settled in an area near Eufaula, Indian Territory, where Mildred was born April 3, 1869.[28]

Mildred McIntosh Childers' family records provide the clarification of the origin of the name of our hometown, 'Broken Arrow', which was from their homeland in Georgia. "When one town became too large to gather around one campfire, the people divided and some would find a new location and would take a new name for their town. One year, some of the Indians of Muscogee town journeyed to the Chattahoochee River bottom where canes grew alongside the banks. This cane was jointed and easily broken instead of being cut, and was found to be suitable for making arrows. They gathered this cane break for the whole town. When they returned after about a year, the camp had grown too large for them to gather around one campfire. They left the established town and began the town of Thlikachka, translated as Broken Arrow, in honor of the cane which broke easily for arrows."[29]

With the Louisiana Purchase of 1803 by the United States government and the movement to settle the Southwest, the Creek Nation felt even more threatened as talk of relocating them west of the Mississippi became reality. With assistance from the Cherokees, their neighbors to the north, the Creeks, tried every political strategy they knew to keep their homeland being taken by the Georgians.

---
28. "Mildred McIntosh Childers," Broken Arrow Hall of Fame: 1990. BAGS,1.
29. Childers, Letters and Papers.

Muscogee Creek Inhabitants

However, even before American Independence, some Creek land had already been ceded to Georgia during the leadership of James Oglethorpe. As relentless pressure continued, the most influential leader of the Lower Creek towns in 1817 was Chief William McIntosh.[30]

As the federal government added pressure to induce the *Five Civilized Tribes* to move beyond the Mississippi, the Creeks stood firm with appeals and protests against the concessions but removal of the Creeks to the west by the United States commissioners continued to gain favor with the Georgians. Although the consensus of Creek leaders was an unqualified refusal, William McIntosh began to advocate an emigration policy. The commissioners, resolved to negotiate a treaty with McIntosh, met secretly in his home. A meeting was then called by the commissioners at Indian Springs, Georgia in order to carry out the plan. The other Creek chiefs refused to attend, having already given their answer.[31]

McIntosh having won the support of some of the citizens of the Lower Creek Towns, signed what became known as the *Treaty of Indian Springs* in 1825. Opothleyahola, a leading Lower Town Chief was present at the council meeting only to witness the signing. Before papers were signed, he warned McIntosh of the death penalty for violating Creek law by seeking to sell Creek Land.

---

30. Rhoades, 5.
31. Rhoades, 6.

Because of the division of the Muscogee Creek Nation, Chief McIntosh met with an untimely and tragic death. He sealed his own fate by signing the *Treaty of Indian Springs*. Since some agreed with the government while the other group staunchly opposed selling Creek Land, the actions were documented as such, "Early one morning McIntosh awoke to find his house surrounded by angry Creek warriors. After calling out members of his family and two white men, who were spending the night in his home, the warriors set fire to the house and shot him as he came out of the door."[32]

The stage was set for the destiny of the Muscogee Creek long before 1830. Some of their tribes' first inhabitants were brought to Oklahoma as early as 1826. As part of the *Muscogee Creek Tribe Removal Agreement*, the Creeks were allotted land in the northeast portion of the territory. Dispute over the land had to be settled with the Osage Tribe when new tribes were moved here.

Some Muscogee Creeks emigrated to *Indian Territory* in 1828 with the first party settling at the *Three Forks* of the Arkansas, Verdigris and Grand Rivers a few miles north of the present Muskogee, Oklahoma. This group was mostly comprised of people from Broken Arrow, Coweta, Big Springs, (Lower Creek towns) in Georgia.

Some Creeks migrated further north when they were

---

32. Rhoades, 6-7.

Muscogee Creek Inhabitants

forced to leave Georgia. Those families were the McIntosh, Childers and Perrymans. They originally settled east of Broken Arrow in Wagoner County around 31st Street. These families played important roles in the development of the Broken Arrow community, with continuing tribal descendency. Later, the Perrymans migrated about fifteen miles west and became well known cattlemen.

The many Creek Indians who came to this area of *Indian Territory* in 1826, settled in what was part of the "old" Broken Arrow - about five miles south of what became the town. They settled on the north side of the Arkansas River and extended from Cedar Creek to Haikey Creek.

As in Georgia, the Muscogee Creeks settled close to rivers. Our Muscogee Creek citizens often settled in areas that were similar to the topography and environment they left behind in Georgia. They retained the old names for these communities. In one sense, their towns were no longer the same, but were now farming communities. Many of the tribes were close blood relationships and had historical ties as well. By 1891, the Creek tribe numbered 431 inhabitants.[33]

As with other Creeks, the McIntosh family story began in Georgia and Alabama. When the Muscogee Creek came to *Indian Territory*, they brought their culture and history with them. Alongside their livestock, tools, and clothes, they also

---
33. Ibid., p. 9-10.

brought heroic stories of their ancestors.

Mildred McIntosh attended *Bacone College* in 1885 and finished at *Carlisle College* in 1891. She also attended *Grayson College* at Whitewright, Texas, and *Texas Normal College* at Denton, Texas.

Mildred taught school at the *Eufaula High School* until she married Daniel Boone Childers (1879-1946), a Creek Indian, in 1898. Mildred became the private secretary for Creek Principal Chief Isparhecker, 1895-1899, while her Father, Roley McIntosh III, was the Second Chief of the Creek Nation. Mildred and Daniel Childers made their home in the "old" Broken Arrow in 1902.[34]

Mildred once stated that the two most important days in her life were when Chief Isparhecker had been called to Fort Smith by Judge Isaac C. Parker on tribal business. Her father, Second Chief Roley McIntosh III, was in Eufaula on business, and could not be located. Therefore, she was vested with temporary authority to sign papers and to deal with all matters officially referred to the Principal Chief by the *Creek Council* then in session. She was the only woman ever so honored by the Creek Nation. In 1932 she was elected a member of the *House of Warriors* to serve in the *Creek Council*. Mildred was later appointed as clerk in the *Creek Citizenship Court* and passed on questions relating to doubtful claims of white persons, freedmen and alien

---

34. Jackson, Effie. "Mildred McIntosh Childers Interview" 12011, *Indian Pioneer Papers*, https://digital.libraries.ou.edu/ 1937.

Indians. Mildred Childers and Alex Posey were among the members of the *Committee of Eighteen* which compiled the *Creek Census*. In 1903 Mildred was elected secretary of the *House of Warriors* defeating David M. Hodge. She was the only woman who had ever held any official position in the *Creek National Council*.[35]

In 1935 Mildred was the only Indian delegate at the convention of the *Women's Missionary Council of the M.E. Church, South,* which was held in St. Louis. Mildred was quite active in the Broken Arrow Indian Methodist Church and the Broken Arrow Methodist Churches. She was chosen by the *Democratic Women's Club of Broken Arrow* to officially receive Mrs. Eleanor Roosevelt, wife of the President, on her visit to Broken Arrow in 1937. She was also active in the town's *Self Culture Club.*

Mildred Childers died on May 13, 1944 and is buried in the *Park Grove Cemetery* in Broken Arrow. Her husband, Daniel B. Childers, died on December 27, 1946 and rests beside Mildred. They had four children: Clarence William Childers, Ruby Mildred (Childers) Bruner Haynie, Kotcha Childers and Eloise (Childers) Boudinot.[36]

(Permission to reprint by Broken Arrow Genealogy Society.)

---

35. Jackson, Ibid.
36. Childers, *Hall of Fame* 1990, 2.

Meet the BROKEN ARROW CENTENNIALS

The Legacy Lives On

Mildred McIntosh Childers was a member of the *Self Culture Club* which began shortly after the establishment of Broken Arrow. Family names such as the Bruner, Haynie, and Boudinot are familiar sounds to many of our current Broken Arrow residents. Mildred and Daniel Childers' daughters, Ruby Haynie and Eloise Boudinot were respected and active members in the community. Fred Haynie, Danny and Steve Bruner, Okema Boudinot Randall and Michelle Boudinot Wolfvoice, Rodney Randall, Shonday Lee Randall and Ashley Wolfvoice Carson are some of her Broken Arrow descendants.

HARRY ALEXANDER SELLS
(ca. 1855 – 1930)

Harry A. Sells, a Creek Freedman, was born in *Indian Territory* around 1855. He was the son of Rose (Kernal) and Jo Sells, who were citizens of the *Creek Nation Freedmen*. Harry Sells married Jane McIntosh (1855-1935) circa 1878. She was the daughter of Harriet (Lewis) and John McIntosh.

As a married couple in the Creek Nation, Harry and Jane McIntosh Sells received separate allotments. Although they did not live in the Broken Arrow area for the majority of their lives, the location of their Indian allotments was considered of importance. Both of the Sells family land tracts in the town of Broken Arrow, *Indian Territory*, were significant pieces of property for the future development and growth of the community.

Jane McIntosh Sells selected a 40-acre tract of land as part of her Creek allotment. The location of this 40-acre tract today is located southeast of the intersection of Kenosha and South Elm Place, where a QuikTrip now stands. The *Arkansas Valley Townsite Company* purchased the Jane Sells' 40-acre tract on August 28, 1903, for $800. R. H. Kello, civil engineer from Muskogee, Indian Territory, surveyed and platted her 40-acre tract which became the *Northside Addition* to the new town of Broken Arrow. Harry Sells selected land to the south of his wife's tract and adjoined hers.

HARRY AND JANE SELLS

Sells was granted a 160-acre tract of land as an allotment in the *Creek Nation, Indian Territory,* on March 30, 1903. His 160 acres were in two separate tracts of 80-acres each. One portion, an 80-acre allotment was located southwest of the *Broken Arrow Townsite* near the historic *White Church and Cemetery.*

The other and more noteworthy part was just north of the original townsite plan, and in the beginning was not part of the original plat for development of Broken Arrow as a new town. However, the *Arkansas Valley Townsite Company* which was promoting the *Broken Arrow Townsite*, purchased this 80 acre tract from Harry Sells on May 12, 1904, for $3,425.

Jane Sells had also selected a 120-acre tract of land south of the town of Tullahassee, *Indian Territory,* allotted to her by the Creek Nation in 1903. There Harry and Jane Sells made their home. Their children were: Joseph Harry Sells, Eliza Jane (Sells) Murrell, Rose Sells, Lawrence Sells, Jacob Sells, Willie Sells and Grace Evangeline (Sells) Ford.

For many years, the Sells family were members of the *Fountain Baptist Church* located east of Tullahassee. It is Oklahoma's first Baptist Church originally founded as a mission in 1832. Descendants of the Sells family continued to attend and to support this church at the time Harry Sells was chosen as a member of *Broken Arrow' Hall of Fame in 1990.*

Harry Sells died at the age of 75 in 1930. His wife, Jane Sells died at the age of 79 in 1935. Their interment was in the *Jamison Cemetery* east of the *Fountain Baptist Church.*

(Permission to reprint by Broken Arrow Genealogy Society.)

Chapter 3

M. K. & T. Railroad

Many Creek Indians who were removed to this area had mixed ancestry from parents in the East. They adopted agricultural methods of farming from the English, Scots and French colonists and were very successful.

Numerous towns west of the Mississippi River were often developed because of trading posts which met the needs of people traveling these thousands of acres of grasslands. Texas cattlemen drove herds from Texas through Broken Arrow. Cattle was herded to Missouri and shipped from there by railroad to eastern stockyards. Among the most well-known and prosperous cattlemen in northeastern Oklahoma were the Perrymans. The Perrymans once lived east of Broken Arrow but migrated and were instrumental in founding *Tulsey Town*, now known as Tulsa.

A well-known trading post of the time was established by William F. Moore in 1874, and was located near the intersection of Tucson and Olive Streets in the vicinity of the *White Church and Cemetery* near the Creek Indian settlements. It was a good location because of the cattle crossing at the old *Wealaka Creek Indian School* where Leonard is located today. Goob Childers, a Creek Indian, operated a ferry to cross the Arkansas River there. This trading post was the site of the first post office in this area. Charles H. Thomas was appointed the first Postmaster.[37]

When the government opened central parts of the *Unassigned Lands of 1889* for non-Indian settlements with the passing of the *Organic Act in 1890*, it was named *Oklahoma Territory*. This was the beginning of the Oklahoma Land Runs, of which there were several. Adventurous people began coming from both northern and southern states to hopefully stake claims and acquire some undeveloped land.[38]

Many of Broken Arrow's early settlers came from several surrounding states. Among the early pioneers were the Hurd and McKenna families from Kansas. The Laws Brothers hailed from Tennessee. The McGechie family migrated from Scotland to Nebraska, then to Oklahoma Territory. Other families came from Missouri. The best-known pioneers who first settled in Elam, in the Aspen and Florence Streets area, came in 1901 from Huntsville, Arkansas. Biographies of the Brooks, Sanders and Williams Brothers' families appear in a later chapter.[39]

Besides a desire to own land, some of the draws that

---
37. Wise, Vignettes, 2
38. Debo, 333 cf.
39. Rhoades, 28.

brought people here were farming, oil, gas and coal mining. Coal mining had just begun by *Adams Creek Coal Company*, which was a subsidiary of the newly organized *Arkansas Valley Townsite Company*. It brought people from as far away as Ohio. The stockholders and board of directors were: Bowman, Darby, Lynde and W.S. Fears. Herman Galbreath was an agent for the company.[40]

Mining in this area was a hot topic of the day. Quality coal was being mined and delivered in Broken Arrow. Almost every issue of the *Broken Arrow Ledger* from 1903 on, mentioned a few lines about these first established coal mines, until their closing in 1946. The coal mining took place even before Elam was fully established. The first pits were located in the Evans community five miles east of Broken Arrow in Wagoner County on Kenosha Street. Some streets in east Broken Arrow were named for those communities.

The *Arkansas Valley Townsite Company* played an important role in the development of Broken Arrow. Provisions were being made, according to the *Creek treaty* of 1866, for another new railroad to be built in *Indian Territory*. Because the *Missouri, Kansas and Texas Railway Company (MK&T)* had built-out the north-south franchise, the Catoosa facility was already in existence. Now an east-west railroad franchise was needed to run toward Tulsa. With this area growing, there be-

---

40. Wise, Donald A., *Myriads of the Past, Colorful Broken Arrow History Told by Pioneers*, by Dora Esslinger, 3.

came more of a demand for shipment of cattle, corn, cotton and coal. Once the right-of-way was secured by *MK&T* to construct a railroad from Muskogee, plans were made to build a branch line which passed through the south part of Main Street in Broken Arrow, from Wybark to Osage Junction. In 1902 three townsites between Wybark and Tulsa were sold to the *Arkansas Valley Townsite Company*.

W. S. Fears, secretary of *Arkansas Valley Townsite Company*, was allowed to select one location of the three. After careful consideration and inspecting the railroad route that was proposed between the two towns, Fears chose a picturesque location near two high mounds, eighteen miles southeast of Tulsa. He named it Broken Arrow in honor of the Indian community by the same name.[41]

Selling lots in the new townsite began immediately. Fears, being well-versed in the law, knew warranty deeds to the property could not be given to the buyer because of restrictions that applied. Therefore, Fears gave a written agreement or quit claim deed to each person buying land. This promised the purchaser a legal title to the property when the Secretary of the Interior gave permission.

The *Dawes Commission* had allotted land to Stephen Franklin, a freedman and Billy Atkins, a Creek. Their

---
41. Rhoades, 25.

land made up a quarter section and was the principal portion W. S. Fears wanted for the new townsite. Because of restrictions about whether Indian allotted lands could be used for a townsite, Fears made a special trip to Washington to discuss the matter of getting legal title with Principal Chief Pleasant Porter and Senator Matthew Quay, a Delaware Indian from Pennsylvania. Fortunately, there was provision in the *Appropriation Act of March 3, 1903* that private parties could enter agreements of surveying and platting at their own expense when the stations were along the lines of the railroads.[42]

On October 16, 1902, the Federal Court at Muskogee approved an original plat and survey map drawn by S.A. Cobb, a civil engineer from the *Townsite Department of the Indian Office* in Muskogee. It is considered to be the date of the founding of Broken Arrow, and celebrated by our hometown as the date of its establishment. However, because of the government's change in procedures concerning the purchase of Indian land, it was one full year before the deed for the townsite was approved by secretary of the interior. The date of the deed reflects a date of October 22, 1903.[43]

---

42. Rhoades, 25.
43. Deeds. Western District, Indian Territory (Wagoner, 1902) I-D, 509.

Meet the BROKEN ARROW CENTENNIALS

WILLIAM SUMMERFIELD FEARS
(1869 – 1955)

William Summerfield Fears was a unique and creative young man. His personality was much more than just adventurous. He had several careers and jobs during his lifetime, two of which were from cowboy to businessman. He was born in Atlanta, Georgia on September 12, 1869 to Mattie E. Tidwell and Stockton Fears, who had served in the *Confederate Army*, was wounded and discharged as a Colonel.

W. S. FEARS

After the Civil War, the Fears family moved to Sherman, Texas where Stockton served three times as mayor. The family moved to Muskogee, Indian Territory. Young Will Fears was first involved with moving cattle herds along the *Chisholm Trail* from Texas to New Mexico with Pat Garrett, the lawman who shot Billy the Kid.

For a short time, young Will played professional baseball in the Texas League. He went to New York City and took several business courses.

He was appointed court recorder for William M. Springer, U.S. Judge for the *Northern District in Indian Territory*. Fears served as a secretary to Principal Chief Pleasant Porter of the Creek Nation. Working for Chief Porter later proved to be an important step in helping Broken Arrow become a townsite. Fears joined the *Rock Island Trust and Investment Company* in Muskogee in 1902 where he was Director and Secretary. This firm was involved in land speculation, developing townsites and resource exploration. To achieve these purposes, they organized the *Arkansas Valley Townsite Company,* the *Verdigris Valley Oil Company,* the *Adams Creek Coal Company* and the *Arkansas Valley National Bank*. Fears was a Director at *Arkansas Valley Bank* and Secretary of the *Arkansas Valley Townsite Company.*

Besides selecting the physical site for the townsite of Broken Arrow in 1902, Fears moved to Broken Arrow in 1903 and was instrumental as the Secretary of the *Arkansas Valley Townsite Company* in developing Fears Subdivision, a 40-acre tract, the first addition made to the town of Broken Arrow. He also served as Vice President of the *Arkansas Valley Bank*, as well as serving on Boards of various companies with his business partners.

In 1907 the holdings of the *Rock Island Trust and Investment Company* were divided. Fears purchased a farm where the Cedar Ridge Addition was later developed. He specialized in raising registered shorthorn cattle. In 1920 Fears became active in the real estate business in Tulsa.

He was married three times. Fears and his third wife, Blanche Randall, had one son, William S. Fears Jr. and a daughter, Mary Kathleen Fears.

W.S. Fears died at the age of 85 years on April 17, 1955, in Tulsa. He was interred in the *Greenhill Cemetery* in Muskogee, Oklahoma.

(Biographical information courtesy of Broken Arrow Genealogy Society.)

M.K. & T. Depot completed in 1903.

Chapter 4

From Elam to Main Street

Elam Historical Marker

At the same time Missouri, Kansas and Texas Railroad was making plans to lay tracks from Muskogee to Tulsa, four businessmen came to Indian Territory from Huntsville, Arkansas searching for new business opportunities. They selected land that William N. "Newt" Williams referred to "as the middle of a cotton patch." It seemed an ideal location, with fertile soil and native timber in abundance. They knew there were oil and gas leases in the area and coal was being strip mined from shallow pits just a few miles to the northeast. This land was owned by Elam B. Hodge, a brother to David M. Hodge and a member of the Perryman family. The businessmen named the settlement Elam in his honor. Elam is located on Florence Street, west of Aspen intersection, across the street from the new *Aspen Creek Early Childhood Center*. As in the business deals with the railroad in the townsite purchase, the U.S. Treaty stated that non-Indians could not acquire legal title to the lands in Indian Territory. It was agreed that Elam Hodge would give them a warranty deed when he acquired a clear title from the government.

These industrious businessmen made plans to build a mercantile store and cotton gin. Their new businesses were named *Brooks, Sanders and Williams Brothers*. The closest railroad facility for purchasing building materials was Catoosa. Lumber was hauled overland from Catoosa to the site of Elam by horse-drawn wagons. The Williams brothers built houses at Elam for their families who had remained in Arkansas.[44]

By 1902, Elam had developed into a self-sufficient settlement. Elam now consisted of a hardware store, two drug stores, a blacksmith shop, two dry good stores, a cotton gin and several residences. A post office was established on September 25, 1902 in the Williams' store and W.N. "Newt" Williams was appointed the postmaster.

W.N. Williams' House

The *MK&T* decided on a different route and tracks were being laid for the new railroad. Because the railroad would be tracking north instead of running alongside the Arkansas

---

44. Rhoades, 21-22.

River, as they anticipated, they were faced with making some important decisions. The business partners quickly realized, in order for their commerce to be successful, they would need to alter their plans. Not to be deterred, they devised a plan to be included in the development of this new township. One of the partners, Nathaniel Sanders was part of the group that surveyed for the railroad. Another partner, W.T. Brooks, had recently made the acquaintance of F.S. (Fitz Simmons) Hurd at a "coincidental" meeting, was also aware of the *MK&T* plans that were going forward.

MAIN STREET LOOKING SOUTH FROM BROADWAY (1903)

W. S. Fears, being a sensible businessman himself, knew the importance of establishing good relationships with experienced merchants. In order to initiate a strong bond among these new pioneers, Fears offered the Elam group their

Meet the BROKEN ARROW CENTENNIALS

choice of lots in the new townsite.

Remarkably, the day before the town plat was even completed, the Brady brothers' *O.K. Restaurant* began serving people before any other business. Taking advantage of the situation, they stretched a tent on south Main Street near the railroad right-of-way and began serving meals to the people who came looking for lots. As quickly as lots were available, people flocked to the new Broken Arrow townsite, ready to buy. The first businesses established were the *K. C. Barber Shop* owned by J.D. Shipman and the office of the *Hammond Lumber Company*. These merchants had begun preparing for this day and opened their stores on October 16, 1902, the same date Broken Arrow declared itself a new town. Within six months after the town plat was completed, more than two blocks of businesses had been opened.[45]

Local historian, Donald A. Wise described the beginnings of the new settlement in this way: "Although the new town of Broken Arrow started with tents which housed families and businesses, the community soon had several wooden buildings and homes completed by 1904."[46]

---

45. Rhoades, 29.
46. Wise, Donald A., *First Census (1904) of Broken Arrow, Oklahoma*, 1.

L-R: MAC, JAMES AND NEWT WILLIAMS

WILLIAM NEWTON WILLIAMS
(1866-1972)

MERIDA CALEB (Mac) WILLIAMS
(1868-1963)

Finding an ideal place in April, 1901, Newt Williams and his brother Mac partnered with Nat Sanders and W.T. Brooks. Avoiding the thousands of longhorn cattle grazing in the vicinity, they chose a site close to a cotton field and named it Elam. Their families remained in Arkansas until they built their businesses and houses. By 1902, they had succeeded in building a mercantile store, cotton gin, post office, homes and a few other businesses. Ironically, Newt was appointed Postmaster of Elam about a month before the new town of Broken Arrow was opened for new settlers.

When the men realized the *MK&T* track was being laid to the north, they knew the better opportunity would follow the railroad. In the spring of 1903, they put their mercantile buildings and homes on log rollers and used a tractor operated by steam to pull them into the new town of Broken Arrow. *Brooks, Sanders and Williams' Brothers Mercantile* building was placed at the northwest corner of Commercial and Main. The cotton gin was moved in 1904 and sold shortly thereafter. [47]

(Permission to reprint copyrighted article by Broken Arrow Ledger, BH Media Group and Tulsa World Media Company.)

NATHANIEL (NAT) L. SANDERS
(1865 – 1927)

From an article in the *Broken Arrow Ledger*, Thursday, February 10, 1927:

"This community was sorrowfully shocked last Saturday morning with the announcement from Tulsa that Nathaniel (Nat) L.

---

47. Wise, *Myriads*, 37.

Sanders had unexpectedly passed away at his desk in the office of the county assessor, where he occupied the responsible position of chief deputy. The summons came entirely without warning....

"Nat Sanders was for many years a highly respected and much honored citizen of Broken Arrow. His residence here dated back to the very organization of the town and continued without interruption until about four years ago when he removed to Tulsa. His residence in Tulsa County commenced at the little inland town of Elam in May, 1901. He traveled by wagon with W.N. Williams, M.C. Williams and W.T. Brooks with whom he associated himself in the mercantile business. With advent of the railroad and the platting of Broken Arrow townsite the firm moved its business here from Elam. A few years later Mr. Sanders disposed of his interests in the firm to R.C. Knight, but later returned to mercantile pursuits by organizing the company known as the *Sanders-Lancaster Company*. Sanders later became County Commissioner and served a two-year term. With the advent of the democratic administration of President Woodrow

"Nat" Sanders

Wilson (c. 1913), he accepted the appointment of postmaster in Broken Arrow for eight years. Although the last four years of his life were spent in Tulsa, he still retained property interests in Broken Arrow as well as a lively interest in community affairs. Among his possessions are the two brick business structures at the northwest corner of Main Street and Dallas Avenue, and the post office." Nat Sanders was 63 years old at the time of his death. His mother was Viola Tranquilla (Polk) Sanders, a direct descendant of President James K. Polk. His wife was Lutie. Their daughter was Ruth L. Sanders Hollingsworth and their granddaughter was Hazel Hollingsworth.

(Permission to reprint copyrighted article by Broken Arrow Ledger, BH Media Group and Tulsa World Media Company.)

WILLIAM THOMAS BROOKS
(1852 – 1940)

William Thomas, (W.T.) Brooks, Broken Arrow's first Postmaster, was around Broken Arrow from the very beginning. He was prominently connected with banking and merchandising. Because of his public life in Broken Arrow, his labors were a vital force in the development of his town. Brooks' life was always one of activity accompanied by gratifying results.

Life began for William Thomas Brooks on December 15, 1852 in Hawkins County, Tennessee. W.T. was the oldest of the eight children of Isabel (York) (1831-1898) and

WILLIAM THOMAS BROOKS

Lafayette Reed Brooks (1829-1899). The family moved to Washington County, Arkansas when he was six years old.

Brooks became a student at the University of Arkansas during the first year of its existence in 1872. He taught in the schools of Fayetteville, Arkansas, but he regarded this merely an initial step to other professional activity. It was his earnest desire and purpose to become a member of the bar. With this end in view he enrolled as a law student at the University of Michigan in Ann Arbor, where he graduated in 1875.

Brooks was in the banking business when he met a school teacher, Sarah Alice Routh (1859-1943). They married on July 4, 1879, in Hindsville, Arkansas, and were parents of five children: Ora Bell (1881-1966); Guy Lafayette (1888-1961); Roscoe Walton (1891-1961); Floy Josephine (1891-1982); and Ina (1894-1948).

Mr. Brooks served several terms as an U.S. Revenue Officer in Arkansas and had resided in six states, including Texas, Tennessee, Oklahoma, Michigan, Missouri and Arkansas. His profession led to his election to the Arkansas legislature, 1883 to 1889, as the only Republican from his district. He was always conversant with the vital questions and issues of the day and as a lawmaker closely studied the problems bearing upon the welfare of the State. During the Spanish-American War, he was commissioned as a colonel in the United States Army, but was not called upon to serve.

After the turn of the century, W.T. Brooks had new ideas as a land-owner and banker. He joined his friends from Arkansas in a new venture as they established Elam in *Indian Territory*. However, reportedly, in December of 1902 he had a chance meeting with F.S. Hurd and John Lonnberg when their buggies met between the new town of Broken Arrow and Catoosa. Brooks and the two Kansas City men agreed right there on the open prairie to start a bank in Broken Arrow. As a result of their meeting Brooks favored this area, perhaps because of the new railroad. Shortly afterward, he built one of the town's first adequate houses.

The postmaster's house was located on West Broadway across the street from the present location of the *Broken Arrow Tulsa County Public Library*. The house was there from 1902 until fairly recently. Charles Sanders, local developer, commented, "The South side of the house had a garage where Brooks kept his horse and wagon that he delivered mail in. The East side of the house had a door with a slot which people could put their mail in for him to deliver." He lived in this home until his death.

Having purchased the first two lots at North Main and Commercial, Brooks opened his first post office one door north of their mercantile store. The U.S. Post Office opened on December 17, 1902 with cracker barrels as mail cubicles. His oldest daughter Ora was his assistant. The rest of his family remained in Arkansas until 1903. The four families became the outstanding business leaders of the community.

DOORS OF OPPORTUNITY

Although William T. Brooks aspired to become a lawyer, his career experiences opened other doors. He saw the opportunity to invest in the Broken Arrow area sooner than the others. He was a wise investor and was talented in banking as well as having a spirit of entrepreneurship.

By 1904 Brooks and his wife built a new brick business building on the lot just north of the original post office. At the same time, Brooks was connected with *Traders and Planters Bank* whose door opened in December, 1902. Because of his acquaintance with F.S. Hurd, he was named Vice President, an office he held for eleven years. He eventually withdrew from his partnership of Brooks, Sanders and *Williams Brother's Mercantile Company* and began a mercantile business of his own.

He was the first President of the *Commercial Club*, forerunner of the *Chamber of Commerce*, when it was organized in 1903 to address the improvement of roads and plans for a schoolhouse. Brooks chaired the first meeting, which met to organize a school through private subscription. He also played a major role in the installation of the city's water system.[48]

It had been a source of pride to Mr. Brooks that Broken Arrow was always known as a peaceful town, lacking the rough elements characteristic of many Oklahoma towns in the early days. Although retired from the mercantile business due to his health, he continued to be avidly interested in all that concerned the city.

When the *Broken Arrow Ledger* reported Brooks' death on Thursday, January 18, 1940, the townspeople mourned this colorful pioneer from Elam to Main Street as a chapter closed on the Elam settlers. Mr. Brooks led a varied life. His proud figure defied his age of 87 years. The article detailed how Brooks passed away quietly at his home at 4 o'clock Monday afternoon. He died in one of his favorite rocking chairs after having made his daily visit and walk to the post office.

His obituary continued: "The funeral was held in the *First Presbyterian Church*, Wednesday afternoon at 2:30 with Rev. J. Edwin Kerry, Wagoner, Oklahoma, and Rev. L. Allen Holley conducting the services. *Barth's Funeral Home*

---

48. Rhoades, 29.

was in charge of arrangements. Burial was in *Park Grove Cemetery,* Broken Arrow. Business houses remained closed from 2:30p.m. to 3:30p.m. in tribute to the oldest pioneer of our town. Mr. Brooks had been a member of the Presbyterian Church for nearly thirty years and his was a consistent Christian life that won him the honor and unqualified regard of all who knew him. To his family he was a devoted husband and father, and to his friends a faithful, loyal companion.

Attending his funeral service were all five of his children: Mrs. M.G. Lewis of Farmington, Arkansas; Roscoe Brooks, Broken Arrow; Guy L. Brooks, who flew here by plane from his home in Pomona, California; Mrs. Floy Greene, Broken Arrow; and Mrs. Ina Kneale, Tulsa. Two sisters, Mrs. Lou Porter of Broken Arrow and Mrs. Ad Patrick of Ozark, Arkansas, were present at the last rites for Mr. Brooks."

The Tulsa scribe wrote of W.T. Brooks, "The world is full of things that man can do, but of them all, there's none more satisfying to an individual than that of helping to settle a new country, to build a city from a wilderness, to establish homes and churches and schools where people may live out their years peacefully and happily. So believed W.T. Brooks…"

Brooks' name could be found connected to about every civic activity for the betterment of our hometown. While in business circles Brooks had an ever-untarnished name. He had been active for more than three decades, and was named to the *1992 Broken Arrow Hall of Fame.*

(Permission to reprint copyrighted article by Broken Arrow Ledger, BH Media Group and Tulsa World Media Company.)

The Legacy Lives On

W.T. and Alice Brooks left a legacy in Broken Arrow. Floy Brooks Greene, Roscoe and Ina were known best by Broken Arrow residents. Roscoe, known more by his nickname "Peck Brooks" was also wellknown here for several decades. They were full of life and quite humorous. Floy and younger sister, Ina graduated from Broken Arrow High School in 1909 and 1910, respectively. Ina was mother to Jane Rogers, who married Clay McPherson. Jane graduated in 1935. Clay and Jane's daughters graduated from Broken Arrow High: Sally McPherson Neas and her husband, John Neas live in this area. Sharon McPherson Matthewson lives in Florida. Brooks' sister, Lou Brooks Porter and her husband, Zeb also raised their children here. Many Porter, Whiteley and Perry families are connected to the Brooks families. One Whiteley descendant, Hazel Whiteley, married H. Cecil Rhoades, who was one of the primary resources for this book.

The Rhoades' three children are the late Sharon Rhoades Mead Foster ('62), Jerry Rhoades ('65) and Janelle Rhoades Robison ('65). This family donated the home place land to the city next to Northeast School. *Rhoades Elementary School*, east of First Place on Midway Street, was renamed in their father's name.

BUSINESSES WERE BOOMING

The decisions these four Huntsville businessmen made proved to be perfect timing. *The Broken Arrow Ledger's* first edition was printed on April 23, 1903. By the time Broken Arrow was six months old, The *Ledger's* list of business houses included two hardware stores, two dry goods and groceries, three drug and gave a list of business houses including two hardwares, two dry goods and groceries, three drug and pharmacy stores, two banks, two lumber companies, a mercantile company, coal and gin company, grain elevator, two blacksmiths, four doctors and one hotel. Among these first businesses are some family names that are still recognizable today. Of course, the *Brooks, Sanders and Williams Brothers Mercantile* made its debut, as well as the *Williams' Brothers Gin,* a separate business.[49]

---

49. *Broken Arrow Ledger,* Broken Arrow, Indian Territory, April 23, 1903.

Cecil Rhoades compiled a roster: Nichols-Raup Hardware, Charles A. Nichols, manager; *Sprague and Parker Hardware; Lancaster and McAnally,* (dry goods, groceries and hardware); *Simmons Hotel,* Joseph Sylvester (J.S.) Simmons; G.L. *Holt Pharmacy; L. Waller Drugs; Broken Arrow Drug* operated by Lewis and Ash; *First State Bank,* L.D. and S.W. Marr; *Traders and Planters' Bank,* F.S. Hurd cashier; *Dickason-Goodman Lumber Company,* A.L. Wilson, manager; *Hammond Lumber Company,* H.H. Hill manager; *Hill Mercantile Company, Coweta Coal and Gin Company, Brown Elevator,* two blacksmith shops; C. Nagel and G.H. Trusler; Sol Jamison, *Elevator*; and *M.K.O., Restaurant.* Doctors were S.C. Parsons; R.S. Plumlee, A.J. Pollard, and F.H. Hollingsworth.[50]

Thus, began a new page of Broken Arrow history and gone were the memories of Texas cattle crossing this prairie land. In the spring of 1903, the community of Elam had begun a difficult but unique trek from their original homes to new adventures a few miles north. On April 16, 1903, the rail line reached Broken Arrow. By May, 1903, Broken Arrow's depot had completed construction. Broken Arrow citizens had two reasons to celebrate on July 4, 1903: America's Independence Day as well as the *MK&T* "Katy" Railroad's inaugural appearance - the first passenger train from Muskogee to Broken Arrow. Mrs. Mac C. Williams especially recalled the excitement as

---
50. Rhoades, 29.

MK & T "KATY" LOGO

a passenger herself on that first offical run. When the train arrived in Broken Arrow at 1:18 p.m., it was the highlight of Broken Arrow's first Independence Day celebration. W.W. Jones, the conductor was from Junction City, Kansas, and helped to make this a memorable day as there were hundreds of people at the station to greet them and celebrate its arrival. Even after that day, Saturdays and Sundays became a tradition and was customary to see who was coming and going, as well as to see who was staying.[51]

FINALE FOR ELAM

As more of the Elam people moved north to Main Street Broken Arrow, the little hamlet gradually dwindled. Mail service was finally discontinued at the Elam Post Office on September 28, 1906. After that, Broken Arrow Post Office provided postal service for the whole area.

BROKEN ARROW THRIVES

These pioneer families and others who came to settle in a new land between 1902 and early statehood, experi

---

51. Rhoades, 24.

THE WILLIAMS BROTHERS' REAL ESTATE OFFICE

enced the immense growth of this former prairie, cattle land, rolling hills and Indian mounds like few Oklahoma towns. The Elam families and many other territorial families from nearby states and further, came in droves when they heard about this new land "of plenty". It was only the beginning of how Broken Arrow came to thrive as well as it has for the last 100 years and longer. People still remember Williams brothers and W.T. Brooks because they lived long and prosperous lives in the new town they developed.

MERIDA CALEB (Mac) WILLIAMS
(1868 – 1963)

Mac Williams was elected mayor for both the 1911-13 and 1921-23 terms. As mayor, he signed the April 3, 1922 ordinance that specified names for Broken Arrow streets. Until then the streets were only called by letters.

He was a member of the local Masonic Lodge, the Presbyterian Church, Akdar Shrine and early-day civic committees. Mac Williams died in 1963.

MERIDA CALEB "MAC" WILLIAMS

(Permission to reprint copyrighted article by Broken Arrow Ledger, BH Media Group and Tulsa World Media Company.)

WILLIAM NEWTON WILLIAMS
(1866 – 1972)

Williams was an alderman in 1906, which was similar to a city councilman. He was also a founder of the *Commercial Club* and elected president of the organization in 1909. He and 21 others raised funds in 1909 to purchase land for *Haskell State School of Agriculture*.

Meet the BROKEN ARROW CENTENNIALS

Williams was postmaster from 1922 until 1934. He led the *Chamber of Commerce* as president in 1933 and 1934 and was elected mayor in 1936. He was active in civic and Republican Party affairs and known as *Mr. Republican*. Williams was a member of the *Methodist Episcopal Church South*.

"NEWT" WILLIAMS

In 1931, Williams became a partner in the community-owned *Ledger Publishing Company*. He was a founder of the *Broken Arrow Building* and *Loan Association* and served as a director for 50 years.

WILLIAM NEWTON WILLIAMS

The Williams brothers' businesses flourished at their new location. Eventually, they sold the general store opened a real estate and insurance office.

Newt Williams retired at the age of 78 and celebrated his 100th birthday at a party given by the community. He voluntarily surrendered his driver's license at age 105 and died at age 106 in 1972. Williams' name was placed in the *Broken Arrow Hall of Fame in 1991.*

(Biographical information courtesy of Broken Arrow Genealogical Society.)

The Legacy Lives On

Mostly everyone connected with *The Museum Broken Arrow* or the *Broken Arrow Historical Society* knows Martha Williams, or at least knows who she is. Martha is the granddaughter of W.N. "Newt" Williams. She is the daughter of their youngest son, Robert. She is well-aware of the many family stories as well as a great deal of Broken Arrow history. She enjoys attending exhibit openings and events at the museum. She is an active historical society member. Martha is a pleasure to know and with whom to work. She is avid about "keeping Broken Arrow history alive".

Meet the BROKEN ARROW CENTENNIALS

Broken Arrow, Oklahoma (1905) Indian Territory

The Town Adds Homes to the Frontier (ca. 1906)

Chapter 5

The First Ladies of Broken Arrow
'City of Roses and Sparkling Water'

The wives of the Huntsville businessmen were definitely good matches for their husbands. Each woman was exceptionally talented. As wives and mothers, they focused their unique abilities in the areas of church, school, and for those in need of financial aid. The new town was in drastic need in all these concerns. And, if that's not enough, they were also amazing entrepreneurs.

SARAH ALICE BROOKS
(1859 – 1943)

Although Sarah Alice Brooks was always referred to as Mrs. W.T. Brooks, she was an influence on the development and progress of Broken Arrow, apart from that of her husband. Once she arrived in Broken Arrow, Mrs. Brooks occupied several social positions and found a variety of her ac-

SARAH ALICE BROOKS

quaintances already here.

Sarah Alice Routh was born in Lincoln County, North Carolina in 1859. She first attended school in Huntsville, Arkansas and afterward was a student in the University of Arkansas at Fayetteville. When her college course was completed, she devoted five years teaching in Hindsville, Arkansas.

On the 4th of July, 1879, W.T. Brooks was united in marriage to Sarah Alice Routh (1859-1943) in Hindsville. Nicknamed Allie, she was the daughter of Martha J. Boyd (1837-1922) and Levi Walton Routh (1833-1900) of Huntsville.[52] After marriage, she taught for about five more years.

Her husband was a financial investor who established the village of Elam with three Huntsville associates. All but Brooks brought their families to *Indian Territory* in 1901. The men then relocated to Broken Arrow, and Mr. Brooks readied a new home. Since there were no schools for white children in the Territory, Allie Brooks waited to bring their children - Ora, Roscoe, Guy, Floy and Ina, until school was out for the summer in 1903. The family was reunited in the home in Block 40 on Broadway, close to the F.S. Hurd home.

Almost immediately after arrival Mrs. Brooks began working to start a school and the Presbyterian Church. She was particularly active in its missionary department. Main-

---

52. https://www.findagrave.com/memorial/10252870/sarah-alice-brooks

ly through her efforts, a *Presbyterian Sunday School* was started. She also assisted her husband in the post office.

Alice Brooks was an organizer and first president of the *Ladies School Aid Society* and helped give many a dinner to raise money for a school. An eloquent speaker, she often read papers at literary meetings. She was an active member of the *American Federation of Women's Clubs,* the *Order of the Eastern Star* and a charter member of the *Self Culture Club*. Besides being very active in organizations that promoted Broken Arrow, she was also an astute business woman. Mrs. Brooks watched Broken Arrow grow from a few straggling shacks and tents. As part of that growth, she became owner of one of the early brick business buildings on Main Street. *Star Jewelers* is now located in the building W.T. and Mrs. Brooks had built around 1904.

Mrs. Brooks went into business on Main Street with Mrs. Mac Williams and Mrs. Nat Sanders, who had moved from Elam. They opened the *Crystal Theatre* where the *First National Bank* parking lot is now located. The theater became the hub of the social life in Broken Arrow for several years. Both Hollywood films and hometown talent shows were presented. Silent films were shown in the early days of the theater. Even graduation exercises were held at the theater. Mrs. Brooks managed the theater until 1933.

Mr. and Mrs. Brooks were parents of three daughters and

two sons: Mrs. M. G. Lewis of Farmington, Arkansas, Mrs. Floy Greene of Broken Arrow, Mrs. A. D. (Ina) Kneale of Tulsa, Guy L. Brooks of Pomona, California and Roscoe W. Brooks of Broken Arrow.

(Biographical information courtesy of Broken Arrow Genealogical Society.)

CLEO E. LOWRY WILLIAMS
(1875 – 1955)

Cleo Williams joined her husband in Elam as soon as he had suitable housing ready. The trip here was by train to Catoosa, followed by a bumpy ride overland to Elam.

Cleo was a talented musician and colorful writer. She helped start the *Presbyterian Church* and was choir director for more than 30 years.

Mrs. Williams was a charter member of the *Self Culture Club, The Order of Eastern Star, Daughters of the American Revolution* and a founder and board member of the library. During a 1955 anniversary program celebrating the 50th anniversary of OES in Broken Arrow, she was presented her 50-year pin.

Her musical talents and creativity were put to use early in the town's history. The first Fourth of July program in 1903 was to feature out-of-town speakers and entertainers. It was the day that the first official passenger train came to town. It rained and every speaker and entertainer failed to come in on the train as expected. A local minister gave an impromptu talk and Mrs. Williams came to the rescue with a musical program. She gathered up youngsters of the new town and they delighted the crowd with their songs.

CLEO E. LOWRY WILLIAMS

As an avid supporter of beautifying our city, Mrs. Williams was chairman of the *Self Culture Club* committee. She helped the club acquire land on Iola Street, between Elm Place and Date Street by paying the back taxes for the property owner. The club purchased additional lots for the park project, then donated the land to the city, which was named for Mrs. Sieling.

Meet the BROKEN ARROW CENTENNIALS

Mrs. Williams was a graduate of Tulsa University. She was a member of the high school faculty as music instructor for several years and did private tutoring. Throughout her career, her girls' high school chorus frequently entertained at social and civic affairs. Among her many talents was use of humor in creative writing. Mrs. Williams wrote a paper for the *Self Culture Club's Pioneer Day* about the history of Broken Arrow in 1907. It has been repeated and published several times through the years. Parts of it will appear throughout this book. Here she described their move:

> "It seems a long time since we moved to Broken Arrow; perhaps it is because there have been so many, many changes; perhaps, because we have had so many ups an downs, principally downs, that time seems so long, for it has been only five years.

> "We moved to Broken Arrow April 11, 1903, when the place was a mere village of tents. We didn't move on the train for there wasn't even a track laid then, and we didn't move in wagons as people usually do in this country, but we moved in our house with all our belongings. We started from Elam, four and a half miles southwest, where we had lived two years. At 9 o'clock one Wednesday morning. A steam tractor was hitched to our two-room house and traveled at the rate of one-and-a-quarter miles a day until we landed safely, Friday afternoon on the lots we now occupy.

"Of the families who were here at that time few are left to tell the tale; perhaps the families of Sprague, Galbreath, Plumlee, Estill, Orcutt, Marr, G.L. Holt, Sanders, Glick and Williams and a few others. Others were coming in all the time, however, among them Brooks, Pollard, Parkinson, Ed Dalton, Allen, Abbot, Hurd and others. Many were the pleasant times we spent together, enjoying each other all the more because we were all strangers in a strange land.

"It was not all smooth sailing either during those first days. There were but few wells, water was scarce, vegetables could scarcely be gotten at all, the meat that we could get could hardly be eaten, there was no school for our children: once in a while church services would be held upstairs over the old store of *Orcutt & Addison* but seldom. Then those of us who had invested in real estate did so with fear and trembling as we could get no good title to our lots and we did not know at what time the *allotment land owner* [sic] would pop up and throw us out of house and home."

Mrs. Williams was a direct descendent of President James K. Polk and is a great niece to Nat Sanders' mother, Viola Polk Sanders.

(Permission to reprint copyrighted article by Broken Arrow Ledger, BH Media Group and Tulsa World Media Company.)

IDA KNIGHT WILLIAMS
(1871 – 1961)

NEWT WILLIAMS AND
IDA M. KNIGHT

Ida Williams came from Huntsville, Arkansas to the Elam area of *Indian Territory* in 1901 to join her husband, Newt, and his brother Mac. The families moved their houses to Broken Arrow from Elam. Furnishings and occupants made the entire trip inside the house.

Mrs. Williams was a charter member of the *Self Culture Club,* on the library board with Cleo Williams, her sister-in-law, and helped establish the downtown *Sieling Park*. She was also a member of the *Pioneer Club*, the *Women's Christian Temperance Union* and *First United Methodist Church*.

Ida Williams brought a refinement to this new town, both in her very proper dress for a lady of that time and as hostess to parties and receptions in her home. She was active in the *School Aid Society* and other fundraising organizations to benefit church and community. When she died in 1961, she had been married to Newt Williams for 71 years.

(Permission to reprint copyrighted article by Broken Arrow Ledger, BH Media Group and Tulsa World Media Company.)

FERN HUTCHINSON SIZER
(1879 – 1966)

This educator is not a familiar name in most Broken Arrow histories but for a decade she helped set the foundation for the society and education of this young town.

Her husband, Dr. L.J. Sizer, was an early-day dentist here. His practice was located over the post office. Mrs. Sizer taught in the high school, was principal from 1907 until she joined the faculty of *Haskell State Agriculture School* as the Domestic Science teacher in 1913.

In 1908 she helped arrange the graduation ceremony at the opera house for the first graduating class of *Broken Arrow High School*. She later returned to the high school classroom as the German language instructor. Soon the tight budget of the school forced the board to drop German and Mrs. Sizer then went to Coweta to teach.

In October of 1912 she organized the first *Camp Fire Girls* group here and later

FERN SIZER

added two more groups. She was the guardian for the older group. When she went to the agricultural school, her *Camp Fire Girls* followed her. A band instructor came to the school in 1913 and formed a girls' band. Fourteen of the sixteen band members were in Mrs. Sizer's group.

Mrs. Sizer was an unsuccessful candidate for *Tulsa County Superintendent* in 1914 An article in later years listed her as a former county school superintendent but this has not been confirmed at this time.

Mrs. Sizer was a charter member of the *Self Culture Club* and was the first one to hold the office of President. She and Mrs. Daniel Boone (Mildred McIntosh) Childers were active in planning dinners to finance the town's first fire wagon and the first library.

Fern Sizer was an orator and vocalist in most of the early benefit and cultural programs.

(Biographical information courtesy of Broken Arrow Genealogical Society.)

LADIES' SELF CULTURE CLUB
(1905 – 1940)

"Social Club organized in 1905 by Broken Arrow women" was the title of an article printed in the *Broken Arrow Ledger* on August 2, 1988 by historian Donald Wise as a Special article. It reads:

"The women of Broken Arrow organized a club in the fall

of 1905 to promote culture and to become involved in local civic affairs.

"Seventeen women met at the home of Mrs. W.N. Williams and adopted a constitution and bylaws for the proposed club. The name selected for this women's organization was the *Broken Arrow Self Culture Club.*

"According to the first published club program book, 1906-1907, meetings were held on alternate Fridays at members' homes from 3-5p.m. They studied and discussed famous authors and poets, their respective books and poems.

"Besides discussions and writings, club members held special observances such as *Presidents' Day, Bible Day, Patriotism Day* and *Sunset Day* for the elderly women and members' mothers.

"Members were restricted to a maximum number of 25 and each member was given an assignment to lead the discussions.

"The aim of the Club was "the attainment of a higher plane of life through broad culture, free discussion and mutual helpfulness." The Club emblem was the Mistletoe and the Club colors were green and white. Their motto was 'There is so much good in the worst of us and so much bad in the best of us that it behooves none of us to speak ill of the rest of us.'

Meet the BROKEN ARROW CENTENNIALS

"The Club members not only enriched their lives with the study of the classics, they also became involved in local civic affairs. The women's husbands were active businessmen and the leaders of the community, so the Club members had some influence in the civic affairs of Broken Arrow.

"One of the Club's first civic projects was to establish a library which eventually became the *Broken Arrow Public Library*. Another project was to purchase a tract of land in 1938 to establish a park named *Sieling Park* in honor of one of their members. This park is located one block east of Elm Place between West Iola and West Hartford Streets. They also participated in a clean-up of the *Park Grove Cemetery* and promoted the building of a better road to it; established a children's wading pool on the portion of the land now occupied by the present *City Hall*, planted trees and roses to help beautify the landscape of the Broken Arrow community.

"As the members became older, some were replaced by younger persons. However, by the 1940's, the Club became defunct. Over the 35 years of operation, the Club had succeeded in bringing some culture to Broken Arrow and had made some lasting contributions to the civic affairs of the community."

(Permission to reprint copyrighted article by Broken Arrow Ledger, BH Media Group and Tulsa World Media Company.)

The First Ladies of Broken Arrow

Photo Courtesy of The Museum Broken Arrow

CULTURE CLUB CHARTER MEMBERS (1905)

Front left: MISS DORA SULLIVAN (ESSSLINGER), MISS FANNIE LACY (GARRETT), MISS LELIA DALTON (BAILEY), W.N. (IDA) WILLIAMS AND MRS. U. J. POLLARD.
Second Row: MESEDAMES SHIELDS, HERSHBERGER, JOHN TENNY *(Treasurer)*, L.J. (FERN) SIZER *(President)*, GEORGE H. FOSTER *(Vice President)* AND A.E. BENSON *(Secretary)*.
Third row: MESEDAMES M. MCCOY, W.T. (ALICE) BROOKS, J.N. SHIPPEY, E.P. HINTON, H.H. SNIDER, N.L. (LUTIE) SANDERS AND ALLEN.
Back row: MESEDAMES C.L. ROBERTSON, M.C. (CLEO) WILLIAMS, J.B. PARKINSON, ED DALTON, MIKE MCKENNA, MRS. E.T. NEIBLING AND MISS ANNIE RANSOM *(primary school teacher)*.
Not pictured: MISS ORA BROOKS, MRS. G.W. HORTON, MRS. WILLIAM KIRKPATRICK, MISS ELIZABETH LOPP, MISS OLIVE SPURR AND MRS. WILLIAM SPRAGUE.

Meet the BROKEN ARROW CENTENNIALS

Main Street Businesses (ca. 1904)
Broken Arrow, Indian Territory

Bower & Brown Elevator (1904)

Chapter 6
Territorial Days

These courageous pioneers embarked upon an exciting venture for their businesses and the families, with visions of a new and brighter future. Their combined foresight gave a cohesiveness to their belief in success, although their plans and ideas may have differed. News traveled back home about this new frontier, and its main sources of income, which in addition to coal mining, included agricultural development, mercantile business and banking. Soon, family members of those who arrived first, joined them. The excitement of new beginnings spread like wildfire, and as if beckoned, they came from near and far.

JOHN ADAM BARTH
(1860 – 1963)

John Adam Barth was born 14 February 1860 in St. Louis, Missouri, the son of German immigrants Elizabeth Ahms and John Barth. He was married to Talitha Herthel on 12 November 1882 in Barton County, Kansas.

For ten years Barth was manager of an *E.R. Moses*

Meet the BROKEN ARROW CENTENNIALS

Mercantile Co. store in Claflin, Kansas. In 1901 his father died while visiting in Germany. Using his inheritance and his business experience John A. Barth came to Broken Arrow, *Indian Territory* in a covered wagon in 1903 and opened a two-story mercantile business on Main Street, between Commercial and Dallas. He carried everything needed to furnish a new home, along with hardware, harness, saddles and guns. The family lived above the store during the first years. In 1905 he enlarged the original structure and in 1906 built a brick front building next door where Mrs. Barth had a millinery shop. A wooden sign from one of the buildings now hangs in the *Broken Arrow Historical Society Museum.*

Barth also sold coffins. As was common in early times the local furniture store was also the funeral parlor. The earliest Broken Arrow death records were recorded by Barth's between 1912 and 1919.

Barth believed in Broken Arrow and influenced Kansas friends to move here. He was a strong supporter of education and was one of the businessmen who signed a bond to borrow money for the construction of *Haskell State School of Agriculture.* He was also a committee member for *Cornerstone Day* in 1910, as well as a member of the *Masonic Lodge.*

John and Talitha Barth were the parents of five children. Lillie who died at the age of three, Talitha Barth Standring (1885-1968); Frankie Barth Woodward (1887-1973); Leon John Barth (1894-1974); and Dorothy Barth Warterfield.

Talitha Herthel Barth died 25 July 1944. Her husband retired from the mercantile store in 1945 and lived in the home on Broadway until his death on 29 January 1963, two weeks prior to his 103rd birthday. He was Broken Arrow's oldest citizen. Services were held at *Memorial Park Cemetery Chapel* in Tulsa. The Barth's are buried in lots John purchased when the cemetery was founded.

JOHN ADAM BARTH

John Barth's daughter Frankie was mother to John's grandson, Donald E. (Woody) Woodward (Broken Arrow,'41) who married Mary Riseling, daughter of Mable Peterson Riseling, and also Charlie Peterson's neice. Mable Riseling was a 1920 Broken Arrow graduate; Charlie was owner of *Warehouse Market*. Mary and her sister, Betty Riseling Kellam (Don) are living at this writing, both in their mid-90's. Mary remembers J.A., Woody's grandfather, as a kind elderly man. Woody and Mary Woodward have two children: Donald E., Jr. and Deborah (Debbie) S. Cordell, whose family lives in town.

(Biographical information courtesy of Broken Arrow Genealogical Society.)

ARTHUR BETSEY (A. B.) HUBBLE
(1880 – 1963)

A. B. Hubble

A.B. Hubble was multi-talented and worked as an engineer, teacher, physician, civic servant and expert fisherman. This same man flipped the switch that turned on the lights in Broken Arrow late in 1906. A. B. came to town to visit his brother in 1904 and stayed to assist in the construction of the electric plant and to string the first lines.

Except for the short time he spent on the Muskogee water

Territorial Days

A. B. HUBBLE IN HIS OFFICE

plant, Hubble was on the job at the *Broken Arrow Electric Light Company,* then later for *Public Service* until his retirement in 1946. At that time, Clayton Bomar came to town to take over as *Public Service* manager.

As a Kentucky lad, Hubble taught country school for three years, then entered *Centre College* for a year and studied medicine for three years. He left school with a temporary permit to practice medicine, which he did for three years. Out of the hundreds of patients treated during that time, only three died. He became discouraged with his practice, slung his pill kit in a corner and back to college he went, this time to study engineering at the *University of Kentucky.*

In 1946 he explained that years ago he gave up medical practice in favor of electricity years ago for two reasons. First, there were too many night calls from the stork and too much bumpy buggy travel. Second, he said that he could tinker with a turbine and if it still didn't go, he could give it a kick and try again the next day. With medical doctoring, he said, "If you lose 'em once, they're lost."

Ninety-six customers took electrical service the first year. By 1910, Hubble was office manager, plant engineer, trouble-shooter, all wrapped up in one. Hubble "trouble-shot" the whole town, lugging his tools around in a wheelbarrow. He read meters, connected service, made ice and was a one-man line crew.

But the "old doctor" didn't get away from night calls. He put in more late night and all-night vigils with sick engines in the old days of the putt-putt generators that he would have as Dr. Hubble.

For eight years, he worked every day until midnight, then went back to the plant at 4:30a.m. to cook up ice in the icehouse at the electric plant. Seldom did he have time to get to the fishing banks of area rivers, his favorite pastime. At one time, the city threatened to cancel the franchise because of the dilapidated state of the ice machinery. In the end, Hubble saved the business for *Public Service* by putting in a new ice plant.

Territorial Days

Through the years, Hubble had his turn as president of the *Chamber of Commerce* and got a "big kick" out of *Rooster Day*. His name was on most every civic committee that was for the betterment of the town. Elizabeth Hubble also had an impact on Broken Arrow. She delivered his supper during those years of almost around-the-clock work. Often, she had to chase him down out on the line. Sometimes helping with the line work. She read meters and took care of collections. She also did her share of civic work and was in charge of the canning kitchen and the school hot lunch program which were sponsored by *Big Brothers* during the Great Depression.

The medical profession's loss was Broken Arrow's gain "Mr. Electricity" kept the lights shining over town for 40 years.
(Biographical information courtesy of Broken Arrow Genealogical Society.)

BROKEN ARROW ELECTRIC LIGHT COMPANY

DR. ONIS FRANKLIN
(1882 – 1963)

The year was 1904 when a young man came to Broken Arrow to begin his career as a medical doctor. That young man was Dr. Onis Franklin, who hailed from Tennessee, where he was born and raised. Dr. Franklin got his medical education at the University of Tennessee Medical College. His parents were David C. Franklin (1855-1937) and Nettie B. Franklin (1862-1917). In 1905 the doctor married Miss Lena Singleton; they had two children, Lois and Ewing.

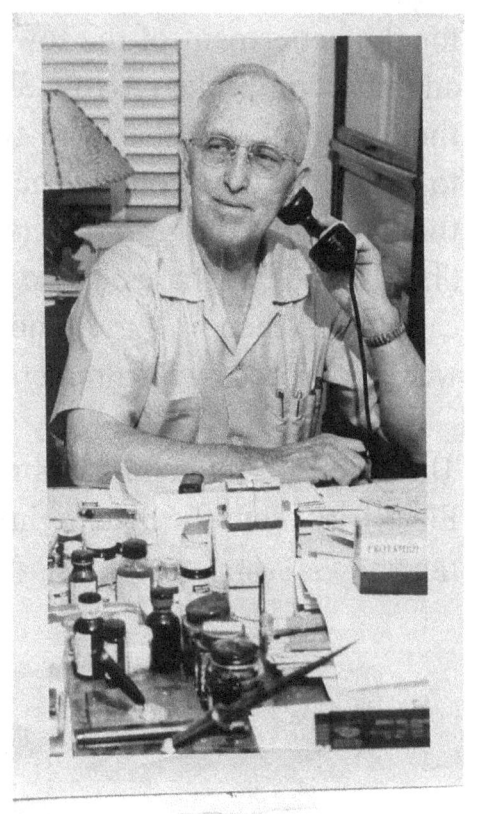

Dr. Onis Franklin

The new Dr. Franklin decided to settle and begin his practice in the *Fry Community,* west of town, but in 1910 moved his family back to Broken Arrow. Dr. Franklin practiced at several locations in the town, the first being upstairs in the new *First National Bank building* at Main and Commercial Streets. Neither of these locations met Dr. Franklin's expectations and after a short time he decided to close them. Although he had an office the majority of his patients were treated in their homes.

It was not unusual for him to perform surgical procedures on the kitchen table under kerosene lamps in those early days, since there was not an adequate hospital yet established in town. He traveled by horseback to his house calls and sometimes drove a wagon. He moved his practice upstairs in a building which later became home of the *Nusho Movie Theater*. He served in the United States Army during World War I as a 1st Lieutenant in the *Army Medical Corp*. After the war Dr. Franklin attended Tulane University for some post graduate work to update new medical procedures.

In 1942 Dr. Franklin and his son, Samuel Ewing (S.E.), now also a doctor, designed and built a modern hospital at 112 North Main in Broken Arrow, which met their every expectation. Dr. Onis continued to serve the Broken Arrow community from this facility until his death in 1963. In fact, while he was hospitalized in his last days, he would get out of his bed and walk through the hospital to treat and care for his patients also in the hospital.

The *University of Tennessee Medical College* recognized his 50 years of service to the community, presenting him with a 50-year pin. He was also honored by his peers from the *Tulsa Medical Association as a Doctor of the Year*. The *Broken Arrow Chamber of Com*merce gave him the title of "Outstanding Citizen" and the City proclaimed "Dr.

Meet the BROKEN ARROW CENTENNIALS

Onis Franklin Day" when he was praised by many of his patients and friends, and his name was added to the *Broken Arrow Hall of Fame, 1991.*

One of Onis Franklin's hobbies was raising and racing horses. Many of his horses won many races at the local fairgrounds and more often than not, brought home the big purse. Dr. Franklin and his son, Dr. S.E. Franklin, practiced medicine and served the community for over 60 years including time at the *Franklin Hospital* on Main Street. The building is now the home of the *Military History Center.*

In the early 1970s a new full-service hospital was built south of town on South Elm and named *Franklin Memorial Hospital* to honor the Franklin doctors. Dr. Onis Franklin died in 1963 and was laid to rest next to his wife Lena, in *Park Grove.* He was also preceded in death by his daughter, Lois Cluck, in an automobile accident in 1930. Dr. S.E. Franklin passed away on August 16, 1977, in Tulsa, due to a heart attack.

Dr. Onis Franklin

(Biographical information courtesy of Broken Arrow Genealogical Society.)

The Legacy Lives On

Dr. S.E. Franklin's son, Samuel Harry Franklin (1938-2016): a gifted engineer, "Sam" worked at Braden Winch then founded Samson Scales in 1971. He designed, manufactured, and sold world-wide. There are still Franklin family descendants in Tulsa area.

OK ERNEST MORROW
(1886 – 1957)

The J.B. Morrow family came to Broken Arrow in 1904 from Tennessee when their son, "OK" was a teenager. Young Morrow worked as a clerk at the *Neibling Store* and later was employed as a typesetter and printer for a contract company, as he traveled throughout the Midwest selling billboard space. In 1926 Morrow purchased a variety store on Main

OK Ernest Morrow

Street and called it *Morrow's Five and Ten Cents Store*. Ernest and Bertha Morrow were well-known in the community.

Business went very well until the Great Depression hit. During those slow times Morrow and a friend, Mr. Turley, who owned a cotton gin, spent hours playing dominoes in the 25 x 90 foot "Five and Dime".

Business was never slow around the time school started - Morrow handled the schoolbooks. Residents often stood in line on the first day of school to get books and supplies.

In his later years Morrow was described as a very distinguished looking man with lots of white hair, who used a long black cigarette holder.

In 1951, Morrow sold his store to his daughter, Verna, and her husband, James Aaron Burdette. Following her husband's death, Verna continued to run the store on Main Street until she closed it in the 1990's. Under the Burdettes the store was associated with the *Ben Franklin Chain*.

The Burdettes added *Globe Office Supply and Copy Center* across the street from *Ben Franklin*. Their son, Jim Burdette carried on the printing tradition of his grandfather at *Globe Office* until recent years. Morrow was added to the *Broken Arrow Hall of Fame* in 1996.

Territorial Days

MORROW'S STORE BECAME BEN FRANKLIN 5 & 10

Ernest Morrow's daughter, Verna, graduated from Broken Arrow High School in 1946. She and her husband, Jim Burdette have three children: Joye Hawkins ('72); Jim Burdette ('74); and Susanne Leonard ('79).

(Biographical information courtesy of Broken Arrow Genealogical Society.)

Meet the BROKEN ARROW CENTENNIALS

FITZ S. HURD
(ca. 1868 – 1955)

December 1902, F.S. Hurd and John Lonnberg drove a team of horses into a struggling prairie community called Broken Arrow, seeking an agricultural community to start a bank. They had previously investigated all of the land from Vinita and Nowata south to Okmulgee and decided Broken Arrow had greater possibilities for agricultural development. Lots were purchased where the *First National Bank* of Broken Arrow now stands.

Fitz Simmons "F. S." Hurd

They returned to Kansas City to buy furniture, fixtures and stationery. A huge square-door safe was also purchased and shipped to Catoosa, the nearest railroad point.

Meantime, *Traders and Planters Bank* established in the townsite company's office was ready for business on December 23, 1902. Hurd was cashier and later was named president of the bank. He took the first shipment of money from the express office, some three thousand dollars in currency and silver, in anticipation of the safe arriving that day. But it did not arrive; the missing strong box spilled in a nearby creek with "the wagon's wheels extending toward the skies." Three days were required to get the safe into the new bank's office. In the meantime, Hurd carried the cash in a satchel, keeping it with him, even when sleeping at the *J.S. Simmons' Hotel*. He slept in a large room surrounded by 20 strangers, all who were sleeping on the floor. He slept with his six-gun in his hand and one eye open all that night.

TRADERS AND PLANTERS BANK

F.S. HURD AT THE TELLER WINDOW

(Permission to reprint copyrighted article by Broken Arrow Ledger, BH Media Group and Tulsa World Media Company.)

ALVIN MARVIN LAWS
(1885 – 1957)

Laws came to Broken Arrow in 1903 with other family members to start a mercantile establishment. He and his brothers Leonard and James were stockholders in all three local banks: the *Arkansas Valley, First National* and *First State*. They built the red-brick business building on Main Street south of the old *First State Bank* in 1904.

ALVIN MARVIN LAWS

Marvin or "Murphy" started as a cashier of *Arkansas Valley* and retired from the bank 53 years later as vice president and director. He retired only six days before his death in 1957.

In 1922 he and his wife, Ruth Harlan (Malone) Laws,[53] moved into their new house at 726 North Main. He walked to work each day and carried coins and candy in his pockets for children he met. He often stopped at the meat market to get scraps for the dogs he saw on the street. He enjoyed playing bridge and fishing.

---

53. Find-a-Grave, Laws: www.findagrave.com/memorial/10256977

LAWS BUILDING — DUNLAP BROTHERS STORE

During the Great Depression he was one of the charter directors of *Big Brothers Club*, founded in 1934 to provide eyeglasses for children. With Laws' help the club grew to provide clothing, medical aid, holiday baskets, free school lunches and a canning kitchen to aid needy families. Frequently he made personal loans to families unable to qualify for bank loans. His father, George Washington Laws, signed the bond in 1909 to secure the loan for the building of *Haskell State School of Agriculture.*

Murphy was grand treasurer *of Broken Arrow Lodge #243, AF&AM* that guided the school's cornerstone laying ceremony. Laws was a member of the *Chamber of Commerce,* inducted into the *Broken Arrow Hall of Fame* in 1993.

(Biographical information courtesy of Broken Arrow Genealogical Society.)

Meet the BROKEN ARROW CENTENNIALS

Marvin and Ruth Laws had a son named Joe whose wife was Betty. Joe and Betty had two sons, Steve and the late Douglas Laws. Joe's boys attended school in Tulsa. Steve and Linda Jones Laws have two daughters. Theresa Laws Kiger and her husband Ky Kiger have two daughters, Kabry and Kally. Andrea Laws Byrd and her husband Bryan Byrd have two sons, Kaden and Troy. Steve is a career builder and developer in the Tulsa and Broken Arrow area. He and his family returned to his roots and has enjoyed restoring his grandfather Marvin's home.

W. P. (WARNER POWELL) FRAKER
(1861 – 1942)

Warner Powell (W.P.) Fraker purchased a controlling interest in a pioneer Broken Arrow bank in its infancy. At a time when a cashier was usually one of the bank shareholders, at age 43, Fraker served as cashier of *First State Bank*. Warner and his wife, Lovina Jane ("Jenny") Wells Fraker (1859-1930) had arrived in Broken Arrow by rail in 1903.[54] Having married in 1889, the couple spent Oklahoma time in Union Township, Canadian County where he had been a

---

54. https://www.findagrave.com/memorial/10256731/lovina-jane-fraker.

merchant before arrival in Broken Arrow.(55)

FIRST STATE BANK — BANK ROBBERY ATTEMPT

The bank was distinguished in the earliest months by an unsuccessful bank robbery attempt. Felons placed so much dynamite to blow open the safe, that it blew out the front windows. In 1904, Fraker moved the wooden structure with its sheet metal front from Main Street to Commercial Street, where he ran his bank until a new structure was completed.

A fine new brick building was built on the southwest corner of Main and Commercial. Then, Fraker must have surprised everyone. Even though he was promoted to president, on December 30, 1911, Fraker left bank management for soil management. This Tennessee native had always wanted

---
55. 1900 Federal Census, Union, Canadian County, Oklahoma, 15.B.

to get out into the open air, out to the bluegrass pastures. In order to do that, he sold a block of bank stock. Economic concerns brought Fraker back into the business for a short time, but he completely closed the doors in 1922, saying "the town does not need three banks."

Fraker then concentrated on the soil he loved with experimental fields of bluegrass and alfalfa and introduced a fine line of registered Shorthorns to the area. He was devoted to helping agriculture students and *FFA Chapter* members. Often county and state fair prize winners, shown by local students, came from Fraker's herd. He was identified with the origination of the *Tulsa County Fair,* which was first held in Broken Arrow.

Better farming methods, finer livestock, better parks, good city improvements, higher educational facilities and better markets all rated high in Fraker's community service. He was a one-man committee to enhance the landscaping at *Haskell Lake Park* with tree and shrub plantings.

At W.P. Fraker's death, his nephew Fred Wells acquired Fraker's 40-acre farm in 1942. Wells was married to Helen Gaddy Wells. She was a native born in the Fry community and is also one of our *100 Legacy Makers.*

(Biographical information courtesy of Broken Arrow Genealogical Society.)

GEORGE A. BROWN
(1871 – 1945)

George A. Brown

George A. Brown was one of the original pioneers who helped establish Broken Arrow. Brown was an investor, grain dealer, elevator owner, cotton buyer and ginner, landowner and behind the scene banker.

Brown's journey began in Greene County, Tennessee. His parents were Martin Van Buren Brown, (1841-1893) and Westie E. Carter (1841-1952). Brown married Mary Coin Dinwiddie (1874-1952) in 1900. Mary was the daughter of Jacob Whitfield Dinwiddie (1838-1897) and Mary Melvina Milburn (1840-1922).[56]

The newly-weds moved to central Oklahoma after the turn of the century, living in a sod house to homestead. They moved first to Union City, *Oklahoma Territory* for the May 1901 birth of their first son, Ivan. The Browns moved again to Hobart where he purchased land in the Kiowa Comanche area of the *Territory*.

---

56. Brown:https://www.findagrave.com/memorial/10244875/mary-c_-brown.

Meet the BROKEN ARROW CENTENNIALS

In search of a permanent place to settle and build a grain elevator, Brown came to Broken Arrow in 1903.[57] W.P. Fraker had also come to the area in the spring of 1903. Fraker was a first cousin to Mary, Brown's wife. It is uncertain who arrived first.

The foundation for the *Brown and Dr. J.S.W. Bower Grain Elevator* was laid in the fall of 1903 to handle arrival of the first crop of corn to the new town. At the end of the first-year harvest, Brown left this work to return to Hobart, to finalize business matters and move his family permanently to Broken Arrow.

His wife Mary returned to her childhood home in Tennessee while their new home was being built on the East side of town. Brown lived in *The Cottage Hotel* when he got back from the *Oklahoma Territory*.[58] Mary arrived in June with their children, Ivan, age 2; and infant James Claude. Youngest child, Mildred, was born a few years after the family had settled, in 1909. Unfortunately, James Claude died from tetanus after stepping on a rusty nail in 1913.

In 1905 the officers of the *Arkansas Valley Townsite Company* opened the *Arkansas Valley National Bank*. Family members say that Brown was one of the initial investors and in 1907 was listed as the vice-president of the bank. The bank later dropped the title "National" changing it

---

57. Brown- Kimbrough, Barbara, personal notes, family history, May 24, 2008.
58. Wise, First Census 1904.

to "State" after Oklahoma's statehood. Shortly thereafter, in 1924, Brown and K.M. Rowe, President of *Arkansas Valley State Bank* opened another bank in Bixby.

E.B. Baxter and Bower joined with Brown in the grain business and their company was known as *BBB*. Their extensive land holdings established grain elevators throughout Northeast Oklahoma. That partnership lasted until 1919 when Bower moved to Muskogee and Baxter left for Tulsa. George Brown continued to invest in the thriving Broken Arrow economy and community.

From the very beginning Broken Arrow was growing so fast that there was a housing shortage ever since the first days of its township. Brown, along with a group of civic leaders, helped to organize and establish the *Broken Arrow Building and Loan Association* to furnish money and encourage home building and ownership of property and houses.

One of the greatest cotton markets that Northeastern Oklahoma had ever seen came in the 1930s and was the moving force behind the *Farmers Gin Company*. In partnership with W.P. Fraker and Harrison Carter, they were able to serve the Broken Arrow farmers through the Great Depression.

People recalled that in Brown's latter years he would purchase a sack of apples on his way home from the office. He greeted people with an apple along the way, often arriving home with an empty bag. That walk was only one block from the bank building.

George A. Brown passed away in 1945. His legacy of establishing *Arkansas Valley State Bank* has continued as the oldest family-owned business in Broken Arrow from its inception. His legacy was first continued through his son, Ivan Brown, also one of the *100 Legacy Makers*.

(Permission to reprint copyrighted article by Broken Arrow Ledger, BH Media Group and Tulsa World Media Company.)

KNOX MCKAY ROWE
(1871 – 1961)

"A cultured manly gentleman" as K.M. Rowe was known, brought his bride from Mississippi to *Indian Territory*. He was the bookkeeper for the *First Bank* in Muskogee. When a group of men from the *Arkansas Valley Townsite Company* decided to open a bank in Broken Arrow, he was named bookkeeper of the new bank.

KNOX MCKAY ROWE

When one of Metzger's dray wagons[59] pulled up to the

---

59. Dray: www.merriam-webster.com: a strong wagon without sides.

Arkansas Valley National Bank on November 11, 1905, he was charged with moving the safe from temporary bank quarters in the *McKeehan Building*. Rowe was one of the first men to open the doors of this new financial establishment. He took a pay cut to come from Muskogee. He wanted to experience small town life on the prairie, and later stated he had only planned to stay a couple of years. Rowe was elected President of the *Arkansas Valley State Bank* in 1916 and with George A. Brown was co-founder of *Citizens Security Bank* in Bixby.

At the 50th Anniversary celebration of the *Arkansas Valley State Bank*, R.D. Patterson, president of the *Broken Arrow Chamber of Commerce*, presented a plaque to Mr. Rowe and said it was very little payment for the efforts of such a great man who helped build the city of Arrow. Rowe was a longtime member of the *Chamber of Commerce* and of the old *Commercial Club* that had preceded it. He steered the bank through the Great Depression and the even earlier state-mandated bank holidays when financial institutions across the state and nation experienced hard times. He especially stressed the importance of caring for the farming community and establishing the town Broken Arrow as a center for trade. He was respected in area and state banking circles and he held several offices, including President of the *Oklahoma Banker's Association*.

During World War II, Rowe was the war bond chairman for Broken Arrow. He led the community and many times surpassed the quota, aiding our troops overseas.

A most exciting and spectacular event occurred July 31st, 1943 when two robbers went to the K.M. Rowe home. They tied Mrs. Gertrude Rowe to the bedstead, then took Mr. Rowe to the bank to await morning when a timer released the bank's safe lock.

K.M. Rowe died on November 10, 1961 and was still President of *Arkansas Valley State Bank* and Chairman of the Board of Bixby's *Citizens Security Bank*.
(Permission to reprint copyrighted article by Broken Arrow Ledger, BH Media Group and Tulsa World Media Company.)

TRACEY MARK HUNSECKER, SR.
(1894 – 1974)

Tracey Mark Hunsecker, known near and far simply as "T.M" was born August 7, 1894, in Solomon, Kansas, near Abilene in Ottawa County. He came to Broken Arrow with his parents, Edward J. Hunsecker (1864-1944), and Mary Vena Thayer (1866-1932) and a brother, Hiram Charles, in the early part of the 20th Century.[60] His parents built the *Vena Hotel* and soon became known for excellent food. They had a steady Sunday trade from Tulsans who came to eat fried chicken.[61]

---

60. www.findagrave.com/memorial/9086355/tracey-mark-hunsecker.
61. Stapleton, Steven L, J.D., *Broken Arrow the First Hundred Years*. Broken Arrow Historical Society: 2002, 169.

T.M. married Florence Hazel Wilborn (1895-1987) and went to work for *Kahn Clothier* in Muskogee. In 1918 at age 22 with $900 in savings, he opened a grocery and clothing store. *Hunsecker's* was one of Broken Arrow's first businesses on Main Street.

To attract customers, T.M. had a drawing for a Shetland pony. For each dollar spent on groceries, he gave the customer a coupon for the drawing. Jack Estes, who later went to work for T.M., won the pony. Jack's father acted as cashier for the enterprise. In later years, he discontinued groceries and sold that part of the business to Charlie Peterson. The store was named the *Warehouse Market*.

T.M. HUNSECKER

T.M. and Florence had two sons, Ralph Uriah Hunsecker (1914-1995), whose professional songwriter name was Ralph Blane, and Tracey Mark, Jr, (1921-1954). Following the death of T.M.'s mother Vena, Edward J. known as Dad Hunsecker, married Widow Hill and moved to her 80-acre farm near the Broken Arrow City Springs on Tucson Street.

Meet the BROKEN ARROW CENTENNIALS

THE VENA HOTEL

During the Great Depression, T.M. had an opportunity to take over control of several other clothing and dry goods stores which were experiencing financial difficulties. By 1945 he owned twelve stores: in Broken Arrow, Bixby, Jenks, Sapulpa, Cushing, Sand Springs Claremore and Vinita and others in northeastern Oklahoma.

Hunsecker's stores provided employment for many Broken Arrow youth during and following high school. T.M. would give a job to any high school graduate who was willing to work. Many went on to become successful businessmen and officials of other companies. They credit much of their business acumen to what they learned while working at *Hunsecker's*.

Hunsecker retired in 1955 and built a country home on an 80-acre farm on South 193rd East Avenue and 141st Street South. He sold his stores to the *Chastain Stores*.

Always a community booster, T.M. was active in both the Broken Arrow and Tulsa *Chamber of Commerce* and in 1969, he was named "Mr. Broken Arrow" by the Broken Arrow Chamber and given the *Lawrence Brewer Memorial Award* for outstanding service boosting the civic and community development of the area.

HUNSECKER DEPARTMENT STORE

He was a former president of *Broken Arrow Savings and Loan* and retired vice-president and director of the *Ar-*

kansas Valley State Bank. He was a Mason and Shriner; a member of *First Presbyterian Church*; and a member of *Rolling Hills Country Club* near Catoosa.

In later years, one of his great loves was pure bred cattle. Along with his son, Tracey Mark, Jr., he established an outstanding registered *Shorthorn Beef* herd on several tracts of land south of Broken Arrow. Later registered *Black Angus* cattle were added to the operation.

T.M. Hunsecker died in Broken Arrow, Oklahoma on September 7, 1974 at age 80.

(Biography by Herb Karner, member of Broken Arrow Genealogy Society.)

B.A. BUSINESSES FLOURISHED

People and businesses continued to flow into this new community. Lumber companies were constantly busy, especially *Dickason Goodman*, the first one in town. With the railroad delivering locally, people no longer had to haul lumber from Catoosa.

Several hotels sprung up to accommodate the needs of men who came first to establish and build a home. Often entire families stayed in hotels while waiting for adequate housing. Several Simmons families were in the restaurant, boarding house and hotel businesses. *J.S. Simmons Hotel,* one of the first in the area, provided shelter for F.S. Hurd, secretly carrying nearly $3,000 before depositing it in the *Traders and Planters Bank*. The *Simmons Cottage House* was also owned by John Milton Simmons, offering housing for travelers and new residents in early 1903.[62]

The Kentucky Colonel Hotel followed shortly, built between 1903-1904. At one time, Simmons owned this hotel and later also operated the *Vena Hotel*. The Hunsecker's *Vena* underwent several name changes such as the *Francis Hotel* and *Mains Hotel*. It was eventually owned by H.A. Jacobs, Broken Arrow mayor, 1941-1947. Located at Dallas and Ash Streets it was beyond saving and is gone.[63]

While the town increased in population and prospered, the community did not support three banks as W. P. Fraker had stated about *First State Bank*. F.S. Hurd, president of *First National Bank* and K. M. Rowe from *Arkansas Valley Bank* met in a friendly session to simply divide the accounts in an alphabetical distribution. Both men were small in stature, but this reasonable and impartial action spoke volumes to the citizens. They appeared to be giants in the eyes of the early-day pioneers. It built trust among the people as these hardworking Oklahomans breathed in anticipation and breathed out sighs of relief and confidence.

---

62. Collins, Jan. *An Oklahoma Original, The Life and Career of Paul E. "Pete" Simmons*. Sand Springs, OK: Bold Truth Publishing, 2015, 27.
63. Stapleton, 169.

Meet the BROKEN ARROW CENTENNIALS

BROKEN ARROW EARLY CHURCHES

First Baptist 1908

First Presbyterian 1910

Haikey United Methodist 1903

Methodist Episcopal South 1904

Broken Arrow Indian United Methodist

St Anne Roman Catholic 1937

Chapter 7

Foundations of a Strong Community
Churches and Schools

Many families who settled here came from communities where churches and schools were a fundamental part of their lives. People were busy building homes and businesses but felt they were missing a vital part of their culture. In 1901 William G. McGechie purchased a six-year lease on land at the outskirts of Broken Arrow. Nothing but green grass and rolling prairie could be seen for miles around. Early one sunshiny morning on the second Sunday in September 1902, McGechie conceived an idea that the place would be ideal for a Sunday School. He called the neighbors together in an orderly fashion and sat down for singing on the ground followed by a prayer and a lesson by Reverend Sylvester L. Morris, a Methodist preacher and missionary.[64]

About the same time, Mrs. William Sprague had already sought out friends and neighbors and began having Sunday school in her home. The group arranged for Reverend Morris to hold the first church service in the home of

---

64. *First Methodist Church. A Centennial Church History: 1903 to 2003.* Tulsa, Oklahoma, The Press Group, 2003, 24, 129.

F.A. Whitmer on Christmas day, 1902. Soon the unified group organized and began meeting on Sunday afternoons in the storeroom of *S.E. Orcutt's Building*. People from all denominations participated.[65] For the next few years, religious services were held in a variety of places, but mostly in the hall over *Hill's Mercantile* store. Once the *Methodist Church* and the first schoolhouse were built, services were held in the new buildings.[66]

First M.E. Church of Broken Arrow, Indian Territory, 1903-1904
(Sketch by Mindy Burdette, 1993)

The town's population was now large enough to establish a church. As W. S. Fears had promised, a lot was given to the denomination that had the largest in attendance, which were the Methodists. In July 1903 the *Arkansas*

---
65. Rhoades, 53.
66. Rhoades, 54.

Foundations of a Strong Community

Valley Townsite Company announced the northeast corner of Main Street and Avenue "C" (later College Street) would be the location. Construction for a 32 by 40 foot wooden-frame building commenced immediately.[67] All denominations agreed to help with the construction of the building because it would be used as a school until a permanent school structure could be built the following year. Other denominations used the church building when it was not occupied. The first service for the *Methodist Episcopal Church* was held on October 8, 1903.[68] By 1904, an addition was made to the original structure and a steeple was added.

The *Methodist Episcopal Church South* became a separate denomination in 1904. The congregation erected a red brick building on the northeast corner of Ash and Broadway (where the *Windstream Communications* building now stands).[69] *M.E. Church South* was dedicated on September 24, 1905, the same day *M.E. Church* rededicated their church with steeple and additions.

Unfortunately, lightning struck the *M.E. Church* in December 1918. The congregation met in the school building across the street for the next two years. New construction used gray brocade brick with Carthage stone trimmings and four Corinthian pillars at the front entrance. It was

---

67. Wise, *Vignettes*, 18.
68. Stapleton, 79.
69. *First Methodist Centennial*, 25.

ornate and shipments of supplies delayed the building until 1920. It was completed with a basement for church dinners and game room. The sanctuary was a large bowl-shaped room with balcony. By this time, the church had become *First Methodist Church* as was inscribed on the cornerstone of the new structure.(70) Church founders' names were on the inscription, including Elmer V. Hartman, Phillip Hartman's father.(71)

Because of economic reasons, the two *M.E. Churches* decided to merge. As described in "The Grand Move" by the *Broken Arrow Ledger* on July 15, 1926, the two churches agreed that the larger and newer *First Methodist Church* would be their new church home.(72)

An educational building was added on a lot next to the sanctuary in 1961. A new sanctuary was built in 1976, and was eventually renamed *First United Methodist Church*. People especially recall the steps of the church because the *Methodist, Christian* and *Presbyterian Churches* joined each summer for *Vacation Bible School* for several years.(73) Broken Arrow citizens enjoyed the majestic structure for the next six decades until it was destroyed by fire January 15, 1982.(74) In place of the old regal sanctuary, a school playground was added, west of the education building.

---

70. Ibid, 26.
71. Hartman, David V. E.V. Hartman details from son of Philip G. Hartman.
72. *First Methodist Centennial*, 26.
73. Collins, 74.
74. *First Methodist Centennial*, 44.

Eventually a large building with a reception room was added. Although it has seen many alterations, it has withstood the generational changes.

First Methodist Church

Other churches soon were added to the community as other denominations were established. The *Missionary Baptist Church* had a unique way of bringing the Gospel to the people. Under the leadership of Reverend J.S. Thomas, a railroad car, *Evangel* was brought in on March 19, 1904.[75] By 1908, a white frame structure with pews and an organ installed, became home for *First Baptist Church* at First Street and Broadway. Later, the *Ladies Aid Society* reached out, purchased a new piano for $450, and added carpet to the pulpit area and aisles. The building

---
75. Wise, *Vignettes*, 18.

Meet the BROKEN ARROW CENTENNIALS

was later replaced by a beautiful rock building in 1951. As *First Baptist Church* grew into a large congregation, they had an opportunity to move to an undeveloped area at the corner of Albany Street and Elm Place.[76]

Missionary Baptist had been the initial name for this congregation, and their namesake was evident as the church expanded and fostered several other Baptist churches in the area. *Arrow Heights Baptist Church* was started in 1955, located in the building that presently houses *Broken Arrow Seniors, Inc.* and *Broken Arrow Community Playhouse*, in the Main Street vicinity of the Broken Arrow Post Office. Other Baptist churches whose members were once part of *First Baptist* include *Calvary Baptist*, 1960's; *Clearview Baptist Church*; Clayton Mission - now *Aspen Park Baptist Church*; and *Forest Ridge Baptist Church*, first named *Oneta Road Baptist*.[77]

In 1903, the Middleton family offered their home for religious services for other Catholic families who came to Broken Arrow. In 1936 a church building was moved from Jenks to their present site on South Lynn Lane and East Dallas. In 1948, *St. Anne's Parish* was established. They added a school in 1954, and the church remains a vital part of Broken Arrow today.[78]

First Presbyterian Church was begun with 17 charter

---
76. Stapleton, 83.
77. Ibid., 84-85.
78. St. Anne's. https://www.stanneba.org/Our-Parish/Parish-History

members in June 1903. The newly organized *Ladies Aid Society* was instrumental in coming to the assistance of several area churches and not just one denomination. This group of women helped secure a $1,000 loan from the *Church Erection Board* for the Presbyterians to purchase a home for the Pastor.[79] The Public School Building was used for worship services until 1910 when a new sanctuary was built. The 80th anniversary of the *Presbyterian* congregation was celebrated on June 22, 1983. As part of the *Rose District* renovation, their 1969 beautiful church structure on West College is now being redesigned into a restaurant and shops.

The congregation of *First Christian Church* started in May 1910 in member homes and in the school building. H. E. Appleby was hired as its first minister. The church building was severely damaged in 1919 by a tornado. In 1932 a new building was completed; in 1950 and in 1977 new additions were made. The church celebrated 75 years in 1986[80] and a centennial in 2011.

The congregation of the *First Evangelical Lutheran Immanuel* began in 1905 when missionaries under supervision of Reverend L.C. Hermerding of Muskogee, came into town by train. A church was formally organized on December 29, 1912 by seven German families. In 1913 *Immanuel* bought two homes in the 500 block of West

---
79. Stapleton, 79-80.
80. Wise, *Vignettes*, 18.

College Avenue, using one structure as a church and school, and the other, a parsonage. In 1956, ten acres were purchased on a prominent *Kenwood Hills* ridge, overlooking Broken Arrow. A new church and education building were dedicated in April 1961. Located near the Lynn Lane exit, the unique hilltop edifice can be seen from the Broken Arrow Expressway. Known as *Immanuel Lutheran Church of Broken Arrow*, the property was sold when the church relocated to Aspen and Detroit in the early 2000's.[81] *Immanuel Lutheran's centennial was in 2012.*

The Assembly of God began as a tent revival in 1909 under the leadership of founding Pastor, Willard Pope. As the Methodist Church was finishing a revival, and the *Assembly of God* rented the tent from them.[81] Official services were held as early as 1912 when the congregation met in the city hall over the jail on Dallas. The first church building began as a wooden frame structure located on the northeast corner of North Main and "D" Street in 1914. That building caught fire and burned down in 1916. A new building was started the same year.[82] According to the charter, after five years of these services, a small group of people voted on May 16, 1917 to become affiliated with the fledgling *Assemblies of God*. In 1949, they replaced the church building with a larger wood-frame structure. That church

---
81. Stapleton, 92-94.
82. Wise, *Vignettes*, 19.

burned completely on November 10, 1952, when *Broken Arrow's Volunteer Fire Department* was unsuccessful in saving it.[83] Rebuilt in the same location within seven months by volunteers, the building's exterior was a masonry block structure. Congregational growth resulted in additions to the church facilities, including a school with a gym. During May 1992, the congregation celebrated their 75th anniversary.[84] The church eventually purchased *The First Baptist Church* at Broadway and First Streets, then built a new facility south of town at New Orleans and Olive Streets.

The school remained at the old *First Baptist* building and continued to grow. The church name has been shortened to *The Assembly,* and the congregation's centennial was celebrated at its new church home in 2017. The original facility at Main and Detroit Streets was torn down, and is being replaced by a large structure with commercial opportunities on the ground level and apartments on the upper levels, as part of the town's revitalization in the *Rose District.*

Broken Arrow has a rich heritage of successful church start-ups in the downtown area. It is quite an impressive record for six churches. The *First Methodist, First Baptist, First Presbyterian, First Christian, Immanuel*

---
83. Fisher, Charles Howard, as told by local historian and volunteer fireman.
84. *Broken Arrow Assembly of God 75th Anniversary.* Wagoner, OK: Arrow Printing Company, 1987.

Meet the BROKEN ARROW CENTENNIALS

Lutheran and the *Assembly of God* Churches have celebrated 100 years in Broken Arrow.

It is a testimony to the foundation of faith in the community. Although the boundaries of Broken Arrow have extended several miles out from the *Rose District*, there are several new churches which have found their place in the town's history. As the founding congregational church, *First United Methodist Church* is the oldest, at the same location for 116 years. *St. Anne's* building has remained in their location for 83 years and has been established as *St. Anne's Catholic Church* parish for 71 years.

WILLIAM G. McGECHIE
(1853 – 1940)

W. G. McGechie, a native Scotsman, came to *Indian Territory* in 1900 because of a drought and grasshopper plague. This Nebraska farmer and pharmacist took a five-year lease on 640 acres of land southwest of the present-day Houston and Elm Place intersection.

When Broken Arrow was established in 1902 the *Ar-*

WILLIAM G. MCGECHIE

kansas Valley Townsite Company promised a free lot to any group who could organize a church. McGechie went to work to raise $500 and enlisted several members for a *Methodist Episcopal Church*. The church building was completed in 1903 The deed for the lot where *First United Methodist* stands today was given to McGechie. He in turn presented the deed and abstract to the minister and trustees of the church.

McGechie was the first Sunday School Superintendent. In 1905 he helped establish the *Methodist Church South*. Later he became a member of the *Presbyterian Church*.

The Nebraska transplant was a director of the township fairs to raise money for a ten-acre city park. A substantial oil well was put down on his land early in town history. McGechie was President of *Farmer's Union* and was General Manager of the association for the town of Broken Arrow, Coweta, Jackson and Porter.

Apparently, he did not practice as a pharmacist after moving to *Indian Territory* but did develop a medicinal concoction, *Animetta*. He applied for a patent in 1916, and the liniment was registered late in 1918. *Animetta* was used to treat certain blood diseases, rheumatism, bruises and skin eruptions. McGechie was added to the *Broken Arrow Hall of Fame in 1993*.

(Biographical information courtesy of Broken Arrow Genealogical Society.)

MARTIN "M.H." BREDEHOEFT
(1890 – 1955)

Martin Bredehoeft, or better known as "M.H.", was a quiet person. During the time he lived in Broken Arrow, his religious, civic, business and agricultural leadership exerted tremendous influence on the growth and well-being of the community.

M.H. BREDEHOEFT

He was born in Sweet Springs, Missouri on November 21, 1890; attended boarding and preparatory schools at Concordia, Missouri and graduated from the *Concordia Theological Seminary* in St. Louis with a ThD degree and was ordained a Lutheran minister. He spent a year in Alva, Oklahoma where he met Martha Kietke. They married on February 11, 1916. Her parents visited then purchased land in the Albany and Garnett Streets' area, and named it Union Gardens; it is now the *Union District*.

In 1915 his denomination assigned him as Pastor of the

newly organized *Immanuel Lutheran Congregation*. His calm, judicious behavior as a community leader was instrumental during World War I in preserving order when anti-German feelings ran high and *Klu Klux Klan* activity was on the rise.

In 1920 Reverend Bredehoeft developed throat problems which forced him to abandon the ministry. He bought and moved to the old Walters Farm on the south edge of Broken Arrow and established a Grade A Jersey dairy. Today the farm is the *Oakcrest Addition*, named for all the oak trees he and his son-in-law planted there.

He was also one of the main businessmen who built a cheese plant in Collinsville, a boon to area farmers and the economy, as it provided an additional outlet for the rapidly expanding milk production. He was later associated with the *White City Dairy* in Tulsa.

Despite the demands of operating a dairy farm, Mr. Bredehoeft became involved with civic affairs, including the *Broken Arrow Chamber of Commerce*; was founding member and director of the *Federal Land Bank Association of Broken Arrow*, an institution that made farm loans in several counties. He was one of the directors on the board of the *Broken Arrow Soil Conservation Association*, organized in 1936. Being a staunch Republican, he ran for *County Commissioner* in the late 1930's but was narrowly defeated by the incumbent candidate. He worked tirelessly on the behalf of his church, both at home, statewide and nationally.

He was known to be an eloquent speaker and was sought by numerous organizations to speak on soil and water conservation matters. Mr. Bredehoeft was a founding member of the *Tulsa Farm Club* in 1939. This organization promoted sound and scientific agricultural practices and was active in the *Farm Bureau Federation.*

M.H. sold his dairy farm during World War II and switched to purebred beef cattle. He became administrator of the *Agricultural Stabilization and Conservation Service,* headquartered in Tulsa and held that post until his death February 5, 1955.

In 1948 the *Tulsa State Fair Board of Trustees* was formed to operate the *Tulsa Exposition and Fair Corporation.* Mr. Bredehoeft was a charter member of the *Trust* and served as its first secretary and later treasurer until 1955.

In 1950 M.H. and his wife Martha sold their farm and built a house on College Street, which remains today. The Bredehoefts had three daughters; Gertrude, married to Arthur E. McCoy; Ruth, Mrs. Herbert R. Karner; and Lavern, married to Albert M. Karner.

(Written by Valarie Karner Kolkmann, Bredehoeft's granddaughter.)

Foundations of a Strong Community

"Martin and Martha Bredehoeft with their children: Ruth, Gertrude and Lavern"

The Legacy Lives On

Bredehoeft, McCoy and Karner were well-known names in the Broken Arrow and Tulsa community, especially Herb Karner, who was *Tulsa World's Farm Editor* and held other titles for many years beginning in the 1950's. Herb is one of the *100 Legacy Makers.*

Prior to statehood, an educational system had been established by the Creek Nation, restricted to their own citizens: Indians and Freedmen. There were also several mission schools operated by teachers who had been sent by various denominations.[85]

---
85. Wise, *Vignettes*, 22.

Meet the BROKEN ARROW CENTENNIALS

As pioneers came into *Indian Territory* from surrounding states, a number of subscription schools were developed to accommodate and provide a basic education for their children. Schools were located at *White Church, Weer* and *Springtown*.[86] Before Broken Arrow had a formal educational system, children received private schooling. In 1897, Minnie McKim Willbanks taught thirty students in the old White Church for $2 or corn-in-exchange, per month.[87]

Mrs. J.H. Wertz opened another temporary subscription school in 1902. The *1904 School Census for Broken Arrow* shows the developing status of the town. Many new residents stayed in local hotels while others could only afford to depend on shelter in tents; fortunate ones stayed with families. The census gave a basis for a school levy.

Because the city was not established until October, there were no tax funds and no building for a classroom.[88] As soon as the "first ladies" of Broken Arrow moved here, they took action. The *Ladies Aid Society* was formed in the spring of 1903, and Mrs. W.T. Brooks was elected president. Having been a schoolteacher in Arkansas Mrs. Brooks understood the value of an education so she began a campaign for parents to make subscription and hired a teacher.

Also known as the *Ladies School Aid Society*, the women

---
86. Wise, *Vignettes*, 22.
87. Wise, *Myriads*, 36.
88. Stapleton, 129.

Foundations of a Strong Community

were creative in their fundraising. According to Mrs. Mary McAnally and Mrs. Josie Sprague, The *Society* served sandwiches, ice cream, plate lunches and presented community plays to raise money for the school fund.[89]

On August 25, 1903, a formal board of education was elected: I.M. Thompson, Thomas Blair, S.E. Orcutt, H.L. Pierce, N.L. Sanders, and G.L. Holt; they selected Holt as the board's president.[90] Mrs. Wertz's school became Broken Arrow's first public school and the school was moved to the *Methodist Church*.[91]

A subscription paper circulated by the *Board of Education* asked residents to subscribe approximately five mills to the dollar on the total value of their personal property. Many activities and fundraisers of the *Ladies School Aid Society* had secured seven hundred dollars. Added to the new levy, the *Society* funds provided enough for the first free public school to open on October 5, 1903. The *Board* hired P.C. Skaggs of Wagoner, Mrs. Wertz and a Miss Patterson to teach. School started with one hundred forty-three pupils and reached one hundred and seventy within two weeks.

The school continued in the *Methodist Church* because it was the only building available. The school was forced

---

89. Rhoades, 57.
90. Stapleton, 129.
91. Wise, *Vignettes*, 22.

to close in January 1904 because of lack of funding, but Mrs. Wertz and Miss Patterson continued to teach on a subscription basis.[92]

Broken Arrow residents remained hopeful and determined it was only a temporary setback. Their commitment to their children's education was firm. The town had already selected an area suitable as a location for their first public school. Known as the *Town Public Square*, it was the northwest corner of Main Street and "C" Street. Three months earlier, Mayor J.B. Parkinson had several trees dug up along creeks in the county to plant in the city. People gathered at the square to plant trees in commemoration of Broken Arrow's first *Arbor Day* on March 18, 1904. According to Mrs. M. C. Williams many of those trees were still standing in the 1950's.[93]

By summer, two major events turned things around. The newly elected *City Council* approved a 2 percent property tax on June 20, 1904 to raise funds for a new building. Also, the *Arkansas Valley Townsite's* president, Guy Bowman deeded Block 30, the 200 block of North Main Street to the school district, on June 23, 1904, in the location the city had hoped: the *Public Square*, directly across from the *Methodist Church*, the school location already familiar to the children. Restrictions still applied if Broken Arrow was chosen as a county seat. Otherwise, it would remain prop-

---

92. Rhoades, 58-59.
93. Rhoades, 59.

erty of the *Broken Arrow Public School District.*[94] Terms were established and the city was required to erect a stone or build a school building at least two stories high.

FIRST SCHOOL BUILDING BUILT IN 1904

Plans were made and a contract was awarded to M.H. Sanders and W. F. Waller for a cost of $4,343. With a combined effort between the city and residents they moved at a rapid pace. The cornerstone was laid on August 7, 1904 and work finished with all specifications in less than three months. The school opened on November 9.[95] It was a beautiful brick two-story building with two rooms on each floor. Enrollment increased to 300 by December. Two more teachers were added to the faculty.

---

94. Ibid.
95. Rhoades, 60.

Meet the BROKEN ARROW CENTENNIALS

Between 1905 and 1908, four new rooms and an auditorium were added. The school received accreditation by the state of Oklahoma in 1905.[96] Broken Arrow's first graduating class was 1908.

Twelve superintendents had oversight of *Broken Arrow Public Schools,* 1904-1925, prior to C.S. Anderson. Although some only served for one or two years, the schools continued to thrive. Five superintendents have been nominated as some of the most influential persons in Broken Arrow history; two are introduced here.

C. S. ANDERSON
(1884 – 1963)

C. S. Anderson was in the office from 1925 to 1933. The following tribute was paid to him in the *1929 Year Book*, dedicated to him. "For any school to be successful one must have a real school man at its head. We have just such a leader in Superintendent Anderson who has been with this school three years and has brought it up to the

C. S. ANDERSON

---
96. Stapleton, 130.

high standard required of good high schools. Under his jurisdiction much progress has been made and classes added. He made a study of curricula of schools which resulted in the organization of a junior high school in which the pupils are now prepared to enter senior high without experiencing that green feeling formerly felt. Each year a class of graduates goes out to seek its fortune in the world, much better prepared for having been in school at Broken Arrow."

C.S. Anderson was joined in life by Effie Alice Drake (1886-1969) whom he had married in Kingfisher County in 1909. Together, they had five sons and three daughters while Anderson spent at least 25 years as an Oklahoma educator. The couple is laid to rest in Tulsa Memorial Park.[97]

ROY DENVER (R.D.) PATTERSON
(1898 – 1988)

In 1927 R.D. Patterson came to Broken Arrow as a high school football coach and math teacher. Patterson received his undergraduate degree from *Northeastern State Teachers' College* and a master's from *Columbia University* in New York. While coaching, Patterson took a summer seminar on coaching techniques at *Notre Dame* under Knute Rockne so he could give his best for his local team.

---
96. Stapleton, p. 130.
97. www.findagrave.com/memorial/157295641/chancy-sevy-anderson

Meet the BROKEN ARROW CENTENNIALS

In 1933 when Patterson was named Superintendent, the district was 30 square miles and had a valuation of about $1.5 million. His salary was $2,000 annually; the total budget was $25,889. As the great depression ensued, the valuation decreased.

Patterson later said, "The money left about the time we came, and it takes money to run the schools."

R. D. PATTERSON

When a fire broke out at the grade school in 1935, Superintendent Patterson joined E.J. Benedict and fireman Charles Fisher to fight the blaze. Patterson opened the 1937 school year with 900 pupils. He notified parents that the school was conducted for the welfare of the children and that it was very important for the child to be on time each day. He knew that often there was not enough money to buy shoes, food and clothes for the children. One of the most difficult things Patterson faced, he said, was seeing his students go off to war knowing that some would never return.

In 1944, Patterson said that there were so many things that had to be done to advance education, and he was

Foundations of a Strong Community

worn out, so he resigned. He became a real estate agent here and worked for 43 years before retiring at age 89. During those years he served the community in several capacities.

Jaycees cited him for his years of support. *The Chamber of Commerce Ambassador's Club* named him as an outstanding businessman. When *Rooster Day* started in 1932, he helped with the event along with the agriculture instructor, L.S. Wortman. On *Rooster Day* 1983 he was named *Honorary Mayor.*

Patterson taught Sunday School at *First Methodist Church* which bore out his philosophy on education: "I believe in education and think it should be as moral as possible. Moral activities are important to the child, too."

Roy clearly understood the life and needs of children, and his wife, Alma Lucille Porter Patterson was also a teacher in the 1930's. Married in Muskogee on May 19, 1928, they were not blessed with children of their own. Both were dedicated to Broken Arrow's success. Lucille was a charter member of the *Rose Garden Club* when it formed in 1946. They are interred side-by-side in *Park Grove Cemetery.*[98]

---

98. Find a Grave: Roy Denver Patterson, memorial 10253493 and Alma Lucille Patterson, memorial 10253498; Park Grove Cemetery.

Meet the BROKEN ARROW CENTENNIALS

THE BEST DAY

The five hundred school children in Broken Arrow were on an unusual holiday, Thursday January 26, 1911. And hundreds more also crowded in from the rural schools, six miles around. A parade down Main Street with the school band brought everyone to the *MK&T Depot*. Merchant and residents' carriages, farmers' wagons and horses lined hitching rails in front of the boardwalk access to stores. Just before 11a.m., the train sounded and a great cheer went up from the crowd. The *MK&T* cars positioned near the platform and the speakers climbed to the loading platform, ready to speak. The guests of honor?

A&M School of Agriculture Exhibition of Livestock and Agricultural Displays (See p. 213)

("Special Train Here Today," Broken Arrow Lodger, January 26, 1911. 1.)

Chapter 8

Politics on the Prairie

The petition was filed with the *U.S. Territorial Court for the Northern (Muskogee) Division of the Indian Territory* on March 30, 1903 for incorporation of the town of Broken Arrow in *Indian Territory*. The U.S. Court approved the petition on May 4, 1903 establishing Broken Arrow as a legal townsite. The Court designated W.T. Brooks, F.S. Hurd and G.L. Holt as authorized agents to act on behalf of the individuals who had signed the petition for a new form of government in Broken Arrow.[1]

Moving rapidly to install city officials, a town meeting was held on Friday, June 26, 1903 to nominate persons to serve on the *Citizen's Ticket*. City fathers realized that there had to be an opposing party to hold a legal election, so men were nominated to run in the *People's Party*. Ironically, three of the names that appeared on the *Citizen's Ticket* were also listed on the *People's Ticket*. Nearly all qualified voters participated and fifty-three

---

1. Rhoades, 39.

votes were cast, electing the following men to their offices; J.B. Parkinson, the first Mayor; Luther Gideon as Town Clerk; W.T. Brooks, Charles Nichols, R.S. Plumlee, R.A. Waller and M.L. Fife as the first Aldermen. The first *Broken Arrow City Council* meeting was held July 10, 1903; the men wrote the first city ordinance to establish rules and regulations for the operation of the new town government. At a subsequent meeting on July 22, 1903, the Council passed ordinances 2 and 3 establishing the offices of town Marshal and Treasurer. T.S. Higgins was appointed Marshal, with a monthly salary of $20. F.S. Hurd was named the first City Treasurer.[2]

Broken Arrow was not birthed without problems to be addressed by the new government from the very beginning. Issues included taxes, road and street improvements, construction of bridges to cross the many creeks in the area, establishing safety rules, fire protection, public health, and a city cemetery.

Also, one of the earliest and possibly the largest political issue to face Broken Arrow was statehood. After the Civil War, there was increasing political pressure to bring *Indian Territory* more formally into the Union. There were two new proposals for states: *Sequoyah* and *Oklahoma*. Broken Arrow and Coweta were

---

2. Rhoades, 40.

the two largest towns in the new Coweta County under the *State of Sequoyah* proposal.

When Broken Arrow was approved as the new *County Seat of Coweta County* on November 15, 1905, the editor of the *Broken Arrow Democrat* prepared a circular to show the building designated as the new courthouse. The town's school, already built and in use during the 1904 first school year, had proven its worth for more than 300 students in attendance. It was expected that if county seat status were granted, Broken Arrow students would be displaced until another school could be provided. The symbolic wreath for the *State of Sequoyah* shown above also embellished the announcement.⁽³⁾

However, in December 1905, David Hodge had heard President Roosevelt reject the proposal for *Sequoyah Statehood*. In June 1906, the U.S. Congress made the first county seat decision null and void. "The passage of the *Enabling Bill* in June 1906 set in motion the process for establishing a new

---

3. "Broken Arrow's Gift to Coweta County," *Broken Arrow Democrat*. Date unknown.

Oklahoma constitutional state government. This directive empowered the people of the Oklahoma and Indian territories to elect delegates to a constitutional convention and to set up a state capital temporarily at Guthrie, in former *Oklahoma Territory*."[4]

W.T. Dalton was elected to represent the *Sixty-Ninth Constitutional District* for the *Oklahoma Constitutional Convention*. The town was partnered with Tulsa as new county boundaries were drawn. Although Broken Arrow was somewhat smaller than Tulsa, its residents still felt confident about being the county seat for several reasons: the convention favored leaving the old Sequoyah county boundaries and county seats intact where possible; Broken Arrow had a new two-story brick building that it was willing to donate to the county for a courthouse; and there appeared to be considerable animosity toward the Tulsa delegate. According to the November 29, 1905, edition of the *Broken Arrow Ledger*, "Tulsa is a regular Ishmaelite in the State Convention as no delegate in any of the districts surrounding that town will lift a finger for her."[5]

After all the efforts to become the *County Seat*, Broken Arrow had to adhere to the decision that Tulsa was ultimately selected as the county seat. Broken Arrow citizens were disappointed by this turn of events. George Foster, Editor of

---

4. The Enabling Act, 1906. www.okhistory.org/publications/enc/entry.php?entry=EN001.
5. Rhoades, 48-49.

the *Broken Arrow Ledger* voiced this bitterness in the November 29, 1906 editorial when he printed this headline: "Governor Haskell is a Traitor." But the town turned its attention to other community developments.[6]

Utilities were gradually established for the new town. In June 1906, the *Broken Arrow Light and Electric Company* was granted a franchise to provide electricity for the town. This company was purchased by the *Public Service Company of Oklahoma* in 1917, continuing ownership and service to this day.[7] About the same time, the *Minshall Oil and Gas Company* was granted permission to provide Broken Arrow with the supply of natural gas. That company stayed in existence until 1927 when it was sold to the *Oklahoma Natural Gas Company* on March 15th.[8]

WATER TOWER NEAR CITY HALL, C. 1910

Water was in short supply, available from a well located at Main and Commercial Streets. This inadequate resource, "salty and carried by citizens with buckets," was a challenge for Mayor C.L.

---

6. Rhoades, Ibid.
7. Rhoades, 47.
8. Rhoades, 44.

Meet the BROKEN ARROW CENTENNIALS

Dalton (1905-1906). Although the *City Council* began discussions about ways to develop a more modern water system, citizens could delay at first since there was a good source from a large spring a few miles south of town. A new system was approved by voters in 1909. It was yet another year before the spring water was pumped and piped from a spring about seven miles south, to the town water tower, located one block east of Main Street between Dallas and Commercial Streets.[9]

Although a telephone service franchise was granted in 1904, it was a primitive system and was installed in very few locations in the town. Phone service in the most private homes was not common until the late 1930s and early 1940s.

The *Mayor-City Council* form of government was used by Broken Arrow from 1903 until April 13, 1954, when the *City Council-City Manager* government was approved by the citizens in a public election.[10] This governing system continues today, with primary authority for ordinances, resolutions, and contracts residing in the Council decisions. Five Council persons are elected by the voters, then the Council elects the City Manager to be responsible for the day-to-day operational functions of the city.

---

9. Rhoades, 47.
10. Wise, *Vignettes*, 14.

JOSIAH BENSON (J.B.) PARKINSON
(1855 – 1929)

Forty-nine-year-old J.B. Parkinson and his wife Emma Benton Parkinson were in Broken Arrow in 1903 or earlier. Their four children were Merritt, Ruth, Lucius (Lute), and Gerald, ranging from nine to two years.[11] Parkinson was also the uncle of another Broken Arrow pioneer, Elmer Hartman.

The first Broken Arrow election chose J. B. Parkinson and the Citizen's Ticket, on Monday June 29, 1903. The term of office was one year, and development of resources and town management presented many weighty questions. The Councilmen had already been business and *Masonic Lodge* associates, but now were united as a government entity. In or out of town office, the men took on an abiding responsibility for Broken Arrow.

J.B. PARKINSON

It might be assumed that the small new community was

---
11. Wise, *First Census 1904*, 20.

normally an orderly place. However, as it happened, the first revenue contributed to the city treasury was a fine collected from a local citizen. He was found drunk on bay rum, disturbing the peace, and was arrested for shooting his gun into the air several times on Main Street. When Marshal Higgins brought the gentleman before Mayor Parkinson, he was promptly fined ten dollars and cost.[12]

The *Broken Arrow Ledger* Editor, M. McKenna wrote, "Owing to the fact that the mayor's office carries with it the duties of police judge, it requires for this responsible position a man with good intellect, quick perception, wide experience and some understanding of law and its applications. Mayor Parkinson seems to be an ideal mayor in these respects."

Josiah B. Parkinson had moved here from Illinois and listed his profession as editor and publisher.[13] He had worked in the newspaper business and served as one of the editors for the local newspaper of Savanna City. It is also recorded that he quickly became active in the civic and religious development of Broken Arrow. He served on the plans and specifications committee for the *Methodist Church*. He was a founding member of the *Broken Arrow Commercial Club* and on the committee to plan the first July 4th celebration.

---

12. Rhoades, 41.
13. *1900 Federal Census, Savanna, Carroll Co, IL*; Josiah B. Parkinson, occupation, Editor, line 1, ED 22; 7.

Just days before assuming governmental responsibilities, Parkinson, Dr. R.S. Plumlee and Frank C. Boles had gathered on May 11, 1903 in the hall over the *Hill Mercantile* on West Commercial across from *Dickason-Goodman Lumber Yard*, to organize a local *Masonic Lodge*. Masonic records show that Parkinson was a charter member, the first Senior Warden; later, a Grand Master in 1912 and secretary for four terms (1914-1917).[14]

J.B. Parkinson was behind the first *Arbor Day* celebration by promoting a city-wide tree planting campaign for the barren streets. Many of the trees were transplanted from nearby creek banks.[15]

Parkinson purchased the *Broken Arrow Ledger* in August 1908. While at the editor's desk he pushed to get one of the Oklahoma's five state secondary schools of agriculture. Broken Arrow won out for one of the schools in 1909, and it was named *Haskell State School of Agriculture.*[16] Other accomplishments that he kept before the public and promoted included the new water supply from the springs, road improvement and expansion of all utilities.

Through the *Ledger,* his pen was active in endorsing *Liberty Bond* sales and reporting about hometown soldiers during *World War I*. Once, when his printing equipment failed, the

---

14. Rhoades, 72.
15. Rhoades, 59.
16. Stapleton, 143-145.

rival *Democrat* Editor, John Wells came to the rescue and printed Parkinson's *Ledger*. In 1918, the *Democrat* plant burned, and Parkinson returned the favor and printed Well's paper at the *Ledger*. Within two weeks John Well's name replaced Parkinson's and the paper was changed to the *Ledger-Democrat*. Wells said that after some hard negotiating he had purchased the paper, but he didn't mention what Parkinson's plans were. Within a short time, however, the Parkinson family had moved to Chicago, where J.B. followed his business interests and became a promoter of oil wells.[17]

CHARLES L. (C.L.) DALTON
(1868 – 1950)

The Broken Arrow Dalton family included three business-minded brothers, William T., (W.T.) Charles L. and Joseph C. Dalton. The oldest brother, W.T., married in 1884 in Illinois and moved to Edgar, Nebraska before traversing to Stillwater, Oklahoma in 1892. Moving on, he was the founder and Vice President of *Coweta State Bank* before arriving in Broken Arrow in 1903.[18]

As often happened, a few family members sought room and board together, or lived in a single dwelling while relocating their entire family to a new and undeveloped area. The *1904 Broken Arrow Census* confirms this to be true of

---

17. *1920 U.S. Federal Census*, "Josiah B. Parkinson, Oil Wells Promoter" Chicago, Cook Co, IL; ED 424, 11A.
18. Rhoades, 29.

brothers "Wm. T. and J.C." who were listed in the household of their youngest brother, C. L. and his wife Ethel Dalton, along with their 6-year-old daughter, Edna.[19]

Courtesy of The Museum Broken Arrow

CHARLES L. DALTON

Two of the Dalton men, W.T., known to his friends as *Bill*, and Charles L. (C.L.) established the *Coweta Gin, Coal and Mill Company,* located on the east side of Main Street near the railroad tracks. This was one of the first enterprises built once the *MK&T Railroad* made plans to establish a station in this area.

Youngest brother, C. L. Dalton became Broken Arrow's third pre-statehood mayor, June 1905 - April 1906, following J. B. Parkinson and H. L. Pierce.[20] By the *1910 Federal Census for Broken Arrow,* Charles L. Dalton, Ethel his wife, and their daughter are shown as residents on "G" Street and Charles' occupation is a "plasterer," a livelihood he contin-

---
19. Wise, *First Census 1904,* 10.
20. Stapleton, 221.

ued for most of his working years.

OIL RIG IN THE DISTANCE DATES THIS PHOTO IN THE EARLY 1920'S.

In the same interval, W.T. Dalton became a representative to the *State Constitutional Convention* in Guthrie. In the discussions about county seat allocation, he probably came to know the fate of Broken Arrow quite early, in its transition from Coweta to Tulsa County. Broken Arrow leaders had favored keeping the original *Sequoyah State* boundaries intact for area counties, but the *Convention* reworked a major part of Broken Arrow into Tulsa County. Ultimately, Tulsa was chosen as the County Seat.[21]

It is likely that the school children were the most elated with

---

21. Stapleton, 153-4.

this news. Their new 1904 two-story brick school building had been designated as the potential county courthouse if Broken Arrow were to be appointed as county seat for the area. Now, their school was secure in its mid-town location at the northwest corner of Main and "C" (later College) Streets. It made all the difference to Broken Arrow's first generation of school children and teachers.

EDNA DALTON BROWNING
(1897 – 1991)

Charles L. Dalton's daughter Edna gave an early-times description, years later. She recalled her beginning school days on Main Street, long after she attended there from first grade until her 1917 graduation. An ever-growing enrollment required added class spaces. She remembered the new 1905 auditorium as a study hall, "although there wasn't much studying going on there." Childhood episodes stayed in her memory, like the water bucket with a dipper which they all used, by the podium at the front. "Some boys were ornery and poured water into the principal's chair. Before long, the principal sat down and jumped right back up, but no one told on the boy who did it." Mr. C.W. Horton was their principal at the time and C.S. Anderson was Superintendent.

At recess, when the girls jumped rope or played basketball, they had to put on black bloomers under their dresses because they didn't wear pants to school like girls do now. Miss Edna said they could play a mean game of basketball in their "bloomer uniforms".

Edna took Latin and Geometry and studied German with Mr. Bredehoeft. One assignment was to attend the *Lutheran Church* once a month where sermons were in German because many families still spoke their original home country language. Students enjoyed attending plays given by the *Self Culture Club* at the *Opera House,* upstairs above the *First State Bank*. She remembered some programs at different businesses through the years, one of which was the *Crystal Theater.*

Graduation ceremonies were held in the *Opera House* as well. The girls designed their class ring, which Edna wore with pride years later. Other girls and one boy in the 1917 graduation class were: Gladys Adleman, Agnes Bullard, Eula Pennington, Gladys Cunningham, and Joe Faull. Edna was reminded that Eula was Virgil Pennington's sister, and Agnes Bullard's father was a drayman who may have pulled many buildings into place those first few years. Still unusual for the time, Edna attended college at the University of Oklahoma after high school.

The crowded first Broken Arrow school became difficult to update. The new 1925 building had several names through the years. Edna probably visited the same place as *North Main* or as *Central Middle School* on different occasions. One specific occasion was in 1985 when Broken Arrow celebrated its 80th year as a school system. She was an honored guest of her granddaughter for the festivities and spoke to middle school students.[22]

One can only wonder how the children's imaginations were piqued as Miss Edna explained that homes and businesses were heated with coal stoves. She shared stories about her 1903 travel with her mother from Kansas to join her father. Their first home was in the back two rooms of the *Coweta Cotton Gin* while their house was being built on Dallas Street. She then lived on "Ice Plant Street" because streets were not yet named, and alphabet designations were used - "A" Avenue, etc. Everyone called the streets by names of businesses located on them.

People walked almost everywhere in town even if they owned a horse and buggy. A few had automobiles, but dusty or muddy streets made riding the train between towns more desirable. She was with her mother the day she met Van Browning, her future husband at the *Wybark* train junction, when he insisted on carrying their luggage. Van had just returned from World War I. She and Van then took their longest train ride during their honeymoon to California, where they lived for a few years.

When they returned to Broken Arrow, they owned and operated *Browning's Gift Shop* at 107 South Main

---

22. Broken Arrow Ledger, 1985.

Street. Many Broken Arrow citizens also remember *Van Browning's Tax Service* which he opened next door.

Edna's parents contributed many successful years to Broken Arrow. C. L. Dalton's death (1950) preceded Ethel's (1959) and they are interred in Park Grove Cemetery.[23]

WILLIAM THOMAS (W.T.) DALTON
(1857 – 1933)

W.T. Dalton,[24] oldest of the three brothers, was born November 7, 1857 in Illinois. He met Miss Minnie Belle Rohrer in Scottville, Macoupin County, Illinois. They were married on January 10, 1884 in the home where she was born and reared as the daughter of James H. and Elizabeth Ann Rohrer.

W.T. and Minnie Belle Dalton built a large white house across the street from the cotton gin, south of the *MK&T* tracks. Its large presence at the northwest corner of Main and Galveston Streets is remembered by

---

23. Park Grove Cemetery; www.findagrave.com/memorial/10253111/charles-l-dalton.
24. "1906, Delegates to Constitutional Convention, Guthrie, Oklahoma." W.T. Dalton 69th Constitutional District, pictured 3rd row from the bottom, 2nd portrait on the left side. https://gateway.okhistory.org/.

many. It also became the last location of the *Broken Arrow Ledger*, where *McGraw Realtors* building now stands. This Dalton family included six children, Clarence, Lela, Bertha, Carl, Ralph and Charles. Bertha graduated from *Broken Arrow High School* in 1909.

W.T. Dalton's House

Through the years, the couple had a busy household while W.T. continued the cotton gin. A Fall 1994 *Broken Arrow Ledger* featured an historic photo in the "Name with Faces" column, in which Minnie Belle Rohrer Dalton was identified with her sisters. Mrs. W.T. Dalton's obituary had appeared in the November 23, 1939 *Broken Arrow Ledger*. She was 79 years old and W.T. (William Thomas) Dalton had preceded her in death in 1933. They lay in repose at *Park Grove Cemetery*.

Meet the BROKEN ARROW CENTENNIALS

The Legacy Lives On

Carl and Ralph, two sons of W.T. and Minnie Belle Dalton have descendants in this area. Carl Dalton married Virgie Shaw, who worked for *Shinn Photography* for many years. They had two children, Buddy and Betty Jean. Betty Dalton married Guy Kinkeade, one of the first three mail carriers in Broken Arrow.[25]

Minnie Belle and W.T.'s granddaughter, Mrs. Betty Kinkeade has shared important information about the Dalton's role in early Broken Arrow's history. At 96 years, she is enjoying living in a senior facility. She and Guy had two sons who both graduated from Broken Arrow, Brent ('66) and his wife, Linda Kindkeade. Brent has a granddaughter, Andrea. The late Gary Kinkeade's ('69) family consists of his wife, Deborah, his son, Patrick, his daughter, Margie and her husband, Reese and two grandchildren, Eleanor and Alden.[26]

Granddaughters of Charles L. and Ethel Dalton who are the daughters of Edna and Van Browning, also live in the area: Beverly Birtell ('46), Patricia Stocker ('51) and Beverly's daughter, Sandy Nation ('75). Several other Dalton descendants attended and graduated local schools.

---

25. Rhoades, 37.
26. Betty Kinkeade interview, family history, March 2020.

Chapter 9

Early Statehood

With the arrival of the *Katy Railroad* more pioneers came looking for land and a new place to settle. It was a warm and dusty day even for November, when a young couple arrived on the train. It took time to unload all their belongings from the luggage compartment, where the man had spent some part of the trip watching over their goods. She welcomed the end of their long journey and prepared to see the town where she knew no one other than her husband.

Suddenly, the new bride was frightened by the loud noise of six-shooters firing rapidly into the air. As she cautiously peered out the window the conductor approached her, announcing that this stop was her destination. And Cora Sanders

CHARLES AND CORA SANDERS

wondered, "What kind of a place has my husband brought me to?"

This northern Kansas farm daughter hesitantly stood and walked to the exit as the conductor followed with her satchel. She worked up the nerve to ask him what was going on, trying not to tremble. "Aw, it's just some of our cowboys; they're all riled up. Excited because today Oklahoma is a State! We're part of the Union now – the 46th State. It's not your regular day, M'am."

What a welcome day for Cora Rich Sanders and her new husband, Charles! November 16, 1907. They adjusted fine to their new farm home and became parents to a son, Orval, within a couple of years.[27] Youngest brother, Ralph was born in 1919, and Edith Marie joined them in 1926.

The *Broken Arrow Ledger* of October 28, 1971 reported a *Cora Sanders Day* in Weer. Her church had surprised her with a "This Is Your Life" party and gifts. They gave some of her family story, that Cora and Charlie had settled just north of Weer on County Line Road. He was a farmer and Cora was a registered midwife during the 1930s, working with several prominent Broken Arrow doctors. The couple were charter members of *Weer Church of God of Prophesy* where Cora was "a pillar of the community and everyone loved her." Charles passed in 1957, and Cora

---

27. Sanders Family; *1910 Federal Census, Boles, Tulsa County, Oklahoma*; E.D. 214, 6A.

had thirty more years in the community. Their son Orval went on to some years in Texas, where he lived until August 1964. Ralph Sanders spent his interesting lifetime in Broken Arrow and is a *Centennial 100* story in a later chapter. Cora and Charles were grandparents to ten, and great grandparents to 13 children.

CATTLE PENS NEAR THE MK&T RAIL LINE, 1905[28]

THE CATTLE STAMPEDE STORY
BY MRS. MAC C. WILLIAMS

The area women often had the most revealing stories of life on the edge of the prairie. Cleo Williams (Mrs. Mac) related her buggy outing with Lutie Sanders (Mrs. Nat). Traveling between Elam and Catoosa; they were caught in a cattle stampede on the way home.[28] The *Broken Arrow Ledger* for November 28, 1907 reported Cleo's story this way.

"… Speaking of cattle reminds me of an incident that happened to Mrs. (Nat) Sanders and myself when we first came to the *Territory*. Of all the things that happened to us, I believe this one affords me more amusement now when I think back over it. This occurred when we lived at Elam, and when life became so monotonous that we longed for a little change and excitement, we would drive 16 miles to Catoosa to watch the train come in. In one of these expeditions, the following circumstances happened.

"Our road lay right through the midst of the 14-mile pasture with cattle - cattle as far as the eye could see. As we were returning from our trip 'twas growing late, and we gave a sigh of relief as we neared our last wire gate between the mounds. The cattle had congregated at this gate, and as we slowly climbed the hill, we felt a little shaky at having to pass them. All at once we heard a tremendous bellow and down the hill toward us came that clatter of thousands of hooves; nearer and nearer came the angry bellows of that mighty herd. It was as we thought, a stampede. Now, Mrs. Sanders does not make loud public protestations of her religion, but rather lives it in her sunny disposition not belonging to any church organization, but as I closed my eyes and resigned myself to my fate, I heard one of the most

---

28. Cattle Pens Near the MK&T Railroad, 1905. *The Museum Broken Arrow Photo Archive.*

humble and pathetic prayers that I ever listened to and I—well, all I could say was, 'Lord, them's my sentiments!'

We arrived home very much frightened but otherwise unharmed. The stampede had been caused by a dog which followed our buggy, and when it tried to escape by running across the pasture, the cattle followed it and thus we were spared. But the dog, alas! His bones repose today in an untimely grave."

GLADYS WALTON TERRY TOMLINSON
(1899 – 1993)

GLADYS WALTON TOMLINSON

Gladys Walton[29] arrived in Broken Arrow as a little girl, and youngest brother William Wilder Walton was born in Broken Arrow, just days after Statehood. Her father was William Wesley Walton (1860-1933) who was to become Judge W.W. Walton, and her mother was Mary Carolyn Huckaby (1874-1959). Older brother Luckey had been born in Arkansas, and Gladys was born in Rector,

---
29. Gladys Walton, Broken Arrow High School graduate, 1918. Photo provided by *The Museum Broken Arrow*.

Arkansas. Her Tennessee-born father moved the family to Elam, then on with the other founders to Broken Arrow.(30)

WILLIAM WESLEY WALTON

Judge Walton was a respected and honored gentleman of the community. He moved his family to Ash Avenue, further south in the town where they could get water. Judge Walton's courtroom was above the jail in the old *City Hall*. It was a multi-purpose room, holding court during weekdays and was an available church-meeting room on the weekends. It was used by several churches through the years while they constructed their own buildings. Judge Walton became Broken Arrow's fifth mayor from 1907 to 1908, during the Statehood year.(31)

As a girl, Zelma Gladys Walton saw *First Methodist* being built, as well as the *Haskell Agricultural College*, and later recounted memories of living in town when only wooden buildings lined Main Street. She could tell the story of a murder on Main Street, about the oil worker who shot his wife as she opened the door of *Hunsecker's Store*. "He ran

---
30. Wise, *First Census 1904*, 24.
31. Mayor W.W. Walton. *Photo Display of Mayors*, Broken Arrow City Hall.

Early Statehood

down Ash and stopped by the picket fence at our house. He stopped and dropped the shells out of his gun, put some more in it and turned around and shot at the crowd. The whole town was chasing him. That was an exciting day in Broken Arrow."

First-hand, Gladys reported that she and her brother went to the silent movie shows. She experienced school picnics by the river, piano lessons with Mrs. Mac Williams, the flu epidemic, gypsies coming to town and hobos that jumped off boxcars. She recalled that during her lifetime, the *Ku Klux Klan* held meetings on the hills north of town. Gladys lived a long life in Broken Arrow, was witness to major events and saw a town grow out of the prairie.

Graduating in 1918, Gladys received a teacher's certificate along with her high school diploma. In 1919 Gladys married Bryan Bland Terry, whom she had met on the way to school one day. In the *1920 Federal Census for Broken Arrow,* both were teachers. Gladys taught for a few years, then went to *Tulsa Business College.* From 1933, Mr. Terry was the postmaster in Broken Arrow for seven years.[32] He also served as president of the *Chamber of Commerce* and as a member of the *City Council.* After Bryan Terry was laid to rest in 1954, Gladys married Bill Tomlinson, an independent livestock trader, but outlived him as well.

Gladys' lifetime loves were flowers and gardening. Many

---
32. Stapleton, 222.

city residents remember her 1920-30's bungalow and garage apartment just south of the railroad tracks, where her home and yard were a beautiful display of constant blooms. Carefully cultivating an assortment of then-expensive and exotic day lilies, she used brilliant color next to green non-blooming foliage. Gladys creatively grouped simple yellow lilies in spots where the sun would intensify their pure color, and allowed brilliantly colored, bold combinations of lilies to unfold as early blooming flowers faded. It was truly a spectacular gardening showcase, and her love of flowers will be remembered forever.

Judge Walton taught Gladys a passionate devotion to God, her family and instilled a love for Broken Arrow in her. To honor him, Gladys gave a most extraordinary gift establishing a substantial Trust Account for the *Broken Arrow Historical Society*. This endowment provides one of the fundamental means to perpetuate the historical heritage of Gladys' beloved community. She had hoped one day the *Historical Society* could build a museum in place of her home and garden.

Gladys Walton Tomlinson's life ended April 24, 1993 at 93 years of age. She was committed to rest in *Park Grove Cemetery* with other members of the Walton and Terry families.

(Biographical information courtesy of Broken Arrow Genealogical Society.)

HELEN GADDY WELLS
(1904 – 1993)

HELEN GADDY WELLS

Two years after her parents came to *Indian Territory,* Helen Gaddy was born in Fry on February 11, 1904. The family rented a farm from Robert Fry, a Creek Indian. This farm girl attended *McCullough School* for eight years, then Broken Arrow where she was valedictorian of the *High School Class of 1921.* She attended *Oklahoma A&M* for a couple of years then worked for various oil companies: *Gypsy, Amerada Hess, Barnsdall, Gulf* and *Sun.* Many of those years, she was an executive secretary, a position she held until her retirement from *Sun Oil* in 1965.

Fred Wells, a local mail carrier for more than a decade, and Helen Gaddy married in 1938. In 1942, during World War II, Helen took a patriotic leave from her office to help with the farm, plant a victory garden and tend to the poultry, sheep, and other farm animals. In 1961 the Wells couple subdivided the farm, and the *Barry Dayton Addition* went up on the land.

Although Fred died in 1973, Helen remained active, in fact took on a new career, taking her real estate board exams in 1974. She joined the *John Bryce Real Estate* firm in 1977 and retired from her second career in 1992.

Helen Gaddy Wells helped form the *Broken Arrow Historical Society*, served as secretary of the *Park Grove Cemetery Committee* and was a member of *Eastern Star*, the *Embroidery Club*, *Rose Garden Club*, *Broken Arrow Seniors*, and *National Association of Retired Employees*. Helen Wells was Honorary Mayor in 1989 and inducted into the *Broken Arrow Hall of Fame* in 1992. She was also a member of *First Presbyterian Church* from 1922 until her death in 1993.

(Hall of Fame, 1992 Biographical information is courtesy of Broken Arrow Genealogical Society.)

CHARLES WAITMAN "SHORTY" COUCH
(1892 – 1968)

C.W. Couch arrived in Broken Arrow from Tennessee in 1907 when he was 15. The son of Thias Porter Couch, who was a widower at the time of the *1910 Federal Census of Broken Arrow*, C.W. had three siblings: Samuel C., and two sisters, Pansy and Opal. In 1915, C.W. married Rotha Olivia Neas, who also had arrived here from Tennessee in the first decade of

Rotha and Shorty Couch

the 1900s. Couch and his bride both were from prominent farm families and invested their lives in farming as well. They raised cattle and crops on their land in the Houston Street and *County Line Area*. He became known as *Shorty* or *Dad* in the community.

FIVE-YEAR CELEBRATION OF BROKEN ARROW, CA 1907

Shorty's wife, Rotha Neas Couch was the oldest child of William H. and Ellen E. Neas. She was quite equal to Shorty's skills for their farm responsibilities. Some family members and a neighbor report that Rotha was the one who posed as *the Pioneer Woman* walking in a *Rooster Day Parade* with her grandson. She rode in many Rooster Day Parades, regarded as "eccentric" for her ease and skill in riding side-saddle. Another grandson said she could rodeo and rope steers better than most men.

Shorty and Rotha later purchased the land on which the early-day, nine-hole golf course lay. The course was located just east of the present-day concrete plant on Houston Street. This couple had two sons, Ralph and Fred. Fred of Broken Arrow, says that his father was an industrious and highly respected farmer, active in the *Broken Arrow Farmers Co-op*.

Both Ralph and Fred acquired their hard-working trait

from their father. Ralph became owner of *Couch Pharmacy* in Tulsa, while Fred continued to farm and to work in agriculture as an employee of the *Farm Home Administration.*

Rotha Couch's sisters and brothers were Pauline, Nora, Bonnie, Joseph, George and Maynard.[33] Her siblings like her parents, were Broken Arrow residents and are now interred in Park Grove Cemetery.[34] Shorty Couch died in 1968 but some of his land remains in the family today.

The Legacy Lives On

> Shorty and Rotha had two sons: Fred ('34) and Ralph ('38). Fred was in the oil supply business, but also helped his dad farm. Fred and his wife, Marie, had two children, Don ('60) and Margaret. Don's children are Megan, Bridgid, Colin and Maureen. Ralph was a pharmacist in Tulsa. He and his wife, Irene, had 3 sons: Stephen, Ernie, and the late Charles Couch. Most of the Couch family still reside in this area and some specifically are in Broken Arrow. Many of Rotha's relatives live in the Broken Arrow area as well.

---

33. Park Grove Cemetery, www.findagrave.com/memorial/6750459/rotha-olivia-couch
34. Park Grove, www.findagrave.com/memorial/10258173/charles-waitman-couch

Early Statehood

SAMUEL PLUMMER
(1863 – 1943)

Early *Broken Arrow Ledger* items show that Samuel Plummer came here in 1904, as confirmed by his granddaughter. He was associated with the *J.A. Dix Elevator,* and in 1908 he opened the *Plummer Elevator.*

A *1908 Ledger* profile of local businesses gives a favorable review. "Mr. Samuel Plummer is one of the pioneer grain men of the state. For many years he extensively engaged in the grain trade in both mill and elevator lines. Top prices, courteous treatment and a square deal all the way through is the Plummer policy, a policy that has made strong friends for the elevator."

His granddaughter, Martha Plummer Roberts of the Bixby area, reports that her grandfather had strong family values. He required that the entire family eat their meals together. She recalls that "even when he did not get home until late at night, the family waited to have dinner with him." A family friend states that the Plummer house was the largest one in town, and one of the nicest.

It is noteworthy that Plummer was born in Ireland on May 26, 1863, and was brought to America by his parents when he was 3. As a young man, he engaged in studies at *Illinois University,* but moved on when his mother died. Before moving here, he had been a rancher with his father and brother in Kansas, worked on the first railroads in Colorado, and had been in wholesale business in Galveston, Texas. He married Catherine Teller in Guthrie on May 8, 1895 but continued to move to new opportunities.

1907 Corn Overflow; Granary Full, Stored Near Kentucky Colonel Hotel, Waiting for *MK&T* to Add More Cars for Shipping.

After an interval in Stillwater at their first mill and elevator, he was associated with the *Stevens-Scott Grain Company* at Wagoner. In addition to milling and elevator business, Plummer was a grower and became one of the largest shippers of alfalfa in the Arkansas Valley. Once he was settled here, he stayed. Even when he built an elevator in Bixby in 1915, he kept his home here. An undated *Ledger* fragment carried an item stating that Plummer was appointed to the *Broken Arrow City Council* while he was out of town on a business trip!

The family was mentioned often in the social, editorial, and school columns of the *Ledger*. It has been reported that the Plummers were pioneers in the formation of the *Episcopal Church* in Oklahoma. When Samuel died in 1943, his funeral service was held at *Trinity Episcopal Church* in Tulsa. When Catherine Plummer died in 1948, her funeral was held in the *Broken Arrow Presbyterian Church*, but the Reverend E.H. Eckel, Jr. of *Trinity Episcopal* officiated at both services. The couple reposes in *Tulsa's Memorial Park Cemetery*.

Although the Plummer home is no longer to be found, it was the homestead for their five children: Paul, Roger, Helen, Lucy Lee and Evelyn. Roger ('19) carried on the family business in Bixby. Lucy Lee ('21) and Evelyn ('21) both taught in Broken Arrow for a period in the twenties. Roger's daughter, Martha Plummer Roberts donated her aunt Evelyn's high school memory book to the *Broken Arrow Historical Society Museum*.

(Roberta Parker Biographical Notes, Broken Arrow Ledger with permission.)

BERTIE ETHEL (NORRIS) GILBERT
(1893 – 1983)

Bertie came to Oklahoma on October 27, 1907 with her

mother, Arminta Caudill Norris and father, John U. Norris and seven siblings. Although originally from Carroll, Arkansas, they had some time in Seymour, Missouri prior to moving to Catoosa.

Bertie recalled a trip taken with her father to purchase corn for their horses in Southwest City, Missouri. That night they camped next to a creek and were visited by Indians, who claimed her father had stolen corn from their field. Mr. Norris denied their claim but offered them a silver dollar if they would leave them alone. The Indians rode off whooping and hollering after getting the ransom money and didn't bother them anymore.

BERTIE ETHEL (NORRIS) GILBERT

John Norris was an expert hunter and trapper and earned money for his family by selling furs and skunk oil, which was determined to be a cure for the croup. John was the first man to receive a trapper's permit in this area. By the *1910 Federal Census, Adams Creek, Wagoner County*, the family of several children was listed with Bertie as the oldest, at age 17. Her years in school were cut short because the family moved several times when she was young, and then by her age 15,

Early Statehood

Bertie's mother had died. She had only a short time in school in the *Konklin Community*. In 1910, her seven siblings were from age 15 to as young as 3 years. She later stated that she knew how to make good cornbread and flour gravy.

Bertie met a young man by the name of John Lee Gilbert in 1910 while attending Sunday School at a small church in *Springtown*. The couple was married in Tulsa in 1912; he was 26 and she was 19. She remembered: "We drove a team of mules hitched to a surrey but there was no fringe on the top." After the wedding they drove back to Wagoner County where they lived for the next 42 years.

John Gilbert was a cotton farmer and carried his harvest to the *Miller Gin* in Broken Arrow. They planted peanuts and Bertie thought they were the first to do so in Wagoner County. Along with farming, her husband and her father, John Norris made coffins, and when there was a flu epidemic, they could hardly keep up.

John and Bertie had five children, but one son and two daughters succumbed early: Audie Lee was killed in a duck hunting accident at 17 years; Myrtle Faye died due to appendicitis when she was only 10; and Lorine Jewell became ill with the too-common childhood dysentery, and lived barely 18 months. The surviving sons Onis Junior and Eugene Norris Gilbert attended *Konklin School* and later graduated from *Broken Arrow High School*.

Meet the BROKEN ARROW CENTENNIALS

Bertie was well known for her beautiful quilts that she pieced together by herself, for as long as she could, and then had to send the pieces to a quilter to complete. Each of her grandchildren now owns one of Bertie's beautiful handmade quilts with her love hand-stitched into each one.

Moving from Konklin area, Bertie and John lived several years in their home on East Broadway Street. They enjoyed a Broken Arrow City neighborhood until her life-long friend and husband, John passed away in 1971, and Bertie passed in 1983. They were laid to rest in Park Grove Cemetery, Broken Arrow.

The Legacy Lives On

Bertie and John's sons graduated from *Broken Arrow High School*. The older son, Onis Junior ('42) has one living son, Jack Gilbert. Eugene (Gene) Norris ('50) and his wife Jo Ann Gilbert, who have lived in the Broken Arrow area almost all their married lives. They have three children who are also Broken Arrow graduates. Ron ('76), Linda ('79) and Tom ('84). Ron and Tom live in this area.

(Roberta Parker Biography, adapted from the Broken Arrow Ledger.)

BESSIE WILSON SMITH
(1904 – 2003)

Bessie Wilson Smith

Bessie Mae Wilson was born March 2, 1904, in Juno, Tennessee to Lillie Maude Patton and Joseph Samuel Wilson. Living in the central hill country, her family moved close to her Patton grandparents, where her father and grandfather farmed. As an adult, Bessie recalled "a simple life on the farm – no rushing around; just getting up before daylight to feed the horse and get ready to go to the field to plow, plant, harvest." Their big breakfast was "country wealth." Biscuits and gravy, ham or bacon and eggs, sorghum, molasses, honey from nearby hives and homemade jams and jellies. The iron stove kept a low fire, fueled by wood that had been chopped the previous night. Bessie's daily chores included drawing well water for family needs. A glow came from coal oil lamps, carried between rooms as needed. And warmth came when neighbors gathered to play fiddles and guitars into the evening hours.

Bessie's maternal grandmother was Rebecca Ann Laws (Patton), whose three brothers, (G.W.) Wash, Len and James Laws came from their Tennessee home to Broken Arrow before 1910. When they were established here, they told Bessie's dad Joseph Wilson, about the great need for carpentry in the area. He was a farmer and carpenter by trade, and this move seemed full of better opportunities for their family.

Bessie recalled the 1913 journey as an adventure, an amazing first train ride across Tennessee. Life after arrival at the *Broken Arrow Depot* was eye-opening as she became aware of gas lights hanging from ceilings and cookstoves fueled by gas. She found that water was piped right into the house, so she didn't have to bail and haul water anymore. The first Wilson home was across the street from the ice plant next to the *Katy Railroad Tracks* on West Dallas Street. Bessie was 11 years old when she got her first ride in an automobile.

Bessie's first day in 4th grade was at the *North Main School*. Her high school years were in the *Haskell Agriculture Building*, which had become a home for *Broken Arrow High School*. She graduated with fifteen classmates in 1922. During her junior year Bessie began dating a football player by the name of Truman ("Pruny") Smith. He would later say that she never missed a game while he was playing.

Bessie went on to *Northeastern State College* in Tahlequah where she prepared to teach. After graduation she taught at the one-room Thomas School for two years. Located six miles east of Broken Arrow, Bessie taught 25 students and all eight grades.

Bessie and Truman Smith married in Springfield, Missouri

on July 19, 1926. Pruny was a mail carrier, having begun this work when he was only seventeen. He delivered mail in the morning and still attended school in the afternoon. He skillfully built his own car for carrying the mail on his rural routes. The couple began immediately to save money for a new house. With a salary of $125 a month they managed to save $1,000 in six years, and in 1931 they started building with her father's help. By the time they finished their home, they had invested $2,500 and were able to borrow $1,200, which they paid off as soon as possible.

First child, Max Edward Smith, was born on August 30, 1932. Like most native Broken Arrow children, Dr. Onis Franklin delivered him in their home. A year later Patricia Sue Smith was born in September and Dr. Franklin was not available, so Bessie and Pruny delivered the baby themselves.

Bessie Smith's career at the *U.S. Post Office* started as a substitute clerk at the window. She was later the first female to serve as a route carrier, from *Alsuma* south to Broken Arrow and then East on Kenosha Street. The *Broken Arrow Ledger* described her route as "miry, muddy roads and when it was dry, they were dusty and rutted out." She experienced flat tires, snow drifts and accidents with wildlife. But she made it a priority to get to know her rural route clients and shared their lives through personal stories and experiences. She kept this work that she loved, for 35 years.[35]

---

35. "Bessie Smith, Oklahoma's First Woman Mail Carrier." *Valor Telcom*, Date unknown, probably 2002.

Sadly, in February 1965, Pruny Smith passed at the age of 65, Bessie's good companion for 39 years. This was a hard adjustment but through leaning on the Lord, her children and many loving and caring friends, she made it. One of her most memorable times was the 1990 *Rooster Days* celebration, when she was proclaimed *Honorary Mayor of Broken Arrow* by the *City Council*. She rode down the same Main Street that she remembered going down when she first arrived in 1913, but oh, how much it had changed since then.

Bessie Mae Wilson Smith passed from this remarkable life on August 1, 2003 in Broken Arrow. Her service was held at the *First Baptist Church* and she was interred in the *Park Grove Cemetery* next to her loving husband, Pruny.

The Legacy Lives On

Bessie and Truman had two children, Max Smith ('50) and the late Patricia Smith Crawford ('51). Max married Judy Ross Smith ('62). Max and Judy have two children, Wade Smith and Darci Smith Delso. Patricia married Wayne Crawford. Their two boys are Bobby and Ricky.

(Adapted from an autobiography by Bessie Smith, assisted by her son, Max Smith.)

MARVIN TUCKER
(1900 – 1978)

MARVIN TUCKER

Marvin L. Tucker was born in December 1900 in Tucker, Missouri, where his father owned the general store and ran the post office for the little town established in 1891. Marvin's mother died when he was young and was one of six brothers and four sisters. At age 10 he lived with his brother William's family on a Ripley County farm in Missouri. He followed several siblings from their home state and settled in Broken Arrow in 1920.

After delivering mail for a short time, Marvin took up barbering for *Boles Barber Shop*. He opened his own barber shop on Main Street in 1923. Marvin and Eula Williams married in 1925, and their children were Bob and Janette. In 1935, Marvin opened a Main Street beauty parlor and was the only male beauty operator in town for eight years. After closing the beauty shop, he kept the barber business until he retired around 1975.

His son, Bob Tucker took over the Barber Shop part time while Marvin continued to barber off and on through the years. It is not unusual to hear town men and women say, "I remember Mr. Tucker cutting my hair when I was young."

In 1944, Marvin Tucker was Scoutmaster for his son's *Boy Scout Troop 104.* An interesting opportunity for the troop came during his barber shop years. Marvin had met Russell Kelce, owner of the *Peabody Coal Company.* Over the next years, the vital coal mining that took place in the East New Orleans Street and County Line Road area played out. The land was to be abandoned and was left treeless and desolate. Marvin convinced Mr. Kelce to donate the 400-acre tract to the Scouts.

JOHN TUCKER, MARVIN'S BROTHER, ALSO WAS A BARBER IN THE MAIN STREET SHOP

Boy Scout Troop 104 began some work that took several years, making the land into what became "the Scout Camp." They cleared land for camping, planting trees and digging a swimming pool. *Camp Russell* has been used by the Boy Scouts and the community for fishing, swimming, boating, hiking, and camping through this present time.

Early Statehood

Marvin L. Tucker retired from the camp in 1972. His death came in October 1978 and he rests at *Park Grove Cemetery* with wife, Eula Williams Tucker. In addition to their two children, Marvin and Eula were grandparents to nine children.

The Legacy Lives On

Tucker is a common and well-known name for many family descendants who still live in this area. Marvin and Eula's son, Bob Tucker (Broken Arrow High '47) and his wife Peggy live in Broken Arrow and have been active with the *Broken Arrow Historical Society* for several years along with their daughter, Teresa. Bob and Peggy's children are Stephanie Tucker Smith ('72) and her husband Steve; Paul Tucker, Anne Tucker ('78), Teresa Tucker ('83), Jill Tucker Norman ('87) and her husband Clay, as well as the late Philip Tucker ('75). Philip's two daughters (Marvin and Eula's grandchildren) are Stephanie ('90) and Megan ('02). Marvin and Eula's only daughter, the late Carol Janette Tucker Kennedy (BA graduate in '52) (1934-1987) had 3 children, Leslyn, Jud and Keli Kennedy. Keli ('78) is the only one still living. Most of the Tucker family reside in Broken *Arrow*.

(Biography and photo courtesy of Broken Arrow Genealogical Society.)

DAVID ALBERT "DEACON" WILSON
(1858 – 1933)

David Albert "Deacon" Wilson didn't make noise – he made news. During just twenty-two years in Broken Arrow, Deacon's impact was so profound that on the day of his funeral in 1933, downtown merchants closed their stores to honor him. Deacon and his wife Caroline came from Wichita, Kansas in 1911. There, he had been a farmer and a dealer for farm machinery, owning a *McCormick Dearing Implement Company*. He was also an operating partner in various oil and gas leases, had served as a Kansas legislator and was on the *Board of County Commissioners for Sedgwick County*.

For his move to Broken Arrow, Deacon rented a railroad car. All the furniture, household goods and clothing were loaded into one end, along with farm equipment, wagons, and a buggy. In the other end, the family's cattle, horse, and chickens were made secure. Deacon assigned two sons to the high adventure of staying in the car to feed and water the livestock for the journey. Deacon, Caroline and another son and daughter rode in the comparative luxury of a passenger car.

In Broken Arrow they bought a 120-acre peach orchard on the northwest corner of Washington and Elm Streets. Just a year later, Harry, their second-born son died, and then in 1918, Caroline became suddenly ill and died. It was later presumed by family that they died of influenza. At age 60, Deacon had been married twenty-seven years and according to those who knew him, it was as though a light went out of his life when she died.

Perhaps because of the memory of deep grief, Deacon was prompted to sell the farm and buy another on the opposite, far northeast corner of Broken Arrow. There, at East Omaha Street and Lynn Lane Road, he purchased 480 acres and tilled the soil with two of his sons, William and David Albert II. *The 1920 Federal Census for Lynn Lane Township* shows that his son William with wife Lula G. and their baby son, Gene, as well as youngest son, David A. Wilson II with his wife Stella, were at home with Deacon on the farm.

DEACON WILSON AND FAMILY (C. EARLY 1930S)

Deacon Wilson also plunged into community service.

Meet the BROKEN ARROW CENTENNIALS

He served two terms in the *Oklahoma State Legislative Assembly,* then without salary. He was the head of *Exchange Trust Company,* a corporation of men who bought property where the current Tulsa Fairgrounds is located. Purchasing the land with their own money, they held it until the *Tulsa County Fair Board* could buy it. Deacon served two terms as director and president of the *Tulsa County Fair Board.*

David A. Wilson III, a grandson and 1936 graduate of Broken Arrow High School, had many years to spend with his grandfather and learn about his life's journey. This David attended the *University of Tulsa* and lived with his own family in Tulsa for several years before moving to Longview, Texas. He remembers his grandfather staying at the fair each year during its entire length. "Then he'd bring us little gifts from the fair, like balloons and games." Robert L. Wilson of Tulsa also remembers that their grandfather stayed in the *Fairgrounds Management Headquarters,* a frame two-story building located on the west side of the fairgrounds. "Grandfather was not the loud, shouting kind. He wasn't a blustery person - I don't remember him ever lifting his voice." Deacon Wilson didn't have to; his actions spoke louder than words. David Albert Wilson was a Quaker, a devout Christian, and his deep faith must have rested on him like a clergy's mantle for he was known simply as "Deacon."

Deacon Wilson was among a group who founded the *Federal Land Bank Association* in Broken Arrow. When making current Broken Arrow land or building purchases, the lien-tracing still uncovers documents signed by Land Bank President, David A. Wilson.

Family members are unanimous, Grandfather Deacon "had a tender heart." His granddaughter, Harriett Courington of Longview, related a glimpse of it: "When Mother was in town and Grandpa was in charge of us, if we became too rambunctious and wouldn't quiet down, he'd chase us out of the house with a fly swatter." She said, "Grandpa was a quiet-spoken man and carried himself with great dignity." Harriet's son, Larry recently agreed that many memorable stories were passed down, and the Longview, Texas family still feels a strong connection to Broken Arrow.

Even David III's daughters, Susan and Barbara recall visits with their grandparents, David, Jr. and Stella in Broken Arrow. At one time, these grandparents had a farm on the southwest corner of Kenosha and Elm as well as later having a home on East College.

The Legacy Lives On

Undoubtedly, Deacon Wilson's delight in his large family carried through to this current generation. His daughter, Madeline Wilson Schmidt (1892-1987) raised her family in Kansas. His sons, William M., "Bill" (1894-

Meet the BROKEN ARROW CENTENNIALS

1964) and David Albert, Jr. (1898-1976) lived their lives in this area, each raising several children.

The oldest son, Bill and his wife, Lula G. Burdette Wilson (1896-1985) had six children, five of whom graduated from high school here: Jean ('37), Charley ('38), Harriet ('39), Alyce Kay ('43) and W.H. "Pete" ('43). Bill and Lula's daughter Margaret died as a child, and son Charles Albert was killed as a Silver Star-decorated Marine in the battle of Iwo Jima (1921-1945). Jean died at age 45, in Texas.

Dave, Jr. and Stella Claire Beardsley Wilson's sons graduated from BAHS. David III, ('36), a petroleum engineer, (Cecil) Mark ('39), a veterinarian in Wagoner, Oklahoma; Robert Lawrence "Bob" ('41) was an engineer at Braden Winch, and Bruce Lamont Wilson ('43) in Oil and Gas Producing, Wilson Resources. Bob was the only son who lived his entire life in Broken Arrow and had one son, Dean Wilson ('63) who served in Vietnam and died as a relatively young man after the war. Dean's mother was Anita Bond Wilson.

Dave Wilson, Jr. served during WWI, and his four sons were active in WWII. David III (1920-2013) was in the U.S. Army Air Corps as a B-17 navigator and bombardier, and later was decorated with the Distinguished Flying Cross and the Air Medal with four Oak Leaf clusters. He retired from the Air Force Reserve as a Lieutenant Colonel and resumed civilian life in Oklahoma, then lived the rest of his life in Texas. Bob (1923-2005) also served in the Air Corps as a First Pilot, completing 27 B-17 raids without injury or loss. Mark (1921-2007) enlisted from 1943-1946 and later established a veterinary practice. Bruce L. (1925-2007) served in the U.S. Navy and lived in Longview, Texas from 1955.

The great-grandchildren still have a close bond. Deacon's grand-children Harriet Courington, David III and Bruce migrated to Texas, where most of their children live. Harriet has two sons, Larry and Greg Courington. Harriet's sister, Alyce Kay, has one daughter, Alyce Fay. David III's daughters are Susan and Barbara. Bruce's children are Kyle, Kent, Allen, David and Laura. Mark's children, Gary, Charlie and Tracy live in the Tulsa area.

(Broken Arrow Genealogical Society and Family Interviews)

HASKELL STATE SCHOOL OF AGRICULTURE
(1909 – 1917)

Haskell State School of Agriculture opened on November 15, 1909 with classes in the *Opera House* on Main Street. The cornerstone for this secondary education building was laid in May 1910 on an 80-acre tract of land on East College Street. Between 150 and 200 students from 15-counties enrolled in the school each year. The primary classroom building was surrounded by poultry houses, a barn, creamery, pastures, grain fields, gardens, vocational shops, and a caretaker's house.

Meet the BROKEN ARROW CENTENNIALS

HASKELL STATE SCHOOL OF AGRICULTURE (1909 – 1917)

The school seemed to be a concession by the new State of Oklahoma to Broken Arrow for its missed appointment as a county seat. In 1905, while living in Muskogee, J.H. Esslinger and several others representing a citizen's group, offered Broken Arrow as a potential county seat for Coweta County in the proposed state of *Sequoyah*. They also lobbied to have one of the six newly proposed *State Normal Schools* placed in Broken Arrow, for educational development and preparation of teachers. Instead of either of these options, the town was notified in September 1907 that the Broken Arrow received approval for a secondary school, a state school of agriculture.

Quickly brought under construction, the primary building of the *Haskell State School of Agriculture* was an impressive three-story brick structure with fourteen rooms, placed in the center of the purchased acreage, and was designed to serve up to 300 students. No dormitories were made during the short construction interval, so students boarded with local families.

The school was named for the first governor of Oklahoma, Charles N. Haskell. Esslinger had been a member of the campaign staff when Haskell ran for state senator. Appointed superintendent of the *Haskell State School of Agriculture* in 1909, J.H. Esslinger was Master of Ceremonies at the campus opening in 1910. Area farmers and residents benefitted from agricultural workshops offered at the school. Within three years as executive of the school, in 1912, the *Oklahoma Board of Agricultural* appointed Superintendent J.H. Esslinger to head the state's *Farm Development Department.*

The *Haskell State School of Agriculture* was closed in 1917, when the State of Oklahoma cut the budget appropriations. A great and well-used opportunity while it lasted, and not an entire loss to the city, *Broken Arrow High School* found a new home in the building, as did the *Broken Arrow Junior High.* Later, the building was renamed, becoming the *Fine Arts Building* for the high school. The third floor became a large study hall room during part of the 1920's and 1930's. During the 1960's the large room became the band room, resounding with marching band rehearsals.

JAMES HOUSTON ESSLINGER
(1870 – 1920)

JAMES HOUSTON ESSLINGER

J. H. Esslinger, son of Alabama parents Katherine Margaret Fennell (1842-1884) and Andrew Jackson Esslinger (1844-1929) was born in Madison County on March 17, 1870. After serving in the Confederate Army, his father resumed farming where James grew up with seven brothers and two sisters. He earned a Bachelor of Science degree from the Winchester Normal School of Tennessee and taught school in Tennessee and Alabama. During that time, he was principal of several schools.

While teaching at Gurley, Alabama he met Nola Katron Sullivan (1880-1907), daughter of Amanda Jane Johnson (1853-1923) and William R. Sullivan (1845-1923). She was born on September 27, 1880 at St. Joseph, Champaign County, Illinois. Her father served in the Union Army during the Civil War and later moved his family to Gurley, Alabama.

James H. and Nola had married on November 10, 1896.

Early Statehood

Four children were born in Alabama, and his young family had moved with him to Muskogee, Indian Territory.

Although a family man and a prior educator, J.H. Esslinger was quickly and deeply involved in civic and political affairs after his arrival in 1904. He was employed by the *Muskogee Times Democrat* and *New State Tribune* which made him well-known throughout the area. He became intensely involved in the formative issues for the new state.

During this same interval, Nola gave birth to their fifth child, Nola Sullivan Esslinger, born June 9, 1907. Still living in Muskogee, the family faced the shock of Nola Katron Sullivan Esslinger's death at her age 26. Baby Nola was just five weeks old when her mother died from "acute heart trouble."[36] She was taken to the Sullivan, maternal grandparents' home, and even after J.H. and the other children moved to Broken Arrow, the *1910 Federal Census for Broken Arrow* shows that "granddaughter Nolie" continued to live with William and Amanda Sullivan.

W.R. Sullivan, James Esslinger's father-in-law, and owner of the local brick factory, handpicked brick for

J.H. AND DORA SULLIVAN ESSLINGER'S HOME

---

36. "Mrs. Nola Esslinger is Dead," *Muskogee Times Democrat*, June 8, 1907.

this house in 1911. The founding president of *Haskell State Agriculture School* first owned this house at the southwest corner of East College and 5th Street. From its completion in 1911, this was James and Dora Esslinger's home.

James had married Dora Sullivan (Nola's younger sister) on May 24, 1908 in Broken Arrow. Dora became responsible for the home and her sister's five children; and later, with James, added Elsie and Frederick to the family. Their seven children had a home here, and the *1910 Federal Census for Broken Arrow* lists: James, wife Dora, and children, Cecil, 12 years, Charles, 10, Houston, age 8, Mable, 5 years and newborn Elsie, 11 months old in May; last son, Frederick would be born in 1915. Nolie Esslinger, age 2, still lived with her Sullivan Grandparents. In 1916, this College President's family home also served as a dormitory for about 30 girls.

After his time at Haskell ended in 1917, J.H. Esslinger later worked as an insurance agent for the *Modern Woodmen of America*, a fraternal organization. He was responsible for establishing new local organizations in many towns in western Oklahoma. An active church member, he was also choir director at the *Methodist Episcopal Church, South,* in Broken Arrow. He was only fifty years old when he died on 20 February 1920 after a prolonged illness. J. Houston Esslinger's grave is marked by a shared headstone with Nola S. Esslinger in Muskogee's Greenhill Cemetery. Both J.H. Esslinger and Dora Sullivan Esslinger were recognized in 1991 as *Broken Arrow Hall of Fame* honorees.

Early Statehood

Nola and J.H. Esslinger Children, Miss Wells, Teacher, ca. 1908
Front Left, 2nd Girl: Mable, Born September 1904
Back Left, 2nd Boy: Houston, Born June 1902

(Biographical information courtesy of Broken Arrow Genealogical Society.)

Meet the BROKEN ARROW CENTENNIALS

ALL TYPES OF BROKEN ARROW BUSINESSES WERE THRIVING

COTTON HARVEST- KENTUCKY COLONEL ON LEFT IN BACKGROUND

Chapter 10

From the Cotton Fields to the Battlefields
"The War to End All Wars"

Broken Arrow's residents were enjoying a unique time with bragging rights as one of the Nation's newest states. Success in business came from area coal mining and general farming, with a primary source of income from processing the acres of cotton grown throughout the region. Families were satisfied with their new community which provided a stable and safe environment with churches, schools, and social groups. However, toward the end of the second decade of the twentieth century the world began to change.

Two deaths in Sarajevo, Bosnia on June 28th of 1914, provoked a widespread European conflict that eventually involved England, and later a "neutral" United States. The assassination of Archduke Franz Ferdinand and his wife sparked a broad European war and "opportunistic despotism" that reordered many countries' borders and forms of government.

Meet the BROKEN ARROW CENTENNIALS

President Woodrow Wilson guided the United States in a neutrality that changed dramatically when a German U-boat sank the *RMS Lusitania* in May 1915. The British liner had departed from New York for Liverpool, and in the explosions, 1,198 people died, including 128 American citizens. In the face of U.S. reaction, Germany promised to forestall further warfare on the seas. However, upon a January 1917 declaration that it would resume unrestricted warfare in war-zone waters, President Wilson declared war on Germany the 6th day of April 1917.[37]

Our Army was unprepared in so many ways. "The U.S. Army had a grand total of 122 thousand enlisted men and 5,800 officers on April 6, 1917. The Army was spread among posts around the American West and on constabulary duties in the Philippines, Puerto Rica, Cuba, and Panama. The National Guard (Reserve) had a grand total of 182 thousand personnel and they were cursed with uneven training and even older equipment than the active force."[38] Less than 310 thousand U.S. troops at hand! Senator Thomas Martin, when he found out that the War Department requested three billion dollars to equip and train our army, responded with: "Good Lord, you're not going to send soldiers over there are you?"[39]

---

37. Keene, Jennifer D., *World War I: The American Soldier Experience*. Lincoln: University of Nebraska Press, 2011, 1-2.
38. Jim Garamone, "April 1917: America Entered the First World War," *DoD News, Defense Media Activity* https://www.army.mil/article/184897/ April 7, 2017. *(Editor: Numbers rounded up to nearest thousand.)*
39. Keene, 11.

From the Cotton Fields to the Battlefields

Another remarkable fact was that our military only had 55 airplanes and some of them were in questionable airworthy condition. There were enough Springfield rifles to arm 850 thousand soldiers but only a supply of ammunition for 220 thousand was readily available. Armored tanks were non-existent at the time.[40]

Experienced military leadership was required. "The Secretary of War, Newton Baker and the President did not want to manage the military and appointed John J. Pershing as the *Commander of the Allied Forces in Europe,* to freely operate and do whatever he had to do to win the war and bring the troops back home. That order perhaps gave Pershing the most freedom to operate than any other commander in the history of the United States Armed Forces."[41]

Who did the town see off to distant shores? Our local boys had become more secure in their achievements since the *Broken Arrow High School* was graduating greater numbers each year after the first 1908 graduation, and *Haskell State Agricultural School* appeared to have a solid future. This farming community grew in its sense of promise for their sons and daughters. However, parents' dreams of success were suddenly challenged when the first of the world-wide-wars altered family plans.

Support for the servicemen was shouldered by a willing

---
40. Keene, 9.
41. Keene, 12.

Meet the BROKEN ARROW CENTENNIALS

1910 - 1911 BROKEN ARROW FOOTBALL TEAM

FRONT LEFT: T.M. HUNSECKER, ERNEST MARTIN, WARREN PEELER, ZEUS JANEWAY, JAMES HUNTER, WESLEY GRUBE,** "LUCKY" WALTON

BACK LEFT: N.H. EDWARDS, CAPTAIN; CHARLES FOSTER, *SHELBY HARLESS, COLLINS LAWS, *BERNHAM DEWEESE, EARL LAWS, *VIRGIL FORD, ERNEST HUNTER

*SERVED IN WWI MILITARY, AND **DIED DURING SERVICE.

American population. New organizations were required; each major town or city came under a state-authorized *Council of Defense* to evaluate and allocate resources. *National War Bond* drives gathered funds from citizens in billions of dollars for new military equipment. Broken Arrow had representatives who already held notable banking roles and assumed responsibility for a Tulsa County and National role in the *Third Bond Drive*. "The *Broken Arrow War Council* was organized in March 1918 under the charge of F.S. Hurd, Chairman representing the *Council of Defense*; with banker Robert B. Mitchell representing the *YMCA* and the *Fuel Administration*; and Charles E. Foster representing the *War Savings Stamps campaign*."[42]

Across the county, *"Four-Minute Men"* gave short speeches to support bond drives and military recruitment, and in Broken Arrow the group of fifteen leaders included W.T. Brooks, Rev. Harry Morgan, W.T. Dalton, F.S. Hurd, Robert B. Mitchell, Dr. W.D. Ownby and a few others.[43] Women also were appointed to the bond-raising efforts through reaching their social and church groups.

Farmers began extra food production and housewives learned new recipes for "meat-less and wheat-less" foods as rationing allowed local-grown beef, pork, and flour to be shipped overseas as meals for troops. Automobiles were stored away when gas rationing required use of public transportation. Scrap metal items were collected by neighborhood boys for recycling into military machines and weapons.

The *American Red Cross* organized a nation-wide volunteer work force which saw their work and sacrifice as

---

42. Lampe, William T., Compiler. *Tulsa County in the World War, An Authorized History*, Tulsa: the Tulsa County Historical Society; 1919, 86-87. Access: archive.org/details/tulsacountyinwor00lamp/mode/2up
43. Lampe, 141.

a means of supporting our boys "over there." Women's groups began sewing hospital items and men's uniforms as well as knitting socks, sweaters, caps, and other items the government had no capacity to provide. Many employers designated five paid hours a week for workers to participate in these activities in storerooms or church spaces set aside for this work.[44] Bandage-rolling hours were posted in newspaper society columns.

RED CROSS WORKROOMS WERE DEVELOPED ACROSS THE COUNTY

The *Broken Arrow Red Cross Branch* was organized in July 1919 with Rev A.J. Reynolds, chairman. Mrs. Lutie (Nat L.) Sanders was one of two women in charge of the work which involved all willing adults, as well as children in the

---

44. Lampe, Red Cross Workroom, 138.

Jr. Red Cross. "Under Mrs. George A. Brown, chairman of the women's work, the work was brought up to a high standard and after her inspection was ready for shipment… this included both hospital and knitted garments."[45]

The entire the nation had a mandate and a moral imperative to serve America in the firmly held belief that this was the *War to End All Wars!* General Pershing followed his orders, and the war came to an end with the *November 11, 1918 Armistice Agreement* and most troops were home by mid-1919. The results of one terrorist's actions five years earlier in Bosnia ended with the loss of over nine million lives worldwide, including 117,000 Americans.[46]

Ultimately, when the war ended, more than four million "Doughboys" had served in the United States Army with the American Expeditionary Forces (AEF). Half of those participated overseas. According to Secretary of War Newton D. Baker, "over 25 per cent of the entire male population of the country between the ages of 18 and 31 were in military service."[47]

During the war, the morale of the citizens here at home wavered at times, but with George M. Cohen's musical talent for writing and performing patriotic songs, he lifted the willing spirit of the country. The lyrics such as,

---

45. Ibid, 133.
46. *America's Wars.* VA Department. www.va.gov/opa/publications/factsheets/fs_americas_wars.pdf.
47. War Department, *Annual Report of the Secretary of War for the Fiscal Year, 1918,* Vol. 1, 1918; 11.

Meet the BROKEN ARROW CENTENNIALS

"Johnny Get Your Gun," the first verse of his most famous song, *"Over There"* voiced courage, and the chorus resounded with needed bravado for hometown people and the troops: *"Send the word, send the word over there ... the Yanks are coming, the Yanks are coming."*[48]

OUR BOYS WHO SERVED, COLLINS AND EARL LAWS.
SEATED LEFT: COLLINS WITH SHORTY WILLIAMS;
STANDING LEFT: EARL WITH T.M. HUNSECKER

"THE YANKS ARE COMING"

As always with our patriotic heritage as Americans, the call to arms was not taken lightly by the citizens and sons of the Broken Arrow community. In all, seventy-five hometown boys enlisted in the Army, Navy, and the

---

48. Cohan, George Michael (1878-1942) composer. *Over There.* Canada: Whaley, Royce and Co. for William Jerome Publishing Corporation, NY, 1917. Made available by the Library of Congress.

From the Cotton Fields to the Battlefields

Marine Corps to defend freedom where needed.

As mothers do for their soldiers, they lovingly prayed for and honored their sons. A unique sign of their devotion is an old scratchy wool Army blanket with Broken Arrow servicemen names carefully embroidered in outline. Many mothers provided an embroidered patch and Mrs. Fitz Hurd (Nancy M. Crandall) assembled the memorial quilt. The blanket was lost for a time, then was discovered in the attic of the *Currell Lumber Company* by Chris Housley. This "must-see" WWI Artifact is displayed in *The Museum Broken Arrow*. One of the exceptional features is that the pieces are from each soldier's uniform pants, worn during his service.

OUR SOLDIER BOYS – WWI MEMORIAL QUILT
THE FULL LIST OF NAMES APPEARS ON P. 201–202

Perhaps the most interesting patch was stitched at the

quilt's center, a sizable piece from General George Pershing's breeches. His distinctive uniform is seen in most of his wartime photos, and this real-life piece was obtained by Mrs. Hurd from his brother in Kentucky.

"TILL IT'S OVER, OVER THERE"

The war cast some of Broken Arrow's finest into the thousands of young men who would serve. Deacon Wilson's (p.178) youngest son, his namesake David, served in the U.S. Navy[49] from May 13, 1917 until August 27, 1919.[50] David returned safely, but his time away from home was all the more difficult because his mother, Harriet C. Wilson made her will in March 1918, and passed away on April 14, 1918 at age 58.

DAVID A. WILSON, JR., DEACON'S SON
1915 BROKEN ARROW GRADUATE

The following biographies reflect typical lives of the era, young men from different backgrounds. Charles Foster and Roy Pauli served during *World War I* and returned safely. Along with Les Randall, Sr. and Ivan Brown, all four became successful Main Street businessmen in the decades after the war.

---

49. Lampe. *"Tulsa County Fighting Men,"* 45.
50. Ancestry.com. *U.S., Department of Veterans Affairs BIRLS Death File, 1850-2010* [database on-line]. Provo, UT, USA: Ancestry.com Operations, Inc., 2011.

OUR SOLDIER BOYS
Embroidered Names on the WWI Memorial Quilt

Cleo Adams	John Archibald	Ernest Bernard
Fred Brooks	Henry Carpenter	Ira Chilton
Dr. Cooper	Arthur Crandall	Carl Dalton
Gomer Davis	Mack Delk	Clarence Douglas
E. Eberhart*	Cecil Esslinger	Reid Estill*
Charles Fisher	Charles Foster	Dr. Onis Franklin
Robert Fry	Wesley Grube*	Fred Hunt
Bryan Hunter	Tom Hunter*	Ernest Hunter

REID PHILLIPS ESTILL

Reid Estill lived in Broken Arrow with his mother Mrs. S.R. Estill, *1910 Federal Census.* "Age 25, clerk *Tulsa Company F. 357th Infantry, 90th Division.* Killed in action in St. Mihiel drive. Cited for bravery."

Thomas F. Hunter. "Age 21, mechanic, Broken Arrow, Company B. 7th Infantry, 5th Division. Died from wounds received in action on French front, October 1918. Mother, Mrs. Minnie M. Hunter. Brother of James and Ernest, *1910 BA Football team.*

THOMAS E HUNTER

Meet the BROKEN ARROW CENTENNIALS

OUR SOLDIER BOYS
Embroidered Names on the WWI Memorial Quilt

Paul Hurd	Fitz C. Hurd	Bruce Isom
Lawrence Johnson	Orville Keller	Marcy Kelly
Ralph Knight	Collins Laws	Earl Laws
Milo Lofton	Russell Malone	Fred Markham
Roy McKeehan	Henry Morgan	Wayne Mikel*
Dr. Francis Myers	Roy Pauli	Orville Pike
Bud Rankin	F.B. Righter	Julian Sanders
Harry Simon	Urie Smith	William Smith*
James Smoot	William Smoot	George Snyer
James Sutton	Harry Toy	Luke Turley
Ernest Vance	Happy Walker	Fred Wells
Claud Whitenack	Will Wilborn	C. H. Wiliams
Gerald Williams	Dave Wilson	Royal Wolf
Alvin Wolf	Walter Wyatt	Elmer Wyatt

WILLIAM W. SMITH

William. W. Smith. "Age 28, Student, Warner. *19th Sanitary Train.* Died at Camp Dodge, Iowa October 11, 1918 of pneumonia. His father, W.T. Smith, Broken Arrow." Influenza was very prevalent in Army training camps.

---

51. Lampe, 52. *Additional Broken Arrow losses, Alonzo Casey, James Kersey, Homer Reid.*

CHARLES E. FOSTER, FIRST GRADUATION CLASS, 1908

CHARLES E. FOSTER
(1892 – 1964)

Charles Foster was a 1908 graduate of *Broken Arrow High School* and was still an outstanding football player on the *Tigers Football Team* in 1910. Early day school teams could include young men from the town. During the next season most of the teammates played for the *Haskell Agriculture School* and were known as a "powerhouse" in Northeastern Oklahoma.

These students were of prime age in May 1917 when President Wilson imposed a wartime conscription draft which required all men between 21 and 30 years of age, to register for military service. And since every state had an obligation to join the national war bond drive to raise funds, Oklahoma's Governor, Robert Lee Williams declared a holiday and named it *Liberty Day*, a proclamation launching the *Liberty Bond Drives* as well as the draft registration of the state's young men for military duty.

Charles would remember June 5, 1917 as the day that he and some classmates signed-up for another team – the U.S. Army; but he was no lad that day, he was 25 years old. Parades were held throughout the nation, launching the *Liberty Day Bond Drive* and encouraging groups of young men to march together to the recruitment office. Two-hundred men registered for the draft on the first *Liberty Day* in Broken Arrow. The *Ledger* reported that all registrants passed their recruitment inspection without any evidence of disorder, drunkenness, or record of arrest.

Charles left behind an anxious wife, Bonnie L. Chilton Foster, from Reynolds County, Missouri, whom he had married on March 10, 1915.[52] His place and dates of service are not known, but leaving home during national war still held an impact of its own.

After the war, one of Charles' first jobs was as assistant cashier at the *First National Bank* when currency was delivered in printed sheets.[53] The U.S. Treasury sheets were taken to the *Broken Arrow Ledger* office where the paper cutter was used to divide them into bills. Charles Foster was the bank official who signed for the cut bills, and there are notes in the bank today with his name on them, as reported by his grandson, Chuck Foster.

---

52. *Oklahoma, County Marriage Records, 1890-1995;* Ancestry.com Operations, Inc., 2016.
53. *1920 Federal Census, Broken Arrow, Tulsa Co, OK;* "Charles Foster," line 14, E.D. 195, Sheet 4A.

From the Cotton Fields to the Battlefields

Charles Foster was later named Vice-President of the *First National Bank,* and in a few years became Vice-President of *Broken Arrow Savings and Loan,* established in 1919. He started out as the secretary of that firm and was eventually in the position of Director.

Foster was a long-time businessman on Main Street who became affiliated with the *Oklahoma Tire and Supply Company,* later referred to as *OTASCO.* Foster transferred his interest in that company over to his son Joe, who continued to operate that business until its closing.

Charles Foster was very civic minded and served on the *Broken Arrow City Council* and was an active member of the *Broken Arrow Chamber of Commerce.* He was an elder in the *Presbyterian Church.* His successful business life belied the struggle of his beginning years, when he came to *Indian Territory* with his mother after his father's death. He made the most of many opportunities and after a long, successful career as a banker, business owner, civic leader, and respected church elder, Charles Foster passed from this life on Christmas Day, 1964. His wife Bonnie lived in Broken Arrow until 1971, and they are both interred at Memorial Park Cemetery in Tulsa.

(Biographical information and 1908 Graduation photo provided by The Museum Broken Arrow.)

Meet the BROKEN ARROW CENTENNIALS

The Legacy Lives On

Charles and Bonnie Chilton Foster became parents of Joseph Lee Foster on March 17, 1922. (1922-1977). Joe L. Foster and Martha Margaret Malone "Pattie" Foster (1924-1966) married on February 7, 1943.

ROY I. PAULI
(1897 – 1977)

Roy I. Pauli

Roy Pauli was born on the 1st Day of January 1897 in a little Kansas settlement. He was the son of John and Edith Pauli of Washington County. At an early age, his father took him to a county farm sale, and when he heard that auctioneer chant, Roy knew that was what he wanted to do. He decided right there he was going to be an auctioneer but wasn't sure just how to accomplish it.

At his age ten, the family moved to Caddo County, Oklahoma, where they lived for five years before moving to Madison County, Arkansas. Now mid-teens, Roy decided there was not much potential for work to earn enough money to attend auctioneer school. After hearing about Broken Arrow from a fellow at work, he decided to write a letter to Mr. R.A. Wallingford, clerk of the *Broken Arrow School Board* and an employee of the *Arkansas Valley State Bank*. In his letter, he questioned whether Broken Arrow could offer a young man a job and opportunity to go to school. When he received Mr. Wallingford's reply, Roy packed his bags and boarded a train for Broken Arrow. He was on his way to his future.

The day he disembarked at Broken Arrow with several other passengers, he headed to the *Kentucky Colonel Hotel*, but found no vacancy. Proceeding to *Harsen Hotel* across the street, the hotel clerk let him sleep in a rocking chair in the office since they also had no room. He was awakened about 3a.m. by a large man walking down the stairs, joining him in one of the other rocking chairs. The man told him it was better to sleep in the chairs since the beds upstairs were infested with bed bugs.

Roy was up early the next morning, wandered down the street and came to *Shorty's Café*. After the visit, he was hired as a cook by Shorty Baxter, and started work on Friday September 13th, 1913. Still just 16, he also started school the following Monday, continuing to work at the café to earn money to live.

Shorty had a lot of faith in this young man and left him in charge of his café when he went to St. Louis to get married.

One of the customers was Newt Williams, who noticed that Roy had more ambition than to be just a cook. Newt asked him what he planned when he was able to get out on his own. That was an easy question for Roy to answer because his heart was set on going to auctioneer school.

Mr. Williams asked if there was an auctioneering school and why Roy had not started going there. When Roy told him that he didn't have the money, Newt told him to go to the *Arkansas Valley Bank* for a loan, which he would co-sign for him. With the loan in his pocket, Roy phoned Shorty and informed him of his decision, then boarded a train headed for Kansas City. The *Missouri Auctioneering School* was a three-week course, after which he returned to *Shorty's Café*. Shorty Baxter had a reliable employee for six years since there wasn't much demand for an auctioneer in those days.

ARKANSAS VALLEY STATE BANK, MAIN AND DALLAS STREETS

From the Cotton Fields to the Battlefields

Roy's lack of experience meant he couldn't land any sales to hone his skills in selling property and equipment. Not finding any opportunity, he headed back to Arkansas where he found another café job in Rogers, Arkansas. He also attended the *Normal School* in Bentonville, from which he attained a teaching certificate. He sought a teaching job, asking $60 a month. The school hired a 13-year old girl for $30 a month, and Roy returned to Broken Arrow.

Pauli found that Shorty was building a new two-story brick and mortar café, using Charles Dalton's company to build it. He went to work mixing mortar for *Dalton Brothers* until the new café was finished. While in Arkansas, Roy consistently paid the monthly interest on the loan that Mr. Williams had co-signed for him. Now, he went to the bank, renewed the note for a 30-day period, then paid it off in two weeks. This

YOUNG ROY PAULI

was the last time he ever had to sign a note with the bank; after that, a handshake was all they needed.

Roy soon became friends with *Uncle Charley Haley*, an established auctioneer in Broken Arrow, forming a partnership agreement that lasted until March of 1916. They had conducted 21 sales, and since Roy conducted

209

Meet the BROKEN ARROW CENTENNIALS

20 of them alone, he decided to go out on his own, sink or swim. The next season he successfully conducted 21 sales, after which he had enough experience to advertise his own auction business.

Roy's local success was interrupted from August 1918 into March 1919, when he served in the *U.S. Army*. At age 24 in 1921, Roy married Kate Johnson, whose family had traveled by covered wagon from Alma, Arkansas, crossing the Arkansas River on a ferry at Fort Smith into *Indian Territory*, and arriving in Weer Community in the fall of 1904.

Always inventive, his early jobs show a variety of employers and business ventures in the subsequent census and other public documents. In the mid-20's the *Democrat-Ledger* often reported "Col. R.I. Pauli's" out-of-town auctions, using the old-time moniker for an auctioneer. Roy commented toward the end of his 58-year experience in auctioneering, "The most rewarding one thing that ever came to me as the sale business grew was the many friends that were made. It is sure certain that friends are more valuable than all the money that was ever the results of the sales."

> **COL. R. I. PAULI**
> "THE MONEY GETTER" Auctioneer
> 15 Years Experience——For Sale Dates Phone
> Office 333——————————Residence 249

From the Cotton Fields to the Battlefields

Near the end of his career, Pauli took a younger man under his wing to teach him auctioneering. Lynn Bertling, Sr. was a family man who began working as a "Ringman," walking among the crowd to catch bids for Roy. Once, at a small livestock sale near McAlester, Roy, Lynn and Bertling's teenage son, Lynn, Jr. were looking over the animals at hand. Young Lynn spotted a registered shorthorn cow already bred, with a young heifer at her side. This was the pair that he wanted to bid on, but he didn't have the funds. Pauli remembered his own experience with Newt Williams, who had helped him get started years earlier, so he made a deal with the boy. They won the highest bid at $360, after which Lynn, Jr. paid Pauli $5 a week until it was paid in full. The heifer won Reserve Grand Champion at *Tulsa State Fair*! Lynn, Sr. later took over Roy's auction company and became known as a successful auctioneer in his own right.

During the lean years of auctioneering, Pauli was industrious enough to know how to earn money despite the economy. He began a business selling farm equipment,[54] and later opened a real estate and insurance business, which he sold to John Bryce in 1973. Roy owned, edited and published a purebred cattle periodical in the 1940s, named the *Southwest Breeder*.

Not only was Roy a successful businessman, he was also a civic leader, serving several terms on the *Broken Arrow City Council* during the 1920s to 1933. He was City Trea-

---
54. *Photo of "Pauli Brothers" sign on the building next to Les Randall's gas station, p. 219.*

surer during the time when many of the original city bonds were being paid off. As a successful shorthorn breeder, Roy was given an award at the National Shorthorn Cattle Association in Springfield, Missouri, which the Bertling men attended with him.

Roy and Kate were First Baptist Church members, where he served as a Deacon and taught classes to young people and the men. The couple did not have any children, but the Bertling's kids were enjoyed as if they were their own. Clearly loving Broken Arrow life, they both were members of the Order of the Eastern Star. Roy was a member of the Masonic Lodge and a 32nd degree Mason. He received his 50-year cap from the Tulsa Akdar Shrine. Roy was also on the Board of Directors of the Arkansas Valley State Bank and was honorary vice-president at the time of his death in 1977.[55]

IVAN D. BROWN
(1898 – 1972)

It's easy to picture Ivan Brown's confidence about life in Broken Arrow. As George A. Brown's son, he watched his father's activity as ownership partner at one of the major grain elevators. Very likely, he observed the workings of the bucket elevator, scooping up grain from a lower level to deposit it in higher storage areas, waiting for off-loading to railroad cars. And that afforded another first-hand experience, watching the men handle the loading, and the

---

55. Biography and Later Years Photo, *Broken Arrow Ledger,* May 31, 1951.

MK&T shipments of tons of local crops. Ivan just *knew* his hometown and the people.

IVAN, TALLEST YOUNG MAN, CENTER, IN A TIE AND SUIT JACKET, AGE 12

Ivan was undoubtedly pleased to represent his town and his school on the *Special Train Day* in January 1911 (p. 134). Even more, he represented his successful father who was also an investor as well as a farmer in the area (p. 98). On the same page in the *1910 Federal Census for Broken Arrow,* George A. Brown and his partners in the *BBB Elevator,* James Bowers and E.B. Baxter, were all listed as "buyers and sellers of grain."

Years later, Ivan Brown was named as a *Broken Arrow Great Graduate* representing the class of 1919. He was a prankster for most of his life. For example, when he was an 11th grader, Ivan was 'expelled' because of an end-of-school-year prank. [He wasn't really expelled but, he was suspended for a full week.] The following year, he graduated with honors and headed off to the *New Mexico Military Institute* in Roswell.

IVAN D. BROWN, NEW MEXICO MILITARY INSTITUTE

The next year he attended *Harvard University* in Cambridge, Massachusetts, continuing his family's tradition of higher education. He also became Broken Arrow High School's first Ivy Leaguer. Ivan later attended the *University of Oklahoma* where he linked up with his old high school buddy, Willard (Willie) Walker.

The two of them experienced many exciting escapades, some of them mischievous. A record of their travels and exploits is revealed in a book that Ivan penned just prior to his death in 1972, called *Willie and I*.[56] It is mentioned that Willie had arranged a blind date for his buddy, and this double date was Ivan's introduction to Estella Lewis. Ivan and Estella married two years later, on September 18, 1926. Ivan always referred to

---

56. Ivan D. Brown. *Willie and I, An Anecdotal Scrapbook Highlighting a Long and Rewarding Friendship.* Broken Arrow: Self Published, 1972.

her affectionately as *Stell* for the rest of his life.

In 1924, Ivan was employed as an assistant cashier at the *Citizens State Bank* in Bixby. His 1926 marriage to Estella Lewis brought together a couple from successful fathers, hers through oil producer, Jesse Lewis and his through George A. Brown, proprietor of a Broken Arrow grain elevator. Jesse I. Lewis, who was a *Spanish American War Veteran*, having served in an Ohio Infantry Unit, and his wife Frances Maud French Lewis, came to *Indian Territory* shortly after their Ohio marriage in 1902.

Ivan eventually became the major stockholder of the Bixby bank as well as Broken Arrow's *Arkansas Valley State Bank*. The rest of his life was devoted to serving the community and helping people. The close ties between the city and one of its leading bankers was confirmed during *Broken Arrow's 2002-2003 Centennial Celebration*, when residents nominated *"100 Outstanding Citizens of the Century (1902-2002)."* Ivan Brown was on that list with multiple nominations.

Old-timers tell the story that customers sometimes would remove their glasses, clean the lens, and take another look with disbelief at the large, artistic words, *"Si's Recreation Parlor"* on the plate glass window of Ivan D. Brown's office at *Arkansas Valley State Bank*. The window, reaching from floor to ceiling had been retrieved by Brown from the downtown pool hall when the business closed. Keeping it was an indicator of Brown's wry wit.

Meet the BROKEN ARROW CENTENNIALS

ENTRANCE TO IVAN BROWN'S OFFICE
ARKANSAS VALLEY STATE BANK

The "Si's" window was popular throughout the time Brown served in the bank's leadership until his death in 1972. During later remodeling, the window was removed and preserved by family members who had been well taught about the need to "preserve history." The window is now displayed at *The Museum Broken Arrow*.

Brown was an old-fashioned banker who recognized that a handshake confirmed a deal. He was known on busy days at the bank to speed up payroll check-cashing time by pulling cash from his pocket for customers who didn't have time to wait in line for a teller. He broke traditions, and people loved it. Ivan passed from this life in 1972, followed by the death of his wife Stell in 2002. Both were laid to rest in Broken Arrow's *Park Grove Cemetery.*

Preserving the community's history was a high priority for this *Great Graduate.* His office and home were filled with artifacts and writings, many of which were donated to *The Museum Broken Arrow.* A major exhibit there is the result of his early effort to save the *Childers Family log cabin* that was built in 1836. Brown's life is too full to summarize in this brief write-up. Recognizing him posthumously as a *Broken Arrow High School Great Graduate,* even 93 years after his graduation, seemed most appropriate.

The Legacy Lives On

Ivan and Estella Brown had one son and one daughter. George Lewis Brown was born in 1929 and Barbara Aloha Brown, born in 1931. George L. married Wanda Mae Martin in 1950 and had one daughter, Georgeanna (Thomas). Barbara married Neely Kimbrough in 1955. They had 3 children, Kelley, Doug and Sally. The generations that follow these Brown Family Pioneers will be introduced in a later chapter.

(Adapted from Dr. Clarence G. Oliver, Jr.'s Great Graduate Biography, 2012 Ceremony.)

Meet the BROKEN ARROW CENTENNIALS

LESTER RANDALL
(1909 – 2002)

LESTER RANDALL

Les Randall, born May 1, 1909 in a log cabin near Keota, Oklahoma, came to Broken Arrow by covered wagon when he was 7 years old. His family moved here with hopes of buying a farm and to join their friends, the Glen Geren family. Randall recalled that the family traveled in two covered wagons; the back wagon had two cows tied to it. The approximately 110-mile trip from Haskell County (as the crow flies) took weeks as they traveled from landmark to landmark following trails of other pioneers. The Randall family chose campsites with water and trees for shade, and found they were so close on the trail of other travelers, that warm coals remained from the last night's campfire.

Randall often told how the family stayed for three weeks in the Broken Arrow wagon yard. It was built like a stockade with stalls for two horses and bunk beds for four persons in each stall. Les and his brother Ralph slept under the wagon with his father Walter, while his mother, Maude M. Turley Lester and sister Pauline slept in the wagon. They moved in with the Gerens for a short time until Walter Randall found an 80-acre farm on Houston Street west of town.

From the Cotton Fields to the Battlefields

There, young Les met another lad, Jack Estes, and the two became life-long friends.

Mainstays on the Randall dining table during those early winters were rabbits and boiled eggs. During the summer rabbits were not safe to eat. At age 13, Randall started in business for himself, delivering groceries by horse and buggy for local merchants. Everyone knew the town and its neighbors and gave directions by landmarks. Later Les worked for the telephone company and at the coal mines.

Lester Lee Randall and Gustava Baker married on April 26, 1929 in Tulsa. The *1930 Federal Census for Jackson County, Missouri* show his early employment as "parts stockman" in an auto manufacturing plant. He returned to Broken Arrow during the *Great Depression* and opened a service station at Main and Broadway. Under his hand, it became a thriving

LES RANDALL'S PHILLIPS 66 STATION
NOTICE "PAULI BROS" SIGN NEXT DOOR.

business, and in 1936 he became owner of a *Phillips 66 Station* at 301 South Main. Of course, gas station services then included tires and tubes, lube jobs, oil changes and automobile hand-wash and wax; and 11 cents a gallon can't be beat!

Les joined the volunteer fire department and became the *Broken Arrow Fire Chief* in 1936. During *World War II* the veteran firefighter was named chief of the 72-man fire department at *Douglas Aircraft in Tulsa*. After the war he returned to the Broken Arrow Fire Department and was again chief until he resigned in 1953.

In the early 1950s, Randall purchased the *Western Auto Supply Store* on Main Street. His wife Gustava, better known as "Dude," was his best "right hand" in the store. Twenty years later they sold their *Western Auto Store*. Randall tried retirement for a couple of years before opening a saw and knife sharpening business.

Randall's [1900s] Hitching Post

This turn of the last century hitching post was originally in front of Les Randall, Sr.'s home. It was common for cowboys who came into town to tie their horses to the post. Rod Randall, Les's grandson gave this old post to *The Museum Broken Arrow*, and it is at the northeast corner of the Main and El Paso Streets' entrance, near the front door.

For almost a decade, Les and Jack Estes spent two weeks every summer at a fishing camp in Canada. He was a member of the *Broken Arrow Scottish Rite* order, a *32nd Degree Mason* and *Past Master of Broken Arrow Lodge No. 243*. Les was also active in the *Broken Arrow Historical Society* and the *Broken Arrow Seniors, Inc.*

Gustava died on April 14, 1991, just 12 days short of the Randall's 63rd wedding anniversary, after a long interval in a nursing home. After Gustava Randall's passing, Les Randall married Betty Rushing.

The Legacy Lives On

Les Randall's son, Lester Lee Randall Jr., is a 1948 graduate of *Broken Arrow High School* and was an outstanding athlete during his school years. Lester Jr. stayed in Broken Arrow, married Okemah Eloise Boudinot ('43) and reared their two children, Rodney ('68) and Shonday. The legacy is carried on by Shonday and her daughter Jordan, and by her brother Rodney and his wife Jennifer as well as their two sons, Mitchell and Tyler Randall.

(Courtesy of the Broken Arrow Ledger, December 6, 2003 edition)

Meet the BROKEN ARROW CENTENNIALS

ALL DECKED OUT FOR A BROKEN ARROW PARADE.

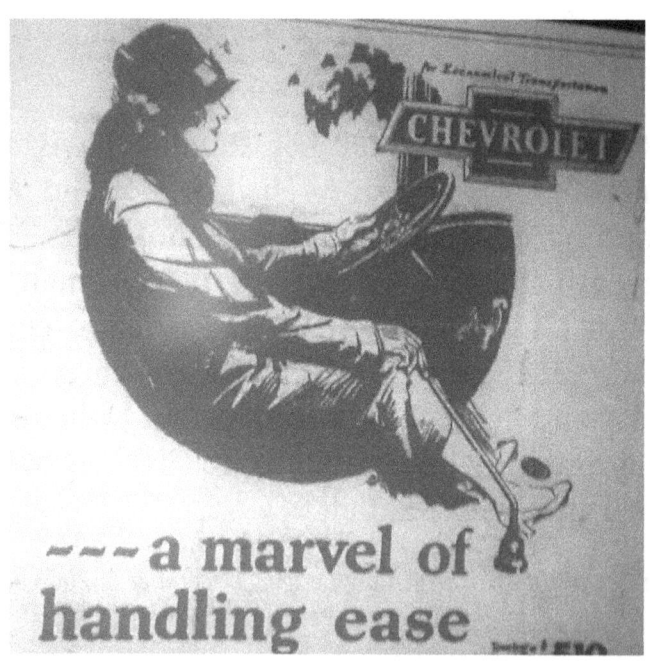

APPEALING TO WOMEN EVEN IN 1920
"LADY IN CHEVROLET" *BROKEN ARROW LEDGER* AD

Chapter 11

Roaring Twenties: A Time of Peace

New inventions followed us right out of the Industrial Revolution into the new 20th Century, changing our world in many ways. Inventions had shortened WWI with aircraft, seaplanes, trucks, and tanks. Farming took strides forward by use of the tractor and other mechanized farm equipment, replacing horse-drawn implements. There was a stronger sense of nation, and a beginning large infrastructure to tie scattered cities and rural areas together. Many soldiers left as sons of the farm and returned as men seeking new employment in large city construction and industries which gave dynamic new opportunity.

Popular songs reflected the new intensity and *Tin Pan Alley* picked up the rhythm. The New York City music haven, with composers and publishers on every corner, took advantage of a changing mood with melodramatic jazz and novelty songs. *"How Ya Gonna Keep 'Em Down on the Farm"* was directed solely to returning soldiers, enticing them toward city life instead of going back to a difficult, routine life of agricultural seasons. Even this song's writers, may not have known the strength of this trend until their song hit the charts as an instant success in 1919.[57]

A pattern of prosperity generally follows war, and during WWI recovery there was a shift in the unique Western culture of America. Immigration was at its height and *meat-and-potatoes Americans* were introduced to new cultures, foods, and lifestyles. Europeans got a taste of liberty and readily sought this new way of life. Many people groups came to Oklahoma seeking new beginnings, often drawn to larger towns and cities to join the working population. In contrast, most Broken Arrow soldier boys were loyal to their hometown, returning with new ambition to their familiar community and their family businesses.

Patriotism showed new strength and Americans were more united, which gave President Warren G. Harding's administration an advantage in bringing back a sense of normalcy. Change often comes gradually, sometimes with hesitation. However, in the 20's many life-changing inventions stirred the desire for other new and different items. Quickly embraced, some 1920's inventions shaped America, preparing our nation for decades to come.

---

57. Tin Pan Alley. www.acousticmusic.org/research/history/musical-styles-and-venues-in-america/.

Roaring Twenties: A Time of Peace

In every area, new patents improved old ideas. With the first automobile electrical ignition system, the telephone and the radio, travel and communication took leaps ahead. Smaller but significant inventions such as the movie camera, the refrigerator, and electrical appliances brought better solutions to typical needs. Two even smaller inventions were welcomed for their convenience. The zipper and the bra, a simple undergarment, were great innovations for women because they brought significant changes in style and cultural appearance, but most importantly, comfort![58] Radio brought new experiences and images of the world into many living rooms. A *1930 Federal Census* question asked each household to report if they had a radio; approximately 40% (12 million) of U.S. households did.[59]

In January 1920, the *Democrat Ledger* announced that street paving would begin just as soon as weather permitted. The dirt-road remedy at present was a water truck that made rounds to keep down the wind-blown dust. New and remodeled buildings filled in the commercial district.

Broken Arrow women were already committed to being in-step with the larger world. Although this town

---

58. New Inventions. www.interestingengineering.com/a-look-at-the-17-most-influential-inventions-from-1911-1920
59. Census questions. www.census.gov/history/www/through_the_decades/index_of_questions/

was in the middle of an agricultural area, the "First Ladies" had gathered in the *Self Culture Club* since its founding. Committed to bringing literature, art, music, and style to local women, they had been encouraged by Oklahoma's vote *for* women's suffrage in November 1918. Followed by the governor's signature to ratify the 19th Constitutional Amendment in February 1920, the full acceptance of the amendment was just months away. National ratification was accomplished in August 1920. In the new decade, the first 1920 meeting of the *Self Culture Club* had presented the topic, "Oklahoma Laws for Women."

However, an indicator of the times is seen in the 1920 *Democrat Ledger*, announcing an August 28th exam for post office clerks. Adults were invited, age 18-45, with healthy male's qualifications described, and this specific note, "Married women will not be admitted to the examination." Another news item also reported that Nat L. Sanders, Postmaster (from 1913-1921) had been instructed that Sunday convenience hours held for those too busy with weekday work schedules, were cancelled per order of the U.S. Postal Service.

Changes were taken in stride; the town's women had already built an impressive record of accomplishments through the *Ladies School Aid Society* and their churches. Following a pattern of other Oklahoma women's clubs, the twenty-five *Culture Club* members presented their own essays about national and social topics, to better inform each other. For instance, in a May 1926 meeting, the *Ledger* reported that "Mrs. J.B. Parkinson was visiting from her home in Chicago and spoke about the Girl Reserve movement here." The *YWCA Girl Reserves* was the fledgling program for teenage girls, with a motto, "Health, Knowledge, Service, and Spirit."

BROKEN ARROW SELF CULTURE CLUB WITH ROSE BOUQUETS
MRS. NEWT (IDA) WILLIAMS IS 5TH FROM THE RIGHT (CA. 1930s)

One wonders if the women addressed each other by their given names during their luncheons, since the public announcements always included the typical lists of several "Mesdames" with their married spousal names. Nevertheless, the group expressed warm greetings to Emma

Parkinson, wife of the first Broken Arrow mayor, J.B. Parkinson. The pattern of meetings also included a roll call to which members responded with something factual, such as "name an amendment of the Constitution," or "give a Community Suggestion."

Mary Talbot, a teacher, had suggested the *Self Culture Club* name after hearing of other communities' literary clubs. The women knew and worked with each other in churches and community groups, but their club project was distinctive and continued for several years. Choosing to advance literacy, they saw the need to begin a *Broken Arrow Library*, especially for the children. By their second meeting in 1905, guests brought their own possessions to the tea for the first collection of 150 books. Charter members, Mrs. (Ida) W.N. Williams, Mrs. (Cleo) M.C. Williams, Mrs. Josie Sprague, and Miss Dora Sullivan were selected to be the *Library Board*.[60]

The *Crystal Theatre* (1925 *Ledger* ad) was one of the few entertainment locations on Main, and was in its heyday during the 20's. "Big City" theater was emphasized on a small scale with

---

60. Roberta Parker. "Library Began with Literary Club Donations," *Broken Arrow Daily Ledger*, Tuesday March 4, 2003.

movies, musicals, live vaudeville acts and local social events. Mrs. (Allie) W. T. Brooks, Mrs. (Cleo) Mac Williams, and Mrs. (Lutie) Nat Sanders were ownership partners of the theater. Taking advantage of the situation, the *Library Committee* solicited the patronage of the public and arranged for the *Crystal Theatre* to designate one night each month as *Library Night*. The committee promised that good music, readings, special numbers, and entertainment that would be well worth the usual admission price.

Cleo Williams, a Broken Arrow music teacher, had the ability to gather students for performances that pleased community parents. Her access to adult church choirs also afforded additional programs at *The Opera House*, on the second floor of *First State Bank*, also a popular place for programs.

CLEO WILLIAMS, TEACHER, 1929

The first 1906 *Broken Arrow Library* itself, was a "shed room" off a Main Street business. By 1908 a Mrs. Stauffer was appointed librarian. Mike McKenna donated two rocking chairs to the library according to a Ledger article, and Mrs. George H. Foster donated a nice Boston fern and six children's books before moving to her new home in Wagoner. Once established, new books were added to the library each year. That same year, nearly $800 was raised and a stove was donated to the library room by Mrs. W.T. Brooks. Other funding came from $1.00 dues collected from the *Self Culture Club* for those who wanted to join the library committee.[61]

The vision for the town's library thrived and was eagerly supported. One of the main proponents for literacy and education was Mrs. J.H. (Dora) Esslinger, a high school teacher for several subjects. Dora was active in many civic causes while serving as the *Self Culture Club* president during 1918-1919. Dora was in charge of the small library started by the club, the forerunner of *Broken Arrow Library*

DORA ESSLINGER
TEACHER, 1929

The *Dickason-Goodman Company* on Main Street joined the library effort by providing space at its office. According to an article in April 3, 1919, an additional circulating collection of over 100 volumes was maintained in the store for free public use. Including novels, books on great wars as well as books for juveniles, this resource was especially popular among rural patrons because of their extended hours after the library was closed.

---

61. Parker, Ibid.

DORA MAHALA SULLIVAN ESSLINGER
(1883 – 1970)

Dora Mahala Sullivan became James H. Esslinger's second wife on May 24, 1908 in Broken Arrow. After the death of Dora's sister, she stepped in to raise the first five children of Nola Sullivan Esslinger and J.H. Esslinger, including baby Nola. With James, they became parents to their daughter Elsie Mildred Esslinger (1909-2007) and a son, Frederick (1915-1988).

DORA SULLIVAN ESSLINGER

After Esslinger's death at age 50 in early 1920, Dora returned to teaching as a widowed single mother with the seven children at home, ages 20 to 4-year-old Frederick. Before her career as an educator ended, she had earned a Master's Degree in Music, and also taught Latin, English and History in Broken Arrow schools for 38 years, retiring in 1951. Dora's daughter Elsie reported that the high school was able to retain accreditation due to Dora's Master's Degree.

Dora Esslinger held several offices in the fraternal organization *Royal Neighbors,* including Recorder and Nobel Grand. She also was active in the *Methodist Church* and the *Broken Arrow Self Culture Club.* She saw the community's educational system through many developments, and kept her advisory role with the library for many years. Dora was 87 when she died February 27, 1970. She is buried in the Esslinger plot in *Park Grove Cemetery.*

James H. and Dora Sullivan Esslinger may be best known as educators, but they are also remembered for their contributions to the community through several Broken Arrow political, social and religious organizations. Their legacy lived on through both their daughter Elsie and son Fred Esslinger. Elsie was especially valuable, contributing to the recorded history of Broken Arrow. Both James Houston Esslinger and Dora Sullivan Esslinger were recognized in 1991 as *Broken Arrow Hall of Fame* honorees.

(Biographical information courtesy of Broken Arrow Genealogical Society.)

City improvements in 1922 included a new fire truck, with a paid Fire Chief. Although still relying on a largely volunteer fire company, improved water sourcing throughout the community allowed greater safety in town. In addition, in January, Fire Chief G.S. Walker brought a proposal to the City Council for renaming the streets to "eliminate the trouble experienced in the past in locating fires." The fireman proposed that Main and Broadway be the dividing line, with Commercial and College Streets retaining their names. Street "D" would become "Dallas" and "E" Street, change to El Paso, and so forth, as is familiar to residents now. Firemen had already given the strategy some sound thinking, and the matter was referred to the Chamber of

Commerce for further development.[62] By April 1922, the Ledger announced community clean-up day as part of posting the new street signs.

1922 Fire Company, Captain J.L Ghere, 1921-1940
Then Captain Les Randall, 1941-1953

Just weeks before this photo, the new *First Methodist Episcopal Church* on Main Street announced that the church was ready for occupancy. Replacing the first-built wooden church of Broken Arrow, this brick edifice took a little more than a year to finish. The building now provided expansive room for Sunday services, classes, and a "downstairs" with a complete kitchen and dining area.

In early April 1922, the *Chamber of Commerce* announced

---
62. "Re-Naming of Streets Proposed by Firemen." *Democrat Ledger*, January 12, 1922.

that Broken Arrow would have a real *City Park* with a caretaker. The town leadership designated April 22, *Arbor Day*, as a transformational event, "creating the park from the cow pasture. Every citizen will be expected to furnish at least one tree to be planted in the park. A free camping ground for the benefit of tourists, with lights, water and fuel furnished, will be established in one section of the park." Tracey Hunsecker was named as the director for the yet-to-be-formed band to give performances in the park.

It is a fact that the original land throughout the region was barren of trees and natural shade except for the creek beds. Residents took the message to heart and began planting. This mighty Elm tree was a 75-cent seedling purchase made by Mrs. Ida (W. N.) Williams as president of the *Culture Club*. Planted in early 1930s on the southeast corner of the City Hall lot, "close to the police station door," this photo shows 35 years of growth. Also, the ladies had no small part in providing and advocating improvement of the road to, and landscape for *Park Grove Cemetery*.

Roaring Twenties: A Time of Peace

The *Broken Arrow School Board* anticipated the 1924 election and bond voting by the community in articles that appeared in May's *Democrat Ledger*. The heating system was woefully inadequate (not even heating some classrooms) and was "blamed" for school children's illnesses and medical bills for families. Further, the annual cost was too much and ever-increasing for heating the high school at $500 and the grade school, $379 a year. The options of a grade-school remodeling, or building a new school were reviewed, and a new school was favored. However, *Bonds for the New School Defeated*, was a large headline in June.

The school board returned to the issue in 1925 and could not vary the $65,000 projected cost for a new school. The *Ledger* showed their expected offset by an $8,000 recovery from salvaging the old building structure, by contracting with a commercial demolition company. In the end, the 1925 bond issue was more expensive so that additional land could expand the property lines.

The 1925 bond proposal was approved and in August, bids for contractors were reviewed in the newspaper, with contractor selections listed. The *Atlas Brick Company of Muskogee* presented the best bid and was accepted for the structure. Also, in August, the community was invited to assist removal of school desks and materials to a number of the area churches, which had offered classrooms without cost. The school year began in those "scattered, nearby locations." A cornerstone ceremony was held in

October 1925, hosted by notables in the State Masons, and represented locally by W.E. Laws and M.C. Williams.

Happy news appeared in March 1926 *Ledger* with a request for community help to return the desks and materials to the new school, permitting classes to begin in the new building "Easter Monday," April 5th. Within a week, the elementary grade students were sending thank you letters to the various churches with glowing descriptions of what their new rooms were like. "Even our best dreams of getting into the new building did not come up to the reality. We spent this week in regular work, but outside of that, we 'fixed our room.' It is lovely and we hope that all the people will come to see the building."

"BROKEN ARROW'S NEW GRADE SCHOOL"
FRONT PAGE LEDGER, JULY 8, 1926

Chapter 12

Dust Bowl, Depression and Draglines
The Challenging 30's

The prosperity of the roaring twenties was in full swing when suddenly, the bottom fell out of the economy. October 29, 1929 was later called *Black Tuesday* due to the crash of the *New York Stock Exchange*. This went well beyond the United States, affecting countries around the world.

Farms and farm towns suffered because of dropping crop prices. Construction, mining and logging operations were crippled with the lack of demand for their products. Although the beginning of this depression impacted Broken Arrow as other communities, our citizens viewed it in a different way. Being an innovative and growing city, many residents saw this challenge as an opportunity to rise up and work together to limit the effect on our town and its citizens.

Our town united and overcame these circumstances in several ways. On March 13, 1933, Governor, "Alfalfa" Bill

Murray ordered all banks in the state to take a 3-day holiday because currency was in short supply. Broken Arrow bank presidents, K.M. Rowe of *Arkansas Valley Bank* and F.S. Hurd from *First National Bank* made it known that their banks were sound and solid. They didn't believe that their businesses should be interrupted, but closed anyway to comply with the Governor's order.[63]

Stories have been passed on within the families most associated with the *Arkansas Valley State Bank*. "I've always heard that during the Depression, in order to keep from there being a run on the bank, they actually took the cash out of the vault and put it on a table behind the tellers so that customers could physically see the money and know it was all right," Kimbrough-Rash said. "I don't know if that was true or not."[64] But from prior reports about Ivan Brown, it seems to be a strong possibility.

Business groups and private companies came to the rescue of our citizens in several ways. The *Broken Arrow Chamber of Commerce* was successful in seeking funding from the *Federal Emergency Relief Administration* (FERA) and from the *Works Progress Administration* (WPA) to employ local citizens to build and work on municipal projects.

Mr. R.C. Beaty, Secretary of the *Seneca Coal Company*

---
63. Elsie Esslinger, *The Museum Broken Arrow* file.
64. Kelley Kimbrough-Rash, Chairman of the Board for *Arkansas Valley Bank*.

was concerned about some families' destitute situations and was determined to do something about it. In 1934 he organized community leaders and established the *Big Brother Club* which provided meals for the families, and eyeglasses for children whose families could not afford to buy them. The *Big Brothers* furnished clothing, toys and food baskets to needy families during the Christmas holidays. Their contributions came from many church and social groups, and from town businesses, along with private donations from citizens.[65] Additional assistance came in the form of credit extended by local businessmen to their customers. Repayment as possible was allowed, even if it took years.

L.S. WORTMAN, 1930 INSTRUCTOR, FFA CLUB, MIDDLE LEFT

The best-known event that sprang up during the depression was the first *Rooster Day Celebration* in 1932. It

---

65. *Depression*, 1930's file, *The Museum Broken Arrow*.

started with an idea from the *Broken Arrow High School Vocational Agricultural* teacher, Leo Wortman, who determined that by removing and changing out roosters in their flocks, the farmers could get better egg production from their farms, generating more revenue for them.

The event was also promoted by local businessmen since they had been operating on a barter system with near-by farmers to help keep their businesses alive. There were three large hatcheries in the area, and egg sales were a major part of Broken Arrow's economy.

The 1930's epic struggle forced many Oklahomans to look for greener pastures and head west to California. A long-term drought added to what would later be understood as poor cultivation practices, caused the *Dust Bowl*. Wheat farmers in the Oklahoma and Texas panhandles, southeastern Colorado and western Kansas were affected by it. The land was simply blown away with the wind. The midday sun was totally obliterated by the huge dark clouds of dust stirred up by high winds, and day turned into night in a matter of minutes. These dust storms reached their peak in the spring of 1935, when a reporter from the *Associated Press* was just traveling through and coined the phrase "dust bowl" in his column.

The name became the familiar way to describe the extreme weather and land conditions. The many Oklahomans who ventured west to California were depicted in John Steinbeck's novel, *"The Grapes of Wrath."* Migrants were referred to as *Okies,* a derogatory term which had a connotation of not only of being poor, but also suggested uneducated and ignorant as well.[66] Those folks experienced tremendous hardship as they traveled unpaved and sometimes uncharted roads leading to California, to what they had heard was *the land of plenty.* Living for weeks in their vehicles and campsites along the way, they were frequently victimized.

F.S. Hurd, Dan Holliday, Don Fisher at Camp Russell.

Aware that many local business and civic leaders also shared financial risk for area farms, sometimes including their own, banker-investor F.S. Hurd became a spokesperson at a whole new level. He became a change agent throughout the state. After substantial activity, he wrote to the *Oklahoma Bankers' Association* noting their work with the state's *69 Soil Conservation Districts.* He reported that "more than 50 meetings have been held where more than 1,200 Certificates of Award were given to District Cooperators ... for an outstanding job of establishing and satisfactorily maintaining a complete soil conservation program."[67]

---

66. Oklahoma Centennial Section, *Tulsa World,* March 25, 2007.
67. *The Oklahoma Banker,* Oklahoma Bank Association, Oklahoma City, OK. May 1945.

Meet the BROKEN ARROW CENTENNIALS

Elsewhere, while the 1930s were known for a calamity of economic events, a contrast is seen in the fact that Broken Arrow was very successfully mining coal. Since early days, the mines had been a focus of resources and income. Even before the railroad, "a small community called Evans grew up around the mine three miles east of Broken Arrow near East Kenosha and South 225th East Avenue. Early settlers used coal fired stoves to heat their homes. They could load their wagons with coal for $2 per ton. Early mining was primarily the work of men with picks and shovels and draft animals, with explosives to speed up the digging."[68]

Old Valcon, 1910

---

68. Wise, Myriads, 18..

In 1910, a steam shovel was introduced into the pit and a drag line operation was incorporated in the strip mining to speed up production. Mine workers nicknamed the shovel *"Old Valcon"* - a massive-sized steam shovel with a large bucket, lifted by a cable attached to an overhanging steel boom. After the terrain was dynamited, the bucket was dropped and dragged down the slope, scooping up the loosened material. This steam shovel was replaced in 1936 with a new and more modern excavator known as an overburden shovel that was more efficient and increased production.

Strip mining was in full swing east of town at the *Seneca Coal Company*, producing over 3,400 rail cars of *"Broken Aro"* coal annually from the Broken Arrow Tipple.[69] The coal was known as the finest bituminous coal for fuel and was undisputedly, the finest preparation for use given any coal, according to Bill Chapman, a retired employee of the company.[70]

This method of mining was extremely detrimental to the landscape which was often never reclaimed by the companies, resulting in deep valleys and mounds of waste material, called overburden. Residents referred to this area of town as the *coal pits* or *strip pits* which filled with rainwater, and many went fishing and swimming there.

The high demand for coal as fuel in the 30s and full pro-

---
69. A tipple is an overhead structure which loads extracted coal for transport, typically into railroad hopper cars.
70. *Broken Arrow Ledger,* September 6, 1992.

duction in these mines provided jobs for area men that boosted the City's base economy. Eventually, *Seneca Coal* merged with the *Sinclair Company*, and later merged into *Peabody Coal*, based in southern Illinois.

When local coal began to play out in the mid-to-late 40s, most of the companies and some of the employees moved on to other locations. However, many families who came here because of the mining jobs available during the difficult depression days still live in our community. The coal companies would often gift the expended land to some of their employees or donate it to local groups such as the *Boy Scouts of America*; for their use.

LEO S. WORTMAN
(1893 – 1970)

During *the Great Depression,* one man was a spearhead for economic improvement in the Broken Arrow farming community. Leo S. Wortman held an important position in the school system as the *Vocational Agriculture* teacher. His role outside the student groups was even more influential in educating local farmers about land conservation and

Leo S. Wortman

methods to improve cattle herds. His work became an informative partnership with a number of the cattle ranchers including Orville Keller, Tracey M. Hunsecker, Sr. and W.P. Fraker. The men established a program of livestock breeding practices which produced purebred cattle in greater numbers and raised their yield at the sale barns.

Leo Wortman directly impacted another area of agricultural management which resulted in the innovative idea that became Broken Arrow's most outstanding annual festival. Thinking of egg production and sales, he taught classes to local farmers to develop poultry flock improvements. Trading roosters between poultrymen was planned for a certain May date in 1931. The poultry handlers gathering was intended to upgrade egg production and quality. It then became a springboard event now known nationally as *"Rooster Day"*. It has been an annual event for 87 years. Many well-known Oklahoma musicians, including Bob Wills and his Texas Playboys, have performed at Main and Commercial on the Grand Stand. Through his success, Leo was asked to serve on several boards of directors for many state poultry organizations.

Bob Wills

Wortman was adamant about soil and water conservation, especially since the Central Plains was experiencing an environmental "Dust Bowl" catastrophe. Locally, the *Civilian Conservation Corp* (CCC) head-quartered east of town worked with the High School *Vo-Ag* Department. He instructed Vo-Ag students to use surveying equipment, and how to select land sites to establish ponds and tree breaks for their long-lasting purposes.

The Vocational Agriculture Terracing Team of Broken Arrow high school. Left to right, Leo Wortman, coach, Lee Smith, Rhinie Wagner, Gene Dillabuny, Loyd Ingle, and Ike Robertson, sitting.

The *Ledger* reported that the students and men started diligently building terraces to prevent soil erosion, and ponds to store water for livestock and crops. Additionally, planting trees throughout the area proved essential in protecting many crops from the prevailing strong Oklahoma winds. Pastureland improved and herds could be grazed in more contained areas, not "walking off their meat." These first-time practices became a great asset, an invaluable improvement for community farms. Area farm owners suffered minimum effects of the drought compared to their fellow farmers in the western part of the state. The results of the techniques taught by Leo Wortman in the early 1930s are still beneficial. Many ponds built during that period are still in the area today, which is quite a tribute to their quality of construction and the foresight of Mr. Wortman's teaching.

Wortman lived a short but significant part of his life in Broken Arrow. Although he was born in Illinois in 1893 and his wife, Gladys L. Richwine was born in Kansas in 1902, they met in western Oklahoma, Woodward County. She and Leo married in Garvey, where their son Leo Sterling, Jr. was born in 1923 and their daughter Mary Belle was born in 1927. The first time Leo is pictured in anything Broken Arrow, it's in the 1929 *Broken Arrow High School* yearbook, named as *Vo-Ag Instructor*. He was also advisor to the *Future Farmers of America Chapter*. During his short time in Broken Arrow (1929–1939), he also served as secretary of the *Chamber of Commerce*. The couple were members of the *Methodist Church*, where he was active in the *Methodist Men*.

By the *1940 Federal Census,* Payne County, Oklahoma, the family was living in Stillwater where Leo was a State Coordinator of the *Soil Conservation Service*. After leaving Broken Arrow he worked for a short time at *Oklahoma A & M College* in Stillwater before accepting a position based in Ft. Worth, Texas, as area director of the *Federal Soil and Water Conservation Service* which had been created by President Franklin D. Roosevelt in 1935.[71]

(Adapted from biography by Herb Karner, BAGS)

---

71. *1940 Federal Census, Stillwater, Payne County, OK*; Leo S. Wortman, age 47, with family. Line 35, E.D. 6-28, p.61A.

Meet the BROKEN ARROW CENTENNIALS

Leo's son, Sterling Wortman graduated in 1943 from Oklahoma A&M (1923-1981) and became a plant geneticist with world-wide impact through the *Rockefeller Foundation*.[72] Their daughter Mary Belle lived in Texas, where she married James D. Spangler and they added two daughters to their family.

WARREN MILTON McCARTY
(1911 – 1981)

On the last working day of 1965, Warren M. McCarty finished a 34-year career as a skilled agronomist with the *U.S. Department of Agriculture, Tulsa District Soil Conservation Service.* He had been District head for 23 years, following a first assignment in 1937 with the local *Camp Hurd Civilian Conservation Corps.*

McCarty worked with CCC's young men who were planting thousands of trees and other soil-holding plants, particularly along the dikes thrown up by strip miners. Some of the land reclamation that he supervised was later turned into the *Boy Scout's Camp Russell.* He promoted the restored property as home sites with attractive wild,

---
72. Saxon, Wolfgang. "Sterling Wortman, Scientist, Dies; Developed High Yielding Grains." *The New York Times, May 27, 1981.*

WARREN MCCARTY

natural-looking beauty with tree-covered hills, private fishing lakes, etc. He also envisioned the reclaimed coal pits as available industrial sites after investing about $100 an acre in the reclamation process.

Also, early in his career, Warren helped write and organize a work program for the *Arkansas-Verdigris Soil Conservation District*, the first of its type in the state. He was the agronomist for the district and later with the *Work Unit Conservation* program. McCarty evaluated nearly every nearby lake, pond, stream, and river for improvements needed. He also gave an expert's recommendation for the Verdigris River to become the water source for Broken Arrow.

One of his personal projects was planting Christmas trees in the abandoned mines area as both a conservation and a commercial measure. For a few years this project added to the city treasury as the trees were harvested for their sale in town during the holiday seasons. He also initiated a city forest at the water springs.

McCarty was a leading Scouter through the years and spent his first weekend of retirement at Camp Russell, holding a winter conservation camp for more than a hundred Scouts. He was a member of the *Indian Nations Council, BSA* in Tulsa.

BROKEN ARROW EXPLORER POST #6 AT PHILMONT SCOUT RANCH, 1955
BOTTOM LEFT: BOB JEPPESON; RIGHT, HARRY LINELL
MIDDLE L-R: GARY NICHOLS, O.T. "ANDY" ANDERSON, EXPLORER ADVISOR; WARREN MCCARTY, SCOUTMASTER; JIMMY HICKS, KYLE DAMERON
BACK L-R: LARRY WHITELEY, DAVID UPDIKE, STEVE PARRISH, DON COUCH [73]

Like Leo Wortman, Warren had lived in Woodward County in western Oklahoma. He graduated from *Oklahoma*

---

73. First photo of Warren McCarty, and this Scouts photo were added to Warren McCarty's internet posting by the late Kyle Dameron on July 12, 2013; see www.findagrave.com/memorial/38330157/warren-milton-mccarty

A&M College in 1933. Warren met and married Mildred Z. Horn (born in Colorado, 1913) on December 31, 1933. Their home was in Hugo, Choctaw County during the birth of their first child, Shirley Warlene McCarty in 1935. Danny Warren McCarty was born in September 1939 in Broken Arrow.

Warren and Mildred are in repose in the *Floral Haven Mausoleum*, in Tulsa. Warren preceded his wife in death by only a few months, he in March 1981 while Mildred died in October 1981.

The Legacy Lives On

At McCarty's death, he was survived by two brothers, Eustace Cole (1907-1988) and Major Dale McCarty (1917-1988); and a sister, Air Force Captain Edna Sprinter (1908-1995) of San Antonio. Warren and Mildred McCarty had two children, the late Danny McCarty (1939-2009) a builder and developer in Broken Arrow, and the late Warlene McCarty Townsend (1935-1995) who lived in Bossier City, Louisiana. Danny's wife, Shelby Jean Reeder McCarty passed away in 2015. They had one daughter, and four granddaughters.

Meet the BROKEN ARROW CENTENNIALS

PHENIE LOU GILLET OWNBY
(1887 – 1954)

First Woman Mayor of Broken Arrow (1931 – 1933)

Phenie Lou Gillet was born in Ely, Fannin County, Texas on November 16th, 1887 to Daniel Gillett and Mabel (Morris) Gillett. Her mother died when Phenie was only 12, and with her Grandmother Morris who lived in the home, she helped raise her four younger siblings. *The 1900 Federal Census*, shows the family living in Whitewright, Grayson County, Texas, where her father was a landlord.

Dust Bowl, Depression and Draglines The Challenging 30's

Phenie was 19 when she married Warren David Ownby on August 16th, 1906, the son of William D. Ownby and Minerva E. (Grable) Ownby. The newlyweds moved to Kirkville, Missouri where Warren attended the *American School of Osteopathy Medicine*. Their first child Byron Gordon Ownby was born in Missouri, May 1907. After Warren's graduation, the Ownby family moved to Broken Arrow and set up his medical practice here. Phenie assisted Dr. Ownby in his practice, and was also a practitioner as a massage therapist. The *Broken Arrow Ledger* carried weekly ads, "Mrs. Phenie Lou Ownby, *Mechano-Therapist,* Treating diseases by Massage and Swedish Movements." Her office was located in their home at 322 West Detroit. The Ownby house is on the Broken Arrow *Register of Historic Homes*.

Phenie was popular among local citizens and to her surprise, she was placed on the ballot in the 1929 city nominations. She was not elected that year but ran for Mayor again in 1931 and won the election as the first woman mayor in Oklahoma and the sixth woman to hold the office of Mayor in the United States. The *Ledger's* headline announced, "*A Woman Mayor for Broken Arrow, City's Highest Office won By A Popular and Capable Lady.*"[74] She is still the only woman to hold the office of Mayor in the City of Broken Arrow.

During the early 1930s many residents were delinquent in paying their water bills. Her recommendation was to

---

74. *Broken Arrow Ledger,* April 10, 1931.

give notice, then cut off water service to those whose ability to pay was evident. Another solution offered by *Mayor Ownby and the Council,* was to let some unemployed, less-able-to-pay patrons work for the City to resolve their debt. Even though there were some uncomfortable episodes in the next few weeks, she received broad national acclaim for her hard line approach to this problem.[75] The measures were effective: the city water department was spared from bankruptcy through her actions and the schools were relieved from the financial burden when their water rates were reduced.

Having resolved the water bill problem, Phenie turned her attention to the local electric company, *Public Service Company of Oklahoma.* She petitioned the power company to lower their rates and to install lower wattage bulbs in the city street lights. Also, to assist the lighting of alleys, and to ease the City's financial burden during the depression, she requested business owners to light the backdoor areas of their buildings, which they did. Mayor Ownby only served one term, but she accomplished great success improving our city functions. Through her leadership, City Ordinances were reviewed and revised and a city-wide clean-up project was initiated. A skating rink and a wading pool were created for the local youth, in addition to building a downtown park.

---

75. Apsley, Marmie. "Phenie Lou Ownby (1887-1954)" *The Broken Arrow Chronicles,* No.1. Broken Arrow Historical Society, 1987, 48-50.

Mrs. Ownby ran for reelection with the other *City Council* members in 1933 but the entire ticket lost their bid in the primary election. With that, Phenie returned to homemaking and worked beside her husband as an assistant in his medical practice. Phenie Lou Ownby lived until age 67, June 19th, 1954 and was followed in death by her husband Warren at his age 75, in 1960; both are interred in Tulsa's *Memorial Park Cemetery*.[76]

Millie Gilliland Marshall *(Broken Arrow Great Graduate '55)* recalls Mrs. Ownby as a sweet, kind, and very interesting person. Phenie loved to cook but didn't like the dishwashing. Millie, who was young and lived nearby, would go to the Ownby home in the evening to wash the dishes that Phenie had laid in the large kitchen pantry. As Millie completed clean up tasks, Phenie enjoyed engaging her in conversations. "Phenie cared a lot about other people and was sincere when she asked me to share stories about myself." Millie had an occasion to prepare a speech when she was the junior high valedictorian; Phenie asked Millie if she could read the speech to her. Millie always felt encouraged, inspired and mentored by Phenie during those years.

Warren and Phenie's granddaughter, Brenda Ownby Griswold, as well as her cousin Ardis Arnold, have fond

---

76. Phenie Ownby: www.findagrave.com/memorial/105812249/phenie-lou-ownby and Dr. David Ownby: memorial 105812287. Tulsa Memorial Park Cemetery.

Meet the BROKEN ARROW CENTENNIALS

memories from their visits to Broken Arrow. Brenda recalls, "Ardis and I had so much fun going to Papa's and Phenie's house when we were young. Papa had an office in Tulsa and on the weekend sometimes, he would go pick up Ardis and me and drive us to Broken Arrow in his old car. Of course, we had to close our eyes as we seemed to "fly" over the hills, especially that big hill west of Sheridan and 71st Street."

"Phenie would be waiting with open arms and lots of kisses. Ardis was 16 and I was 14. We had a great time since our grandmother would give us both a little money and let us walk downtown, only a few blocks away. We hit the dime store, the drug store for comic books and a *chocolate coke*, and then stopped on our way home for a malt at *Dairy Queen*. We loved hearing my dad, Gil's ('31) memories about his job as a soda jerk in high school when he met our mom. The 50s were the good times with our grandparents. I never knew she was a Mayor until her funeral when we witnessed people lining the downtown streets. To us, she was just our Grandmother."[77] The granddaughters have since become aware of her fame, "We have an article stating that Phenie went to NYC and was a guest on the radio *Today Show*."

(Biography for Hall of Fame, 1991; courtesy of Broken Arrow Historical Society)

---

77. Interview with Brenda Lou Ownby Griswold, 2020.

The Legacy Lives On

The Ownby's had three children: Byron Gordon Ownby, was born May 24, 1907 in Missouri and died, 1999 in New Orleans, Louisiana. Byron and his wife Lucille had no children. Secondly, Monica Belle Ownby Arnold was born January 25, 1911 in Broken Arrow and died in Tulsa, 1998. Monica and her husband, Clayton Arnold had one daughter, Ardis; she and her husband Frank Arnold had no children. Ardis currently lives in a nursing home.

The Ownby's youngest son, Warren Gillette Ownby ('31) married Yvonne Lowden ('35). Yvonne had moved to Broken Arrow to live with her aunt Ola Lowden Hart after her dad died. Her cousin, Edith (Hart) Alldredge ('29), six years older, welcomed Yvonne into their home. Gillette and Yvonne are parents to four children, Brenda Lou Ownby Griswold and husband, Stephen Griswold; the late Betty Sue Ownby; David Gil and wife, Kathleen Tinsley Ownby; and Mark Warren and wife Faith Ann Broussard Ownby. There are seven great-grandchildren and three great-grandchildren in this family's heritage.

PAUL FRANKLIN MILLER
(1908 – 1996)

Paul F. Miller came to town in the spring of 1932 and purchased the *Broken Arrow Ledger* newspaper. The previous owners were a group of local businessmen and women who had kept the paper alive to serve the community above monetary profit. That group consisted of J.W. Walton, Mrs. Walton, J.B. Briggs and W. N. (Newt) Williams in partnership with the *Dexter Publishing Company* in Tulsa.

PATTIE AND PAUL MILLER

Miller's first publication of the *Ledger* was on May 12, 1932, and he announced his acquisition of the paper. This occurred one week before the first community *Rooster Day Celebration*. Miller's parents, B.F. and Adella Miller were long time publishers and had owned newspapers in Needles, California where Paul was the editor and manager of the *Needles' Nugget*. The family also had ownership in the *Perkins' Journal* and the *Coweta Times-Star* prior to arriving in Broken Arrow. They also managed the *Hope Dispatch* in Kansas for many years.

Born in Green River, Utah in 1908, Miller was still relatively young, but clearly experienced when he wrote his 1932 introduction. In his first edition of the *Ledger* he stated what his vision of a hometown newspaper should represent: "As a home newspaper, supporting the ideals and ambitions of Broken Arrow and surrounding community will be placed uppermost in our plans at all times. *We believe that Broken Arrow is the center of the finest territory in all Oklahoma and will work at all times on the theory that the best is none too good for our readers and patrons.*"[78]

Paul Miller owned the *Ledger* longer than any previous publisher. J.B. Parkinson had been the owner for nearly 10 years in the early 1910s – teens. Miller was in the *Ledger* office for 15 years. The new editor helped Broken Arrow organize many relief programs to combat the downturn in local business. He was instrumental in work with Leo Wortman to assure the success of the *Rooster Day*, promoting an annual celebration. He also served on committees to support the ongoing *Cotton Jubilee* for many years. Miller reported about many relief measures that the unified town population promoted to help the city through the difficult years of *the Great Depression* and *Dust Bowl* era.

He held subscription contests with great prizes for the school-age and young adult advocates who canvassed the town and nearby farms for new readers. He reduced the price on editions and annual subscriptions, and when a special event was held, he distributed free editions of events, contests, and prizes. The write-ups made the peo-

---
78. Paul F. Miller. *Broken Arrow Ledger,* May 12, 1932

ple want to be there! The look and content of the news was more informative than ever. Miller was instrumental in acquiring Bob Wills for Rooster Day.

Paul Miller and Patti Faries (1900-1993), a Coweta native, married in 1934. They had no children. They lie at rest at *Vernon Cemetery* in Coweta, Wagoner County.[79] Their legacy is remembered by their great nieces, Jane Carlile Bond, Carol Carlile Lenaburg, Nancy Jane Goddard Roberts and great nephew, Stephen B. Goddard.

(Adapted from article by Broken Arrow Ledger, BH Media Group and Tulsa World Media Company.)

JOHN WILBUR (JACK) WALTON
(1885 – 1963)

JACK WALTON, 1945

Broken Arrow received a fully experienced man when Jack Walton arrived from Mason City, Iowa on the 1st of October 1920 and purchased the local phone exchange. His *1918 World War I Draft Registration* shows him as "telephone worker" with the *General Electric Phone Company* in Mason City. And by the

---

79. Patti Faries Miller and Paul F. Miller; www.findagrave.com/memorial/60593021/paul-f_-miller.

time this 35-year-old man came to our town he had additional experience and most recently had been "general plant superintendent for a large group of properties of the *Bell System* in Northern Iowa."

Oklahoma had nothing to compare at that time, but by 1929 Jack was credited with installing the first independent automatic dial system in Broken Arrow – as the third of its kind anywhere in the state. Metropolitan centers, like Tulsa and Oklahoma City were the only other locations with this service.

His parents were living in Enid, Oklahoma during his time here, but he clearly chose his own path, marrying Grace Elizabeth Ross in 1909 in Leavenworth, Kansas then moving on to Iowa for the phone company opportunity. Grace and Jack had no children, but Broken Arrow life absorbed them into many responsible and social roles. Jack served several terms as *President of the Oklahoma State Telephone Association*, and in Broken Arrow he was a member of the *Oddfellows* and became a *32nd Degree Mason*. In August 1945, when he announced his retirement as General Manager of the *Oklahoma Phone Company*, Jack said his retirement included "looking forward to managing three farms, intending to make Broken Arrow his permanent home."[80] Retirement was a "relative term" for Jack.

---

80. "Jack Walton Resigns," *Broken Arrow Ledger* August 2, 1945.

Meet the BROKEN ARROW CENTENNIALS

J.W. (Jack) Walton was a true pioneer in early in Oklahoma, by his dedication and devotion in getting telephone service established throughout the state. There were other titles and "firsts" for Jack Walton, such as when he served as President of the *Oklahoma Utilities Association* and was the first "telephone man" to do so. He also served as a member of the Board of Directors of the *United States Independent Telephone Association*. In 1948 Jack was recognized for his untiring work and assistance in pioneering telephone systems in this area by the *Oklahoma Telephone Association* in Oklahoma City. He was awarded a golden plaque with the following resolution:

> "Whereas, this member has accomplished many things for both the telephone industry in Oklahoma and in the United States and has continued to go forward with foresight, endurance and perseverance in establishing in Oklahoma a modern telephone exchange and whereas, the people of the State of Oklahoma, the telephone industry of this State and the United States owe to the honorable, J.W. (Jack) Walton."

His enthusiasm for Oklahoma business opportunities showed up again in July 1947, when he was President of the *Broken Arrow Chamber*, and was among 160 businessmen and city representatives who took a 17-day, "old fashioned" *Booster Train Ride* through many states and important eastern cities. Imagine the trek through Chicago, Detroit, Buffalo, Boston, New York City, Philadelphia and Pittsburgh. He said a great cheer went up from the tired men when they pulled out of Cincinnati to return home. "We kept a 6 a.m. to after-midnight schedule; this was not a vacation!"

Jack said even if a contract for business did not come directly from this tour, the Oklahoma men had impressed eastern businessmen, and had learned that the in-state network they established on the journey would serve them well. "This group's recommendations to the (State) Legislature in the future will have profound effect."[81]

The Legacy Lives On

Although Jack and Grace did not have children, he came from hardy stock. John Wilbur "Jack" Walton, was born in Kansas along with 2 brothers and 3 sisters. His father had been a confectioner and merchant in Daviess County, Missouri in 1900 and by 1902 the family was living in Enid, Oklahoma. His father had been a musician in the *29th Iowa Infantry, Union Army*. His father passed away in 1923, and some of the family continued in Enid where Jack's mother, Hannah continued to live into her 90's. Both of Jack's parents are interred in *Enid Cemetery*, Garfield County. Those were Jack's "roots."

---

81. "Tough, But Worth It, Walton Says of Trip," *Broken Arrow Ledger*, July 17, 1947.

Meet the BROKEN ARROW CENTENNIALS

HENRY ALEXANDER (H.A.) JACOBS
(1887 – 1967)

Henry and Bertha Cordelia (Hames) Jacobs moved to Broken Arrow during the summer of 1938 to manage a *Glencliff Dairy* outlet in the McKee Building. *Western Creameries of Tulsa* purchased the building on the northeast corner of Dallas and Main from Allie McKee for a location to market *Glencliff* ice cream, buttermilk, butter, cheese, and cream. The sale was a major news event of the year and a boon to Broken Arrow's economy during the final years of the Great Depression.

Henry, his wife Bertha and his mother Sarah moved into a "comfortable" remodeled apartment over the store. There is no doubt that this new owner was hard at work for his business, since the *1940 Federal Census* listed the 84 hours of work in the last week of March. Jacobs opened the retail shop at the front of the building and built an ice dock at the rear. In conjunction with the store he operated a wholesale business and a cream station to purchase cream from local dairymen. On opening day September 1, the first 200 customers received a free nickel package of ice cream.

Three years after his arrival, Jacobs was elected Mayor. He won by a five-vote margin over the Democratic incumbent Jesse I. Miller in 1941 and held the mayoral post until Spring, 1947. As mayor, Henry Jacobs carried the city through *World War II* and its shortages, then a post-war housing boom and the beginning of industrial growth. He participated in *War Bond* and *Boy Scout* fund drives. He improved the city by helping to arrange twice-a-week Main Street sweeping, and promoted a $98,000 bond issue to fund sewer, water, and street projects.

While he was at the helm of city government, *Gardener Canning and Meat Packing Plant* opened. *Broken Arrow Casting and Foundry* began operating, and *Braden Winch* started production at *Arrow Gear*. His partnership with Jack Walton, as Chair of the *Chamber of Commerce,* helped bring these companies, as well as newly built furniture factory to the area. The chicken hatchery business was also booming.

In a city which had changed mayors at each one-to-two years' election, Jacobs held the post for six years, losing his bid for a fourth term in 1947 to an Independent, Ray E. Dotson. During Jacobs' tenure, he served on the committee to promote a new *City Charter* and a *City Manager and Council* form of government. In February 1947, the *City Charter* had been voted down, although approved at a later election.

Later that year, the jovial gentleman with horn-rimmed glasses announced that he was leaving the company and his apartment after nine years and moving into his new home on East Freeport. He kept the ice business and the two ice trucks that he owned. When he came to Broken Arrow after being a merchant in Searcy, Arkansas, he had two ice-cream cabinets. When he left the company, there were six. He had expanded the dairy business from nothing to around $100 dollars a day.

Although *Glencliff*[82] tried to entice the former Broken Arrow manager with other business offers, he said "I think we've got the best town in Oklahoma. So, no matter how attractive the offers get, I don't think I'll leave here."

Henry Jacobs later owned and managed a rooming house on the northwest corner of Dallas and Ash that had previously been the *Vena Hotel* (*Mains Hotel* in the 1930's.[83]

Henry A. and Bertha Jacobs (1889–1972) became parents to their two daughters in Searcy. Willie Lucille Jacobs (1911–1995) was teaching in Arkansas when her parents and grandmother moved to Broken Arrow. In 1945, she married Russell Gordon

---

82. A Tulsa Memories blog shows Glencliff milk bottle; *http://tulsatvmemories.com/icecream.html*.
83. Stapleton, 169.

Charles (1906–1988) also an educator. They moved from Arkansas to Tulsa where Russell became a faculty member at *Tulsa University*; Lucille taught at *Edison High School* and later at *Nimitz*, becoming Teacher of the Year at *Nimitz Junior High* in 1967, where she stayed for several years.[84]

The Jacobs' second daughter, Sybil Monteen Jacobs (1915-1992) married William Thomas Mills (1907–1987) while living in Searcy in 1936. They lived for a time in Austin, Texas but were laid to rest at *East Lawn Cemetery* in Searcy. No grandchildren for H.A. and Bertha Hames Jacobs have been identified.

(Adapted from a BH Media & Tulsa World article.)

F.A. "PAT" PETRIK
(1913 – 1998)

Florian Anton (F.A. "Pat") Petrik was born in Grant County, Oklahoma on May 10, 1913 to A.F. "Tony" Petrik and Anna *(Skalnik)* Petrik. Raised as their only child, F.A. went to school in a small one room Grant County schoolhouse. This could have been difficult for him since he only spoke Czech.

F.A. "Pat" Petrik

---

84. "U.S., School Yearbooks, 1880-2012"; Nimitz Junior High School; Year: 1967. *Ancestry.com data base.*

His grandparents had immigrated to Oklahoma from the Czech village of Nincini, in the old Austro-Hungarian Empire. They were part of the *Cherokee Strip Land Run of 1893*. They established a homestead and farmed their land developing a strong work ethic for their grandson.

After completing his high school education and graduating from *Caldwell High School*, Petrik arrived in Tulsa to begin his quest to become a lawyer. He attended *Tulsa Law School* which at the time was located in the basement of the *Central High School* in downtown Tulsa.

While studying in the same building he met Margaret Naylor, a senior at *Central High,* born in Tulsa February 27, 1914. The couple were married on November 9, 1935. F.A. graduated and passed the bar exam that same year and went to work for his uncle, Charles Skalnik in his Tulsa law firm. While working there he had heard the nearby town of Broken Arrow needed an attorney. Recognizing this as an opportunity, F.A. and Margaret Petrik promptly moved to Broken Arrow, which had a population of less than 2,000.

Petrik opened his office on Main Street between Dallas and El Paso. Making a living could be really tough during those *Great Depression* days. He said there was a time when he and Margaret only had a dime between them, and they took turns on who carried it. Being a young and resourceful new attorney in town he would accept fees in the form of eggs, fruits and vegetables from local citizens.

One time in exchange for a large fee he accepted a side of beef for his services. His daughter Marilyn remembers walking to the Warehouse Market to get the weeks' supply of meat out of the freezer lockers. As they say, "Tough times don't last, but tough people do." Petrik focused his practice to probate and real estate issues and was eventually able to purchase his own building for his firm.

Mr. Petrik became a familiar face in numerous community and civic organizations during his lifetime. He worked hand in hand with the *Broken Arrow City Council* spanning a period of 11 Mayors. He served as the *Broken Arrow City Treasurer* (1937 to 1947) as well as the *City Attorney* from (1937 until 1981). As a member of the *Broken Arrow School Board of Education* (1947 to 1992), he also served as the *Treasurer* and *Attorney*. Petrik was active with the *Broken Arrow Chamber of Commerce* and served as its President three times in 1940, 1950 and again in 1951.

He was a lifetime member of both the *Oklahoma State* and *Tulsa County Bar Associations*. Active with the local youth from farming families he was also a member of the local *FFA Chapter*. In 1981 during the annual *Rooster Day Festival*, Pat Petrik was proclaimed "Honorary Mayor" for the day. Along with that recognition, the City announced that June 20, 1981 would be called "F.A. Petrik Day". He received the *Outstanding Citizen of the Year Award* in

Meet the BROKEN ARROW CENTENNIALS

1983, from the *Chamber of Commerce*. In 1993 the *Broken Arrow Historical Society* inducted Mr. Petrik into the *Broken Arrow Hall of Fame*.

One of Pat's hobbies was woodworking at which he was very accomplished, according to his granddaughter. When he wasn't working in his law office or with his civic duties, he could be found in his workshop. He was an avid supporter of the *Broken Arrow Tigers* football team and was a season ticket holder all his life. As he grew older he had to get his seats a little lower in the bleachers to eliminate a few stair steps, but he was always on the 50 yard line! Scoutmaster of *Troop 104 (1937–1940)* and *Vice-President of the Boy Scout Indian Nations Council,* he was given the *Silver Beaver Award.*

When F.A.'s son, Tony purchased *Jones' Drug* and renamed it *Petrik Drug and Soda Fountain,* it became the usual place for F.A. to have lunch. He was found there often. Many can recall seeing Pat walk down Main Street always wearing a felt hat in the fall and winter and a straw one in the spring and summer.

Perhaps the only thing greater than his love for Broken Arrow was his love and dedication to his family, their two daughters, Marilyn and Gayle and his two sons, Tony and Tim. F.A. Petrik summed up his life in Broken Arrow in these words: "Broken Arrow has been awful good to me. I don't know where I could have gone to do any better than

I've done here." Broken Arrow lost a real treasure when Mr. Petrik passed from this life on December 12, 1998. He was preceded in death by his wife Margaret on May 6, 1982, and both are buried in *Park Grove Cemetery*.[85]

The Legacy Lives On

F.A. had a special regard for his devoted wife, Margaret, who was very active as one of the last living members of the *Self Culture Club* and was a charter member of the *Rose Garden Club*. All of their children and many of their grandchildren graduated from *Broken Arrow High School* and have continued to be a big part of the community.

F.A. and Margaret's daughter Marilyn Petrik Hillenburg ('59) and her husband, the late Harold Hillenburg, Jr., ('59) have two children, Kimberly Lindsay ('79) and Andy ('84); their daughter, Gayle Petrik Smith ('63), and her son, the late Ben Petrik; as well as F.A. and Margaret's oldest son, the late Tony Petrik ('66) and his wife Sharon Kay Stevens Petrik ('66) have one daughter, Kay Petrik ('87). The youngest son Tim Petrik ('72) and spouse Debbie Blair Petrik

---

85. Petrik in www.findagrave.com/memorial/10263242/florian-anton-petrik; see also his son, George Anton Petrik.

have one son, Matthew, and live in the Tulsa area. They have four great grandchildren and two great-great grandchildren.

The Petrik family has continued to be successful in their professions, and business ventures. The entire family participated in the success of Pat's grandson, Andy Hillenburg, a well-known race car driver in the Tulsa area. He raced with the *World of Outlaws* all over the U.S. for almost 20 years. His sons followed him in racing for a while. The Petriks and their extended family enjoyed making this a family affair.

(Adapted from granddaughter, Kay Petrik's biography of F.A. Petrik.)

WILLIAM GERALD HUDSON
(1905 – 1981)

W. Gerald Hudson was born in 1905, Indian Territory just south of Broken Arrow on a farm near New Orleans and Aspen. His parents, Burl C. Hudson (1878-1911) and Willie Lee (Finley) Hudson (1883-1966), came to Oklahoma prior to the birth of their first child. Their children, Ruby Lee (Hudson) Loyd, William Gerald, Harold Jay, Opal Mae (Hudson) Lea and Elizabeth (Hudson) Snyder, all born in Broken Arrow.

W. Gerald Hudson

Gerald was about six years old when his dad died. His mother was only 27 and only had an 8th grade education. She was industrious enough to lease out their river bottoms farm and move to town. She invested in a large 2-story boarding house in northwest Broken Arrow. That provided some income and also space for the children. She also sold Christmas cards, fresh eggs, and dressed out chickens. Fortunately, the school was within walking distance for the children's education.[86]

Gerald played sports throughout school and graduated from *Broken Arrow High School* in 1923. He was a talented athlete, and a diligent student, and earned a Scholarship to *Northeastern State Teachers' College* in Tahlequah. He especially excelled in football, lettering all four years, but also participated in other sports.

He was selected to the *All-Oklahoma Collegiate Conference* three consecutive years. In 1928 he was recognized by *Who's Who in American Sports* as "One of the greatest athletes in the country," by *The Spaulding Guide*, a national sports publication as among the nation's best ballplayers.[87]

After graduation in 1928, he accepted his first teaching position at *Connors State College* in Warner, Oklahoma. While working there Gerald developed the first athletic department and coached all sports. In 1930, Gerald

---

86. Personal interview with daughter, Janice Hudson Anderson
87. *BA Ledger* 10/26/1981

met and married Nina McCullough and they moved to Haskell, Oklahoma where he became the high school principal.

HUDSON BROTHERS MOTOR COMPANY

With his family roots being in Broken Arrow, Gerald and Nina moved here in 1935, where he and his brother Harold purchased the local Ford agency from John Brooks. The new firm became known as *Hudson Brothers Motor Company*. It was located at the northwest corner of Main and El Paso. Their dealership was a full service business that provided a modern and well equipped repair shop with the latest tools and machines to maintain their customer's cars. They even had a radio repair technician to make sure that the Philco radios installed in the Fords worked perfectly. They had a gas station in an adjacent building and eventually added a *Frigidaire Appliance Dealership*, as demand grew for more modern electrical appliances. Gerald purchased his brother's interest in 1950 and operated the Ford dealership until 1960, when he sold it to Jim Nelson. *Arkansas Valley Bank* is now located in the original location of Hudson's dealership, which is north of *The Museum Broken Arrow*. Gerald purchased an oil lease in Coweta after he retired from business and operated it for several years.[88]

Hudson was a very civic minded individual and involved himself in the *Broken Arrow Chamber of Commerce* as a member and served as President of that organization for two terms. He continued to serve on the *Chamber* board of trustees after that. He was instrumental in establishing the first *Little League Baseball Program* in Broken Arrow and was a board member of the local *Boy Scout Troop*. When *The Boys Club* was built in Broken Arrow, Gerald supported it financially, as an enthusiastic promoter of the *Salvation Army's* efforts in guiding young men's lives in our community.[89]

Hudson was a devoted lifetime member of the *Northeastern State College Alumni Association* and served as its President for two years. Gerald was awarded the *Citation of Merit* from the *Northeastern State University Alumni Association,* in 1973 and again, posthumously in 1986, recog-

---
88. *Broken Arrow Ledger,* March 19, 1935.
89. *Broken Arrow Ledger* 10/26/1981

nizing him for his outstanding service, gifts and courtesies to the association and its programs. Mrs. Hudson accepted the award for her late husband.[90] *NSU* honored Mr. Hudson again in January of 1989 when they inducted him into the *Northeastern State University Athletic Hall of Fame*.[91]

Gerald and his wife Nina were members of the *First Christian Church* for 45 years, where his mother "Willie" was a charter member. He was a deacon there for several years.[92]

The Legacy Lives On

From the early 1900's, perhaps because of their mother, the Hudson family had a strong presence in Broken Arrow, active in business and community. Ruby married Elmer Loyd, grocer and school board member; Harold ('25) married Bonnie McKinney; Opal ('26) married Carl Lea, who had a *Pontiac* dealership in Broken Arrow, and Lizzie ('28) married Harold Snyder.[93]

Gerald and Nina's three children, Jack ('53), Janice ('54) and Surilda ('63), as well as their grandchil-

---

90. *Broken Arrow Scout*, 10/08/1986
91. *Broken Arrow Ledger*, 1/26/1989
92. *Broken Arrow Ledger* 10/26/1981
93. https://www.findagrave.com/memorial/10253066/william-gerald-hudson

dren, graduated from *Broken Arrow High School*. After finishing high school, the late Jack Hudson (1935-2017) graduated from *Vanderbilt University* where he also played football. His sons, Burl and Walter, graduated from *Oklahoma University* and *Vanderbilt*, respectively. Both were in the military. Burl will retire this fall as a Colonel from the *United States Marine Corps*.

Janice Hudson ('54) met Andy Anderson at *Oklahoma University* and married. They made Broken Arrow their home in 1965. Their two daughters, Gerri and Holly, graduated from *Oklahoma State University*. Andy served on the school board for *Broken Arrow Public Schools* for 17 years. Continuing as active members of *The Museum Broken Arrow*, Andy and Janice have held the offices of president and treasurer. Nina and Gerald were Charter Members of the *Broken Arrow Historical Society* in 1975. (94)

Part of Gerald and Nina's legacy through their family was the creation of Broken Arrow's newest event park, *Chisholm Trail South Park*. The park is located on New Orleans just east of the Creek Turnpike. It can easily be seen from the turnpike from the *NSU* exit.[94]

(Adapted from an article by Broken Arrow Ledger, BH Media Group and Tulsa World Media Company.)

---

94. Personal interview with daughter, Janice Hudson Anderson

A.L. (AL) GRAHAM
(1903 – 1966)

AL GRAHAM

The *Broken Arrow Ledger* announced in its April 10, 1941 edition that after 36 years, F.S. Hurd was stepping down from the presidency of the *First National Bank* and becoming the Chairman of the Board of that long time Broken Arrow institution. Mr. A. L. Graham, had purchased controlling interest in the bank and would be taking over the office of President. Mr. Graham came to Broken Arrow with considerable background experience in banking and financial matters. He was associated with banks in Dennison, Texas and Durant, Oklahoma from 1927 to 1932. He moved to Tulsa in 1932 and had been the investment manager with the *Central Life Assurance Society* prior to taking the reins of the *First National Bank*[95]

Graham was a product of his pioneering generation always remembering his past frontier heritage and looking to the future to building a thriving Broken Arrow community. Local town folk when referring to Al Graham

---
95. *Broken Arrow Ledger*, April 10, 1941.

believed that he not only was the owner but he WAS the *First National Bank*. When he arrived in Broken Arrow it was a small country town, still reeling from the effects of the *"Great Depression"* and the *"Dust Bowl."* Through the support and leadership of his bank, he watched Broken Arrow become a growing and prosperous metropolitan city. His methods were sometimes controversial but he wasn't concerned about political correctness, he usually got right to the point. If something was profitable to his institution or the city, he would agree to it. If it wasn't, he would fight it and more times than not, he would end up being in the right with his decision. One of the ways that he showed his dedication and love for Broken Arrow was when the coal companies started shutting down. Al lead the way to help expand the *Braden Winch Company* and to get the *Gardner Canning* facilities to locate here to boost the city's economy. Always looking to the future Al was a big proponent of the *Arkansas River Navigation Proposal*. He served as the director of the *Arkansas Basin Development Association*. He had the foresight to believe that some day Broken Arrow could have its own port constructed along the *Verdigris River* east of town.

Mr. Graham was a friend to Roy Turner, Governor of Oklahoma; he appointed Al to serve on the *Oklahoma A & M College, Board of Regents*. He served the city in many civic organizations. He was a member of the *Broken Arrow Masonic Lodge* as a *32nd Degree Mason*. He was a member of the *Magic Empire Quarter Horse Association* and the *Oklahoma Cattlemen's Association*. He was active with the *Broken Arrow Chamber of Commerce* and served as President in 1959-60. In addition to being a member of the *Tulsa Chamber of Commerce.*, Al was also a member of the *Oklahoma Bankers Association*.

AL GRAHAM AND HIS SISTERS

He never lost his love for good horses and strong healthy cattle, coming from his boyhood experiences of being born on a ranch near Collinsville, Texas. He owned and operated a cattle ranch just east of town in the Oneta area.

Al Graham was born March 12, 1903 to Averil and Lula (Scott) Graham. He married Grace (Lee) Graham (1910-1940), daughter of prominent Durant banker,

Lawrence F. Lee (1872-1965) and Fannie Lee (1876-1951). Al and Grace had one child, but she passed away at the early age of 30 and was buried in *Highland Cemetery*, Durant, Oklahoma.[96]

When Graham died unexpectantly, it was a shock to the community. *Broken Arrow Ledger* Editor, C. A. McWilliams, wrote in his newspaper the day after Al's death the following statement: "Dynamic comes to mind when you think of Al Graham. So does shrewd, honest, frank, energetic and friendly. He was our friend and our city's friend. We grieve his passing."[97]

As his obituary stated, Graham was preceded in death by his first wife, Grace. At the time of his death in 1966, his surviving family members included Scott and his wife, Anne (Fulenwider), and their children. Graham's surviving spouse was Emma Lew (North) Graham as well as his stepson, Carl North. At his funeral service, Al Graham was honored by the attendance of many businessmen in Broken Arrow. Traveling from out of town were his two sisters, Mrs. Harold Moneriefand and Mrs. Marshall Davis both of Collinsville, Texas. Graham was buried in *Floral Haven Memorial Gardens*.[98]

---

96. https://www.findagrave.com/memorial/59041890/grace-graham
97. *Broken Arrow Ledger,* December 8. 1966.
98. https://www.findagrave.com/memorial/96296199/a_-l_-graham

Meet the BROKEN ARROW CENTENNIALS

The Legacy Lives On

Scott Lee Graham, was born to Al and Grace Graham on June 23, 1935. Grace passed away when he was only 4 years old. Sue Ann (Saltsman) Graham (1908-1989) married his father and became Scott's stepmother when he was six years old and raised him as if he were her own child. Mrs. Sue Ann Graham was the retired director of the *Wagoner County Department of Human Services.* Sue Ann passed away on August 31, 1989 and is interred in the *Greenwood Cemetery,* Eufaula, Oklahoma.[99]

After college and law school, Scott returned to Broken Arrow to work alongside his dad at *First National Bank.* Because of his father's untimely death, Scott became the bank President and Chairman of the Board much sooner than intended. Scott, his wife, Anne (Fulenwider), have four children, Frank Dixon Graham, Gregory Scott Graham, Leslie Graham and Claire Graham-McDonnell.[100] Scott will be highlighted in a later chapter in the next book along with the family.

---

99. https://www.findagrave.com/memorial/37599133/sue-ann-graham
100. Personal interview with Mrs. Anne Graham, 2020.

L. RUSSELL KELCE
(1897 – 1957)

Russell Kelce was a fourth-generation coal miner, and the 5th President of *Peabody Coal*. His great-grandfather and grandfather were German coal miners and their skills were passed down to his father, to him and his brothers.

Kelce's father entered the Pennsylvania coal mines at the age of 9 years, in 1877. He later operated his own small mine when he was 21 and was injured in a mine explosion in 1911 that took all that he owned. His sons picked strawberries to earn money to support their family while he was recovering from his injuries. Since his father was unable to work, Russell quit school and went to work in the underground coal mines when he was 15 with the high ambition of being a mine superintendent and someday owning his own mine.

L. RUSSELL KELCE

When *World War I* broke out and it interrupted his plans temporarily. Returning from the war with a higher ambition of owning a mine, he remembered that his father had told him about a surface mine located near Tulsa. Dad Kelce had previously worked there in 1890, operating a team of horses, pulling a scraper. It wasn't long after that Russell headed toward Oklahoma and found that the surface mine was just as his father had remembered and he started buying leases for their mining rights. Kelce and a partner opened the *Magic City* surface mine in 1918 near the area that is known as Dawson in East Tulsa. Their big problem was that they needed cash, $230,000 to be exact, to buy the equipment to excavate the coal from the ground. Kelce learned that the *Public Service Company* was planning to build a large coal-fired power plant near there and he saw a way to get his finances to get started mining. Russell met with Fred Insull, President of *PSO*, and negotiated a contract with him for fuel and part of the funding that he needed for the operation of his equipment. Insull was obviously impressed with this young man's ambition and helped him raise the rest of the money through associates of his in the Tulsa oil industry.

His next venture brought him to Broken Arrow where he purchased leases in 1927. Although his father was told that he would never be able to mine again, he became the pit boss at the *"Broken Aro"* mine, also known as the *Seneca No. 2*. His two brothers, Ted and Merl, joined him and his father in running the mine. It turned out to be a family affair with all of them working together to get that black gold out of the ground. The *"Broken Aro"* brand was considered to be one of, if not the finest bituminous coal fuels processed into top grade lump form, sometimes called egg form. The Kelce father and brothers had built their business to the extent that it made Broken Arrow the leading point in shipping coal in the state of Oklahoma. They produced over twenty-five hundred railcar loads in 1935 that were shipped from here. They wanted the buyers to know that the coal they were getting was from Broken Arrow so they put 30 stickers that read *"Broken Aro"* coal in every ton of coal loaded out. Due to the large demand of coal to support the war effort in *World War II*, the coal played out a lot sooner than anyone had expected. The newly named *Seneca/Sinclair* mine shut down and moved out in 1947, but continued to still produce the *"Broken Aro"* brand at other operating mines.

L. RUSSELL KELCE IN HIS OFFICE

Meet the BROKEN ARROW CENTENNIALS

In 1935, Kelce was invited to be the keynote speaker at the *Broken Arrow Chamber of Commerce* annual banquet, to honor him and the many employees and mines of the *Seneca/Sinclair* mining business. He had become the Vice-President and General Manager of the *Sinclair Coal Company*, whose offices were in Kansas City, Missouri. In his speech he reminisced: "We thought enough of Broken Arrow to name our coal for the town. The *"Broken Aro"* trademark was advertised from Nebraska to the Gulf of Mexico in 58 papers, over six radio stations and other media. The *Seneca Mine* spent a million dollars locally in labor and materials since its conception in 1927." At one time the *Chamber of Commerce* erected a large sign on Highway 51 at the north end of Main Street advertising the *Seneca Mine* and the *"Broken Aro"* brand.

Russell Kelce is remembered for his gift of 400 acres of abandoned strip pit land in 1944 to the local *Boy Scout Troop 104*. In his honor they named that land *Camp Russell* and it still provides facilities for scouting activities today under that same name.

Ahead of the times, the Kelces brought forth a land reclamation project that they called, *"Operation Green Earth"*, years before government regulations requiring reclamation were put into place. Unfortunately due to an early death, he was not able to see the end results of this project but his two brothers persevered to see it through to its completion. Russell, Ted and Merl Kelce were all inducted posthumously into the *National Mining Hall of Fame* at a ceremony in Las Vegas in 2002.[101]

(Adapted from Peabody Coal Company, (1893-1973), Ninety Years of Pioneering. 1973 Celebration Brochure).

The Legacy Lives On

Lee Russell Kelce married Gladys Agnes St. John, a teacher, in September 1920 when each was living in Pittsburg, Crawford County, Kansas. Their son, Robert David Kelce was born in Tulsa County, August 22, 1928. Robert and Patricia Diane Robison were married in Jackson County, Missouri on May 29, 1951. L. Russell Kelce passed away on June 30, 1957, at the age of 59. Both he and his wife Gladys lie in repose at *Highland Park Cemetery* in Pittsburg, Kansas.[102]

In 1963, Mrs. Gladys Kelce provided funds to build a planetarium in Yates Hall, a Math and Physics building, on the campus of *Pittsburg State College*, in Pittsburg, Kansas. Mrs. Kelce gave a gift of remembrance permitting acquisition of a much needed addition, a star projector for the planetarium. The *L. Russell Kelce Planetarium* opened its doors in July of 1964

---

101. https://mininghalloffame.org/inductee/kelce-1
102. https://www.findagrave.com/memorial/43994842/l-russell-kelce

Meet the BROKEN ARROW CENTENNIALS

and serves as a memorial tribute to her late husband. The University reported 10,000 visitors in the first year of operation. The planetarium is still open today and is used to support schools, churches, and university students with public programs. Each tour of the planetarium provides a view of the night sky and is visited each year by thousands of people. Recently, the space projections captured by the *Hubble Telescope* were screened there.[103]

ALFRED DUENSING AND JACK DEARSTONE

BROKEN ARROW LEDGER AD

DAD KELCE AND 3 SONS

COAL MINE TIPPLE
1918 - 1947

---

103. https://www.pittstate.edu/physics/Planetarium.html

Afterword

It is almost certain that an author reflects back on particular stories after the book is finished. That did not occur as just a "moment" at the completion, but several times throughout this book's journey. A question that may be asked is, "What was your favorite part of writing this book?"

There are several memorable parts, but my absolute favorite is researching, finding and connecting with the descendants—the family members I met or with whom I renewed an acquaintance. Although many descendants I have not yet met face to face, each time I found a new family member, a descendant that seemed almost an impossibility to find, I felt an instant connection. Could it be the "Broken Arrow genes" run strong no matter where a person's family lives?

For our Broken Arrow natives, my desire is when you delve into this book, you will find stories deep in the recesses of your mind. Whether or not you actually knew a character in a biography firsthand, or heard hometown people relaying stories from long ago, something will resonate with you as "this is what makes Broken Arrow special". For our B.A. "newbies," I invite you into my world. Whether you come to us from a former city, suburb or rural area, I sincerely hope each of you can find stories and people with whom to relate.

There are many wonderful things to say about each of our

Afterword

Legacy Makers. You have just read Part One, which is the basic foundation of Broken Arrow's history and heritage. Part Two will begin with the 1940's. It will consist of educators, bankers, business owners, leading women in their professions and military veterans.

You will not want to miss reading about these very special people who are part of our original 100. Learn for yourself why we are celebrating their legacy by reserving a copy of our second book as quickly as it is released. I am not only looking forward to sharing more of our hometown's finest. I believe you will enjoy reading about the 'Legacy Makers', those who have left footprints on our community.

You may very well have known or do know some of these who are continuing to leave a legacy in our hometown. Now you have a glimpse of "What Makes Us Broken Arrow Proud!"

About the Author

A native Oklahoman, Jan Collins and her husband Ken, reside in Broken Arrow, Oklahoma and are the  parents of two grown children and six grandchildren. They are active in their community by volunteering at the *Museum Broken Arrow*, the *Military History Center* along with the *Broken Arrow Historical Society*.

Jan holds a *Bachelor of Science Degree in Education* and a *Master's Degree* as a Reading Specialist from *Northeastern State University* in Tahlequah, Oklahoma. Jan has teaching experience from pre-school to college. While in the *Masters Program*, she wrote her first children's book. Jan has written four other books: **An OKLAHOMA ORIGINAL; The Life and Career of Paul E. "Pete" Simmons; Mandy's Move** (also available in a Spanish version); **Caught Away;** and an unpublished work titled: **BRIGHT PATH A Children's Book about Jim Thorpe.**

Because of her interest in history, Jan is planning to write a complete series of children's books about famous Oklahomans.

Appendix

Roberta Jean Parker
(1933-2012)

Mrs. Roberta Parker was born to Fred and Agnes Jennings, in Worth County, Missouri. She earned a B.S. in Journalism from the *University of Missouri*. She married James (Jim) D. Parker. She lived and worked almost 50 years in Broken Arrow. Balancing home with employment, Roberta was a reporter for *Broken Arrow Scout/Ledger* for *Retherford Publishing* for about 30 years. During that time, she was Retherford's Periodic Interim Editor for and wrote the popular column entitled Cornerstones for the Broken Arrow Ledger. Roberta was honored at Broken Arrow's *Woman of the Year* once. She was a faithful member of *Broken Arrow Church of Christ* for 48 years, a community service volunteer for BACOC and a Bible School teacher. Other organizations Roberta was involved in are *Oklahoma Christian Women's Association, Broken Arrow Historical Society* and *Broken Arrow Garden Club*. She also enjoyed photography, gardening ad genealogy research as hobbies.

Roberta was survived by her husband, (the late) Jim Parker, her sister, Freida Jennings Roberts, sister-in-law, Marge Parker and children, Nathan Parker, Hannah (Jim) Hoffmeister, Reece (Holly) Parker, Joel (Linda) Parker, Jeanne (Allan) Lay and thirteen grandchildren, many still in this area.

Appendix

H. Cecil Rhoades
(1900-1960)

H. Cecil Rhoades was a native of Galla, Arkansas, he was born to John Henry and Bettie Rhoades. He married Hazel Whiteley (1907-1996) and came to Broken Arrow about 1935. He earned a B.A. degree from *Northeastern State College* in Tahlequah, Oklahoma and later a master's degree from *Oklahoma State University* in Stillwater, Oklahoma. As a partial requirement for fulfillment of his graduate degree, Rhoades wrote a thesis entitled "Establishment and Development of Broken Arrow, Oklahoma". Broken Arrow had become his new hometown, which he held very dear to his heart. His thesis became a book and published in our country's Bicentennial year. Rhoades was the first principal of Broken Arrow's *Southside Elementary School,* located on Houston Street, just west of Main Street. It was the first elementary school to be built after *North Main Elementary* (1924), that was erected to replace the original school on Main Street which housed all of Broken Arrow's students in the early days. Rhoades was the current principal at *Southside* at the time of his death in January, 1960. His death was a devastation to Broken Arrow.

He was survived by his (late) wife, Hazel, daughter Sharon Rhoades Mead Foster, son, Jerry and (Lauri) Rhoades, daughter, Janelle Rhoades Robison. Grandchildren: Corey Mead, Robert and Rachel (Rhoades?), Brad and (Renee) Diggs and great-grandchildren, Ana Rhoades, Peter, Cayce, Ben, Nate and Noah Diggs.

Bibliography

- Apsley, Marmie. "Phenie Lou Ownby (1887-1954)" *The Broken Arrow Chronicles*, No.1. Broken Arrow Historical Society, 1987, 48-50.
- Bryce, J. Y. *"Beginning of Methodism in Indian Territory,"* Chronicles of Oklahoma, VII, December 1929. 475-486.
- Collins, Jan. *An Oklahoma Original: The Life and Career of Paul E. "Pete" Simmons*. Sand Springs, OK: Bold Truth Publishing, 2015.
- Coss, Richard H. *"Jim Henry,"* Muscogiana 3 (Fall, 1992) 55-63.
- Debo, Angie. *Road to Disappearance: A History of the Creek Indians*. Norman: University of Oklahoma Press, 1967.
- First United Methodist Church of Broken Arrow, Oklahoma: *Journeys Through Faith for Ninety Years: 1903-1993*, Broken Arrow: Burdette Printing Company, October 1993.
- Foreman, Grant. *Indian Removal, The Emigration of the Five Civilized Tribes of Indians*. Norman: University of Oklahoma Press, 1932.
- Halbert, Henry Sale and T.H. Ball. *The Creek War of 1813 and 1814*. Chicago: Donahue and Henneberry Printers and Binders, 1895.
- Horton, Chad. *"James McHenry." ArtEFacts*. Broken Arrow Public Schools, OK: Graphic Arts Department, 1990.
- *Record of Deeds, Western District, Indian Territory*. U.S. Territorial Court for the First (Muskogee) Division of the Indian Territory. 3/1/1889-3/1/1895. Deeds, Wagoner I-D, 509. 1902
- Rhoades, H. Cecil. *Establishment and Development of Broken Arrow, Oklahoma*. Self-published: Moongate Enterprises, 1976.
- Smith, Tash. *Capture These Indians for the Lord*. The Arizona Board of Regents: University of Arizona Press, 2014.
- Stapleton, Steven L, J.D. *Broken Arrow the First Hundred Years*. Broken Arrow Historical Society. Virginia Beach, VA:

Bibliography

The Donning Company, Publishers, 2002.
- Wise, Donald A. *Broken Arrow Vignettes, Brief Local Histories.* Broken Arrow, OK; ReTvkv'cke Press, 1989.
- Wise, Donald A. and June Wise. *A Centennial History of the First United Methodist Church in Broken Arrow;* Published by the Church, 1903.
- Wright, James Leitch. *Creeks and Seminoles.* Lincoln: University of Nebraska Press, 1941.

Broken Arrow Hall of Fame; Broken Arrow Genealogical Society

Broken Arrow Hall of Fame: 1900-1997; Broken Arrow, OK: The Broken Arrow Genealogical Society. Series was published annually with various contributing authors; their sources are cited in the original articles. Listed here alphabetically by Surname.

- "John Adam Barth," in *Broken Arrow Hall of Fame: 1995.* Broken Arrow Genealogical Society, 1995.
- "William Thomas Brooks," in *Broken Arrow Hall of Fame: 1992.* Broken Arrow Genealogical Society, 1992.
- "Mildred McIntosh Childers," in *Broken Arrow Hall of Fame: 1990.* Broken Arrow Genealogical Society, 1990.
- "Dora M. Sullivan Esslinger," in *Broken Arrow Hall of Fame: 1991.* Broken Arrow Genealogical Society, 1991.
- "James Houston Esslinger," in *Broken Arrow Hall of Fame: 1991.* Broken Arrow Genealogical Society, 1991.
- "William Summerfield Fears," in *Broken Arrow Hall of Fame: 1990.* Broken Arrow Genealogical Society, 1990.
- "Dr. Onis Franklin," in *Broken Arrow Hall of Fame: 1991.* Broken Arrow Genealogical Society, 1991.
- "C. Benjamin Haikey," in *Broken Arrow Hall of Fame: 1991.* Broken Arrow Genealogical Society; 1991.
- "David McKellop Hodge," in *Broken Arrow Hall of Fame:*

Bibliography

1990. Broken Arrow Genealogical Society: 1990.

- "Fitzsimmons Hurd," in *Broken Arrow Hall of Fame: 1992*. Broken Arrow Genealogical Society, 1992.
- "Alvin Marvin Laws," in *Broken Arrow Hall of Fame: 1993*. Broken Arrow Genealogical Society: 1993.
- "William Grant McGechie," in *Broken Arrow Hall of Fame: 1993*. Broken Arrow Genealogical Society: 1993.
- "Reverend James McHenry," in *Broken Arrow Hall of Fame: 1990*. Broken Arrow Genealogical Society: 1990.
- "OK Ernest Morrow," in *Broken Arrow Hall of Fame: 1996*. Broken Arrow Genealogical Society: 1996.
- "Phenie Lou Gillett Ownby," in *Broken Arrow Hall of Fame: 1991*. Broken Arrow Genealogical Society, 1991.
- "F.A. Petrik," in *Broken Arrow Hall of Fame: 1993*. Broken Arrow Genealogical Society: 1993.
- "Harry Alexander Sells," in *Broken Arrow Hall of Fame: 1990*. Broken Arrow Genealogical Society, 1990.
- "Helen Gaddy Wells," in *Broken Arrow Hall of Fame: 1992*. Broken Arrow Genealogical Society, 1992.
- "William Newton Williams," in *Broken Arrow Hall of Fame: 1991*. Broken Arrow Genealogical Society; 1991.

Newspapers Published in Broken Arrow; Broken Arrow Genealogy Society Microfilm

- *Broken Arrow Democrat,* Indian Territory, September 1905 – November 1907
- *Broken Arrow Democrat,* Oklahoma, (Statehood in November 1907) December 1907 – March 1918

Broken Arrow Ledger

Broken Arrow Ledger had varied editor – publishers through the years, and the masthead varied in presentation, but day the pri-

Bibliography

mary title has been referenced through the years as the Ledger.

- *Broken Arrow Ledger,* Creek Nation, Indian Territory June 16, 1904 – September 21, 1906
- *Broken Arrow Ledger,* (Statehood in November 1907) December 1907 – December 21, 2016
- *Broken Arrow Democrat,* Oklahoma, (Statehood in November 1907) December 1907 – March 1918
- *Broken Arrow Democrat-Ledger,* Weekly, April 4, 1918 – September 3, 1925
- *Broken Arrow Daily Ledger,* April 2, 1979 – February 28, 2007
- *Broken Arrow Scout,* January 4, 1989 – February 9, 1994

On-Line Articles, or Manuscripts and Loose Papers

- Childers, Mildred McIntosh. *Private Letters and Papers.* Broken Arrow, OK: The Museum Broken Arrow files.
- Jackson, Effie. *"Mildred McIntosh Childers, Interview #12011." Indian Pioneer Papers,* https://digital.libraries.ou.edu/. 1937
- Lewis, Lori. *"Looking Back at James McHenry,"* Broken Arrow Ledger; news@baledger.com; June 30, 2016.
- Wilson, Linda D., *"Twin Territories: The Indian Magazine," The Encyclopedia of Oklahoma History and Culture,* https://www.okhistory.org/publications/enc/entry.php?entry=TW002.

Photographs not otherwise credited, *The Museum Broken Arrow* Photograph Archives.

On-line Data Base Collections

- Ancestry.com. *1900 United States Federal Census* [database on-line]. Provo, UT, USA: Ancestry.com Operations Inc., 2004. Original data: United States of America, Bureau of the

Bibliography

Census. *Twelfth Census of the United States, 1900*. NARA microfilm publication T623, 1854 rolls, National Archives and Records Administration, Washington, D.C.

• Ancestry.com. 1910 United States Federal Census [database on-line]. Lehi, UT, USA: Ancestry.com Operations Inc, 2006. Original data: Thirteenth Census of the United States, 1910; NARA microfilm publication T624, 1,178 rolls. Records of the Bureau of the Census, Record Group 29. National Archives, Washington, D.C.

• Ancestry.com. *1920 United States Federal Census* [database on-line]. Provo, UT, USA: Ancestry.com Operations Inc., 2010. Images reproduced by FamilySearch. Original data: *Fourteenth Census of the United States, 1920*. NARA microfilm publication T625, 2076 rolls. Records of the Bureau of the Census, Record Group 29. National Archives, Washington, D.C.

• Ancestry.com. *1930 United States Federal Census* [database on-line]. Provo, UT, USA: Ancestry.com Operations Inc., 2002. Original data: United States of America, Bureau of the Census. *Fifteenth Census of the United States, 1930*. Washington, D.C.: National Archives and Records Administration, 1930. T626, 2,667 rolls.

• Ancestry.com. *1940 United States Federal Census* [database on-line]. Provo, UT, USA: Ancestry.com Operations, Inc., 2012. Original data: United States of America, Bureau of the Census. *Sixteenth Census of the United States, 1940*. Washington, D.C.: National Archives and Records Administration, 1940. T627, 4,643 rolls.

• Ancestry.com. *Oklahoma and Indian Territory, Dawes*

Bibliography

Census Cards for Five Civilized Tribes, 1898-1914 [database on-line]. Provo, UT, USA: Ancestry.com Operations, Inc., 2014. Original data: Enrollment Cards for the Five Civilized Tribes, 1898-1914; (National Archives Microfilm Publication M1186, 93 rolls); Records of the Bureau of Indian Affairs, Record Group 75; National Archives, Washington, D.C.

- Find-a-Grave Home Page: http://www.findagrave.com/ Referenced herein for vital record dates through use of cemetery headstone images. Many individual *Find-a-Grave* records include family historical and relationship information This publication references the headstone and family information when dates and places are found to be compatible with other sources in the biographical sketch.

- Jackson, Effie. *"Mildred McIntosh Childers, Interview #12011."* *Indian Pioneer Papers,* https://digital.libraries.ou.edu/. 1937

- Lewis, Lori. *"Looking Back at James McHenry,"* *Broken Arrow Ledger;* news@baledger.com; June 30, 2016.

- Wilson, Linda D., *"Twin Territories: The Indian Magazine,"* *The Encyclopedia of Oklahoma History and Culture,* https://www.okhistory.org/publications/enc/entry.php?entry=TW002.

Index

NOTE: *Photo of the person is indicated by small p.*

Adleman, Gladys 148
Ahms, Elizabeth 79
Alexander, "Dolly"; Mrs. W. McHenry 17, 18
Alexander, Kizzie 18
Alldredge, Edith Hart 257
Allen, Mrs. 77p
Anderson, C.S. 130p-131, 147
Anderson, Effie A. Drake 131
Anderson, Janice Hudson 273
Anderson, O.T. "Andy" 250p
Appleby, Rev. H.E. 117
Arnold, Ardis 255-257
Arnold, Clayton 257
Arnold, Monica Ownby 257
Atkins, Billy 38
Bailey, Lelia Dalton 77p
Baker, Gustava; Mrs. Randall 218-219
Barth, Dorothy; Mrs. Warterfield 81
Barth, John Adam 79-82, 81p
Barth, Frankie; Mrs. Woodward 81
Barth, Leon John Barth 81
Barth, Lillie 80
Barth, Talitha Herthel 80-82
Baxter, E.B. 101, 213
Baxter, Shorty 207-209
Beardsley, Stella C.; Mrs. D. Wilson, Jr. 182
Beaty, R.C. 238
Bemore, Bertha Haikey 19
Bemore, Douglas 19
Benedict, E. J. 132
Benson, Mrs. A.E. 77p
Benton, Emma; Mrs. J. Parkinson 77p, 141-144
Berry, Lutie; Mrs. N.L. Sanders 50, 67, 77p, 155-156
Berryhill, Henrietta McHenry 15
Bertling, Lynn Jr. 211

Index

Bertling, Lynn Sr. 211
Birtell, Betty Browning 152
Blair, Debbie; Mrs. Tim Petrik 271, 272
Blair, Thomas 127
Blane, Ralph Uriah Hunsecker 105
Blanket, WW I Memorial 199p-202
Boles, Frank C. 143
Bomar, Clayton 83
Bond, Jane Carlile 260
Boone, Mildred M. Childers 74
Boudinot, Eloise Childers 31, 32
Boudinot, Okemah; Mrs. Randall, Jr. 32, 221
Bowers, Dr. James S.W. 78, 100-101, 213
Bowman, Guy 128
Boyd, Martha J.; Mrs. L. W. Routh 66
Bredehoeft, Gertrude; Mrs. McCoy 124, 125p
Bredehoeft, Lavern; Mrs. A. Karner 124, 125p
Bredehoeft, Martha Kietke 122-125p
Bredehoeft, Rev. Martin M.H. 122p-125p, 148
Bredehoeft, Ruth; Mrs. H. Karner 124, 125p
Briggs, J.B. 258
Brooks, Alicc; Mrs. Wm.T. 65p, 77p, 126, 229 330
Brooks, Floy J.; Mrs. Greene 51, 56, 66, 68
Brooks, Guy Lafayette 51, 55, 66, 68
Brooks, Ina; Mrs. Kneale 51, 56, 66, 68
Brooks, Isabel; Mrs. L. R. Brooks 50
Brooks, Lafayette Reed 51
Brooks, Miss Ora 77p
Brooks, Ora; Mrs. M.G. Lewis 51, 53, 66, 68
Brooks, Roscoe Walton "Peck" 51, 55, 56, 66, 68
Brooks, Sarah Alice Routh 51, 56, 65-68, 126
Brooks, William Thomas "W.T." 45, 47-57, 51p
Brooks, William Thomas "W.T." 67, 135-136, 195
Brown, Barbara A.; Mrs. B. Kimbrough 217
Brown, Estella Lewis; Mrs. Ivan Brown 212-217
Brown, George A. 58, 78, 99p-103, 213, 215

Index

Brown, Ivan D. 212p, 213p, 216p
Brown, Ivan D. 100, 102, 212-217, 238
Brown, James Claude 100
Brown, Martin VanBuren 99
Brown, Mary D. Coin; Mrs. G.A. Brown 99-102, 197
Brown, Mildred 100
Brown, Wanda Martin; Mrs. G.L. Brown 217
Brown, Westie Carter; Mrs. VB Brown 99
Browning, Edna Dalton 145, 149-149, 152
Browning, Van 147-150
Bruner, Ruby M. Childers Haynie 31
Bruner, Steve 32
Buckner, Rev. H. R. 9
Bullard, Agnes 148
Burdette, James Aaron, "Jim" 90, 91
Burdette, Jim 91
Burdette, Lula G.; Mrs. Bill Wilson 182
Burdette, Verna Morrow 90, 91
Candler, Bishop Warren 19
Carson, Ashely Wolfvoice 32
Carter, Harrison 101
Carter, Westie E.; Mrs. VB Brown 99
Caudill, Arminta; Mrs. John U. Norris 168
Chapman, Bill 243
Charles, Russell Gordon 267-268
Childers, Clarence William 31
Childers, Daniel Boone 30-32
Childers, Eloise Boudinot 31, 32
Childers, Goob 36
Childers, Kotcha 31
Childers, Mildred McIntosh 8, 25-32, 25p
Childers, Ruby M. Bruner Haynie 31, 32
Chilton, Bonnie L.; Mrs. Chas E. Foster 203-206
Cluck, Lois Franklin 88
Cobb, S.A. 39
Coin, Mary D.; Mrs. G.A. Brown 99-102, 197

Index

Couch, Charles Waitman "Shorty" 162p-164
Couch, Don 164, 250p
Couch, Fred 164-165
Couch, Opal 163
Couch, Pansy 163
Couch, Ralph 164-165
Couch, Rotha Olivia Neas 162p-164
Couch, Samuel C. 163
Couch, Stephen 164
Courington, Harriet Wilson 181-183
Crandall, Nancy M.; Mrs. F.S. Hurd 199p
Crawford, Patricia Smith; Mrs. Wayne C. 174
Cunningham, Gladys 148
Dalton, Bertha 151
Dalton, Betty Jean; Mrs. Guy Kinkeade 152
Dalton, Carl 151-152
Dalton, Charles (son of W.T.) 151
Dalton, Charles L. "C.L." 139, 144p-150, 152, 209
Dalton, Clarence 151
Dalton, Edna; Mrs. Van Browning 145, 147-150
Dalton, Ethel V. Ditch 145
Dalton, Joseph C. 144-145
Dalton, Lela 77p, 151
Dalton, Minnie Belle Rohrer 150-152
Dalton, Ralph 151-152
Dalton, Virgie Shaw; Mrs. Carl Dalton 152
Dalton, William "W.T." "Bill" 138, 139, 144,150p-152
Dameron, Kyle 250p
Dearstone, Jack 288p
Deweese, Bernham 194p
Dinwiddie, Jacob Whitfield 99
Dinwiddie, Mary Melva Milborn 99
Ditch, Ethel V.; Mrs. C.L. Dalton 144-149
Dix, J.A. 165
Drake, Effie Alice; Mrs. C.S. Anderson 131
Duensing, Alfred 288p

Index

Eades, Joe Cleveland 19
Eades, Naomi Haikey 19, 21
Edwards, N.H. 194p
Emarthla, Eneah 11-12
Esslinger, Andrew Jackson 186
Esslinger, Cecil 188
Esslinger, Charles 188
Esslinger, Dora Interviews (ed. Donald Wise) 37
Esslinger, Dora M. Sullivan 186-189, 228, 230p, 231p
Esslinger, Elsie Mildred 188, 231
Esslinger, Frederick 188, 231
Esslinger, Houston 188, 189p
Esslinger, James H. "J.H." 184-186p-189, 231-232
Esslinger, Katherine M. Fennell 186
Esslinger, Mable 188, 189p
Esslinger, Nola Katron Sullivan 186-187, 189
Esslinger, Nola Sullivan "Nolie" 187-188
Estes, Jack 105, 221
Estill, Reid 201
Evans, Hope; Mrs. Herbert C. Haikey 19
Faries, Patti; Mrs. Paul F. Miller 258p-260
Faull, Joe 148
Fears, Blanche Randall 42
Fears, Mary Kathleen 42
Fears, Mattie Tidwell; Mrs. S. Fears 40
Fears, W.S., Wm. Summerfield 37-42, 40p, 45, 112
Fears, William S., Jr. 42
Fennell, Katherine M.; Mrs. Andrew J. Esslinger 186
Fife, M.I. 136
Fisher, Charles Howard 119, 132
Fisher, Don 141p
Ford, Grace Evangeline Sells 34
Ford, Virgil 194p
Foster, Bonnie L. Chilton; Mrs. C.E. 203-206
Foster, Charles E. 194p-195, 200, 203-206
Foster, George H. 138

Index

Foster, Joseph Lee "Joe" 205-206
Foster, Martha "Pattie" Malone 206
Foster, Mrs. George H. 77p, 229
Fraker, Lovina J. "Jenny" Wells 96-98
Fraker, Warren Powell, "W.P." 96-98, 101, 109, 245
Franklin, David C. 86
Franklin, Dr. Onis 86p-87, 88p-89
Franklin, Dr. Samuel Ewing, "S.E." 86-89
Franklin, Lena Singleton; Mrs. O. Franklin 86-88
Franklin, Lois Cluck 88
Franklin, Nettie B.; Mrs. David C. Franklin 86
Franklin, Samuel Harry 89
Franklin, Stephen 38
Fulenwider, Anne; Mrs. Scott Graham 282
Gaddy, Helen; Mrs. Fred Wells 98, 161p-162
Galbreath, Herman 37
Garrett, Fannie 77p
Geren, Glen 218
Ghere, J.L. 233
Gideon, Luther 136
Gilbert, Audie Lee 169
Gilbert, Bertie E. Norris; Mrs. John L. 167, 168p-170
Gilbert, Eugene Norris 169-170
Gilbert, Jo Ann 170
Gilbert, John 169
Gilbert, John Lee 167-170
Gilbert, Lorine Jewell 169
Gilbert, Myrtle Faye 169
Gilbert, Onis Junior 169-170
Gillet, Mabel Morris; Mrs. Daniel Gillet 252
Gillet, Phenie Lou; Mrs. W.D. Ownby 252p-257
Goddard, Steven 260
Grable, Minerva E. 253
Graham. A.L. "Al" 278p-282
Graham, Anne Fulenwider, Mrs. S. Graham 282
Graham, Emma L. North; 2nd Mrs. Graham 281

Index

Graham, Grace Lee; Mrs. Al Graham 280-282
Graham, Scott Lee 282
Grayson, Maisie; Mrs. B. Ben Haikey 18
Greene, Floy Josephine Brooks 55, 56, 66, 68
Griswold, Brenda Ownby; Mrs. Stephen 255-257
Grube, Wesley 194p, 197
Haikey, Alpha 19
Haikey, B. Benjamin 18
Haikey, Bertha; Mrs. D. Bemore 19
Haikey, Betty Jean 21
Haikey, Birdie 19
Haikey, C. Benjamin 8-9, 18-21, 18p
Haikey, Clarence W. 19
Haikey, Freida Young 19
Haikey, Herbert C. 19
Haikey, Hope Evans 19
Haikey, Kizzie Alexander 18
Haikey, Louisa Chisolm Sunny 19, 20
Haikey, Maisie Grayson 18
Haikey, Maymie 19
Haikey, Naomi; Mrs. J.C. Eades 19
Haley, Uncle Charley 209
Hames, Bertha C.; Mrs. H.A. Jacobs 264-267
Harless, Shelby 194p
Hartman, Elmer V. 114, 141
Hartman, Phillip 114
Haskell, Governor Charles N. 23, 139, 185
Hawkins, Joye Burdette 92
Haynie, Fred 31, 32
Haynie, Ruby Mildred Childers Bruner 31, 32
Henry, Jim 9-13
Hermerding, Rev. L.C. 117
Hershberger, Mrs. 77p
Herthel, Talitha; Mrs. J.A. Barth 80-82
Hicks, Jimmy 250p
Higgins, T.S. 136, 142

Index

Hill, H.H. 58
Hillenburg, Harold 271
Hillenburg, Marilyn Petrik; Mrs. Harold 271
Hinton, Mrs. E.P. 77p
Hodge, David McKellop 8-9, 21-25, 22p, 43, 137
Hodge, Elam B. 43
Hodge, Nancy Ann McKellop 22
Hodge, Nathaniel 22
Hodge, Susan Yargee; Mrs. D.M. Hodge 22
Holley, Rev. L. Allen Holley 54
Holliday, Dan 241p
Hollingsworth, Dr. F.H. 58
Hollingsworth, Ruth L. Sanders 50
Holt, G.L. 58, 127, 135
Horn, Mildred Z.; Mrs. W.M. McCarty 248-251
Horton, Mrs. G.W. or Mrs. C.W. 77p, 147
Housley, Chris 199
Hubble, Arthur Betsey "A.B." 82p-85
Hubble, Elizabeth Rhyne; Mrs. A. Hubble 85
Huckaby, Mary C.; Mrs. Wm. Walton 157, 158p-160
Hudson, Burl C. 272
Hudson, Harold 272, 274, 275
Hudson, Jack 276, 277
Hudson, Janice; Mrs. Andy Anderson 276, 277
Hudson, Opal: Mrs. Carl Lea 272, 276
Hudson, Ruby; Mrs. Elmer Loyd 272, 276
Hudson, Surilda 276
Hudson, William Gerald 272p, 272-278
Hudson, Willie Lee Finley 272
Hunsecker, Edward J., "Dad" 104-105
Hunsecker, Florence H. Wilborn; Mrs. T.M. 105
Hunsecker, Hiram Charles 104
Hunsecker, Mary Vena Thayer 104-105
Hunsecker, Ralph Uriah 105
Hunsecker, Tracey Mark, Sr, "T.M" 105p, 104-108
Hunsecker, "T.M" 194p, 198, 233, 234, 245

Index

Hunsecker, Tracey Mark, Jr. 105, 107
Hunter, Bryan 201
Hunter, Ernest 194p, 201
Hunter, James 194p, 201
Hunter, Mrs. Minnie M. 201
Hunter, Thomas F. 201p
Hurd, Fitz C. 202
Hurd, Fitz Simmons "F.S." 92p-93, 109, 135-136, 195
Hurd, Fitz Simmons "F.S." 45, 52-53, 58, 238, 241p, 278
Hurd, Mrs. F.S.; Nancy M. Crandall 92-93, 199p-202
Hurd, Paul 202
Hutchinson, Fern; Mrs. L.J. Sizer 73p-74, 77p
Isparhecker, Principal Chief 30
Jacobs, Bertha Cordelia Hames 266
Jacobs, Henry Alexander, "H.A." 109, 264-267
Jacobs, Willie L.; Mrs. Gordon Charles 266-267
Jacobs, Sybil Monteen; Mrs. Wm. T. Mills 267
Jamison, Sol 58
Janeway, Zeus 194p
Jennings, Agnes Roberts; Mrs. N. F. Jennings 291
Jennings, Freida Roberts 291
Jennings, Roberta Jean 291
Jeppeson, Bob 250p
Jimboy, Rev. William 19
Johnson, Amanda J.; Mrs. Wm. R. Sullivan 186-187
Johnson, Kate; Mrs. Roy Pauli 208-212
Johnson, Lawrence 202
Karner, Albert M. 124
Karner, Herbert R. 124
Karner, Lavern Bredehoeft; Mrs. A.M. 124, 125p
Karner, Ruth Bredehoeft; Mrs. H.R. 124, 125p
Keene, Jennifer D. 192, 193 see Ref. 37
Kelce, David "Dad" 283-285, 288p
Kelce, Gladys A. St. John; Mrs. L. Kelce 283-288
Kelce, Lee Russell 176, 283p-285p-288p
Kelce, Merl 286, 288p

Index

Kelce, Ted 286, 288p
Kellam, Betty Riseling; Mrs. Don Kellam 82
Keller, Orville 202, 245
Kenale, Ina Brooks 55, 68
Kennedy, Carole J. Tucker; Mrs. D. Kennedy 177
Kerry, Rev. J. Edwin 54
Kietke, Martha; Mrs. M.H. Bredehoeft 122-125p
Kimbrough, Neely 217
Kimbrough-Rash, Kelley 238
Kinkeade, Betty J. Dalton; Mrs. Guy Kinkeade 152
Kirkpatrick, Mrs. William 77p
Knight, Ida; Mrs. W.N. Williams 72p, 227-228; 234
Knight, R.C. 49
Kolkmann, Valerie Karner 124
Lacy, Miss Fannie 77p
Laws, Alvin Marvin "Murphy" 94p-96
Laws, Betty Jean Martin; Mrs. Joe W. Laws 96
Laws, Collins 194p, 198p, 202
Laws, Earl 194p, 198p, 202
Laws, George Washington 95, 171
Laws, James 94, 171
Laws, Joe Wilson 96
Laws, Leonard "Len" 94, 171
Laws, Mary F. Wilson; Mrs. G.W. Laws 95, 171
Laws, Ruth H. Malone: Mrs. Marvin Laws 94-96
Laws, Steve 96
Lea, Opal Mae Hudson; Mrs. Carl Lea 272, 276
Lenaburg, Carol Carlile 260
Leonard, Susanne Burdette 91
Lewis, Estella; Mrs. Ivan Brown 212-217
Lewis, Frances M. French; Mrs. Jesse I. Lewis 215
Lewis, Harriet; Mrs. John McIntosh 32
Lewis, Jesse I. 215
Lewis, Martin Grundy "M. G." 55, 68
Linell, Harry Jr. 250p
Lonnberg, John 52, 92

Index

Lopp, Miss Elizabeth 77p
Loughridge, Dr. Robert McGill 9, 21, 22,24
Lowden, Yvonne; Mrs. Warren G. Ownby 257
Lowry, Cleo E.; Mrs. Mac Williams 68, 69p-71, 229p
Loyd, Ruby Lee Hudson 272, 276
Malone, M. M. "Pattie"; Mrs. Joe L. Foster 206
Malone, Ruth Harlan; Mrs. A.M. Laws 94-96
Marr, L.D. and S.W. 58
Marshall, Millie Gilliland 255
Martin, Betty J.; Mrs. Joe Wilson; 2nd Coppage 96
Martin, Ernest 194p
Martin, Wanda Mae; Mrs. George L. Brown 217
McAnally, Mrs. Mary 127
McCarty, Captain Edna Sprinter 251
McCarty, Danny Warren 251
McCarty, Eustace Cole 251
McCarty, Major Dale 251
McCarty, Mildred Horn; Mrs. W. McCarty 248-251
McCarty, Shelby J. Reeder; Mrs. D. McCarty 251
McCarty, Shirley Warlene 251
McCarty, Warren M. 248, 249p-250p-251
McCoy, G. Bredehoeft; Mrs. Arthur McCoy 124, 125p
McCoy, Mrs. M. 77p
McCullough, Nina; Mrs. Gerald Hudson 272-277
McGechie Family 36
McGechie, William G. 111, 120p-121
McHenry, Charles "Chuck" 12
McHenry, Henrietta Berryhill Sarty 15
McHenry, "Dolly" Alexander; Mrs. Walter 17,18
McHenry, Rachel Smith 15-18
McHenry, Rev. David J. 16
McHenry, Rev. Eli 17
McHenry, Rev. James 10p, 8-18
McHenry, Rev. Lewis 15-16
McHenry, Walter 13, 16-18
McIntosh, Chief William 25-28

Index

McIntosh, Harriet Lewis 32
McIntosh, Jane; Mrs. Harry Sells 32, 33p
McIntosh, John 32
McIntosh, Mildred; Mrs. D.B. Childers   8, 25p-32
McIntosh, Roley III 25, 30
McKellop, Nancy Ann 22
McKenna Family 36
McKenna, Mike 142, 229
McKenna, Mrs. Ethel Shaw McKenna 77p
McPherson, Jane Rogers; Mrs. Clay McPherson, 56
Micco, Eneah 11-12
Middleton Family 116
Milborn, Mary Melva; Mrs. J. Dinwiddie 99
Miller, Adella; Mrs. B.F. Miller 258
Miller, Patti Faries 258p-260
Miller, Paul Franklin 258p-260
Mills, William Thomas 267
Mitchell, Robert B. 195
Moore, William F. 35
Morgan, Rev. Harry 195
Morris, Rev. Sylvester S. 111
Morrow, Bertha Marie Pallisard 89-91
Morrow, OK Ernest 89p-91
Morrow, Verna; Mrs. Jim Burdette 90, 91
Mouzon, Bishop Edwin D. 19
Mowbray, Rev. George 19
Murrell, Eliza Jane Sells 34
Nagel, C. 58
Naylor, Margaret; Mrs. F.A. Petrik 267-271
Neas, Bonnie 165
Neas, Ellen E.; Mrs. William H. Neas 164
Neas, George 164
Neas, Joseph 164
Neas, Maynard 164
Neas, Nora 164
Neas, Pauline 164

Index

Neas, Rotha; Mrs. Shorty Couch 162p-164
Neibling, Mrs. E.T. 77p
Nichols, Charles A. 58, 136
Nichols, Gary 250p
Norris, A. Caudill; Mrs. John U. Norris 168, 169
Norris, Bertie E.; Mrs. John Gilbert 167, 168p-170
Oliver, Dr. Clarence G., Jr. i, ii, iv, 6, 217
Opothleyahola 27
Orcutt, S.E. 71, 112, 127
Owen, Robert L. 23
Ownby, Brenda Lou; Mrs. S. Griswold 255-257
Ownby, Byron Gordon 253, 257
Ownby, David Gil 257
Ownby, Mark Warren 257
Ownby, Minerva E. Grable; Mrs. W.D. Ownby 253
Ownby, Monica Belle; Mrs. Clayton Arnold 257
Ownby, Phenie Lou   252p-257
Ownby, Dr. Warren David 195, 253-257
Ownby, Warren Gillette 257
Ownby, William D. 253
Pallisard, Bertha M.; Mrs. OK Morrow 90
Parker, Hannah; Mrs. Jim Hoffmeister 291
Parker, James D. "Jim" 291
Parker, Jeanne; Mrs. Allan Lay 291
Parker, Joel and Mrs. Linda Parker 291
Parker, Marge 291
Parker, Nathan 291
Parker, Reece and Mrs. Holly Parker 291
Parker, Roberta Jennings: Dedication, iii, 4
Parker, Roberta Jennings; Mrs. J.D. Parker 291
Parkinson, Gerald 141
Parkinson, Mayor Josiah B. 128, 136, 141p-145, 259
Parkinson, Lucius "Lute" 141
Parkinson, Merritt 141
Parkinson, Emma B.; Mrs. J.B. 77p, 141-144; 227-8
Parkinson, Ruth 141

Index

Parrish, Steve 250p
Parsons, Dr. S.C. 58
Patrick, Mrs. Ad Brooks 55
Patterson, Alma Lucille Porter 131-133
Patterson, Miss 127, 128
Patterson, Roy Denver "R.D." 131, 132p-133
Patton, Lillie M.; Mrs. Joseph Samuel Wilson 171
Patton, Rebecca Ann Laws 171
Pauli, Edith and John 206
Pauli, Kate Johnson; Mrs. Roy Pauli 208-212
Pauli, Roy I. "Col" 200, 202, 206p-212, 209p
Peeler, Warren 194p
Pennington, Eula 148
Perryman Family 29, 35, 43
Pershing, Commander John J. 193, 200
Peterson, Charlie 81, 82, 105
Petrik, Anna Skalnik; Mrs. A.F. "Tony" Petrik 267
Petrik, Florian Anton, "F.A." or "Pat" 267p-272
Petrik, Gayle; Mrs. Smith 271
Petrik, George Anton "Tony" 270, 271
Petrik, Kay 272
Petrik, Margaret Naylor; Mrs. F.A. Petrik 267-272
Petrik, Marilyn; Mrs. Harold Hillenburg, Jr. 271, 272
Petrik, Tim; Mrs. Debbie Blair Petrik 271, 272
Petrik, Tony; Mrs. Sharon Stevens Petrik 271
Pierce, Bishop George 13
Pierce, H.L. 127, 145
Plumlee, Dr. R.S. 58, 71, 136, 143
Plummer, Catherine Teller; Mrs. Samuel 165-167
Plummer, Evelyn 167
Plummer, Helen 167
Plummer, Lucy Lee 167
Plummer, Paul 167
Plummer, Roger 167
Plummer, Samuel 165-167
Polk, Viola Tranquilla; Mrs. Sanders 50, 71

Index

Pollard, Dr. A.J. 58, 71, 77p
Pope, Rev. Willard 118
Porter, Alma L.; Mrs. R.D. Patterson 131-133
Porter, Lou Brooks; Mrs. Zeb Porter 55, 56
Porter, Principal Chief Pleasant 23, 39, 41
Porter, Thias 162
Posey, Alex 31
Quay, Senator Matthew 39
Randall, Blanche; Mrs. W.S. Fears 42
Randall, Gustava Baker "Dude" 219-221
Randall, Lester "Les" 218p-221, 233
Randall, Lester Lee, Jr. 221
Randall, Maude M. Turley; Mrs. Walter 218
Randall, Okemah Eloise Boudinot 221
Randall, Pauline 218
Randall, Ralph 218
Randall, Rodney 32, 221
Randall, Shonday Lee 32, 221
Randall, Walter 218
Ransom, Miss Annie 77p
Reeder, Shelby Jean; Mrs. Danny McCarty 251
Reynolds, Rev. A.J. 196
Rhoades, Bettie; Mrs. John Henry Rhoades 292
Rhoades, H. Cecil: Dedication, i, 6, 56-57, 292
Rhoades, Janelle; Mrs. Robison 56-57, 292
Rhoades, John Henry 252
Rhoades, Lauri; Mrs. Jerry Rhoades 56-57, 292
Rhoades, Sharon Mead Foster 56-57, 292
Rich, Cora; Mrs. Charles Sanders 153p-155
Richwine, Gladys L., Mrs. Leo Wortman 244-248
Riseling, Betty; Mrs. Don Kellam 82
Riseling, Mable Peterson 81-82
Riseling, Mary; Mrs. Woody Woodward 81
Roberts, Martha Plummer 165, 167
Roberts, Nancy Jane Goddard 260
Robertson, Mrs. C.L. 77p

Index

Rohrer, Elizabeth A.; Mrs. James Rohrer 150
Rohrer, James H. 150
Rohrer, Minnie Belle; Mrs. W.T. Dalton 150-152
Roosevelt, Mrs. Eleanor 31
Roosevelt, President Theodore 24
Ross, Grace E.; Mrs. John W. Walton 261
Ross, Judy; Mrs. Max Smith 174
Routh, Martha J. Boyd; Mrs. Levi Walton 66
Routh, Sarah A.; Mrs. Wm. T. Brooks 51, 56, 65-68
Rowe, Gertrude; Mrs. K.M. Rowe 101-104
Rowe, Knox McKay "K.M." 101, 102p-104, 109, 238
Rushing, Betty; 2nd Mrs. Les Randall 221
Sanders, Charles F. 52
Sanders, Charles A. 153p-155
Sanders, Cora Rich; Mrs. Chas. Sanders 153p-155
Sanders, Edith Marie 154
Sanders, Lutie; Mrs. Nat L. Sanders 50, 67, 77p
Sanders, Lutie; Mrs. N.L. Sanders 155-156, 196, 229
Sanders, M.H. 129
Sanders, Nathaniel L. "Nat" 45, 47-50, 49p, 226
Sanders, Orval 154
Sanders, Ralph 154
Sanders, Ruth L.; Mrs. Harvey Hollingsworth 50
Sanders, Viola Tranquilla Polk 50, 71
Schmidt, Madeline Wilson 181
Sells, Eliza Jane; Mrs. Murrell 34
Sells, Grace Evangeline; Mrs. Ford 34
Sells, Harry Alexandria 8, 32-34, 33p
Sells, Jacob 34
Sells, Jane McIntosh 32-34, 33p
Sells, Joseph Harry 34
Sells, Lawrence 34
Sells, Rose 34
Sells, Willie 34
Shaw, Ethel; Mrs. Mike McKenna 77p
Shaw, Virgie; Mrs. Carl Dalton 152

Index

Shields, Mrs. 77p
Shipman, J.D. 46
Shippey, Mrs. J.N. 77p
Simmons, John Milton 109
Simmons, Joseph Sylvester 58, 93, 108-109
Singleton, Lena; Mrs. Onis Franklin 86-88
Sizer, Dr. L.J. 73
Sizer, Fern Hutchinson 73p-74, 77p
Skaggs, P.C. 127
Smith, Bessie Mae Wilson 171p-174
Smith, Harriet C.; Mrs. Deacon Wilson 178-183, 200
Smith, Judy Ross 174
Smith, Max Edward 173-174
Smith, Patricia Sue; Mrs. Wayne Crawford 173
Smith, Rachel; Mrs. James McHenry 15
Smith, Truman "Pruny" 171-174
Smith, William W. 202
Snider, Mrs. H.H. 77p
Snyder, Elizabeth Hudson 272
Spangler, Mary Belle Wortman 248
Sprague, Josie Zingre; Mrs. Wm. 77p, 111, 127, 228
Springer, Judge William M. 41
Spurr, Miss Olive 77p
Standring, Talitha Barth 81
Stauffer, Mrs. 229
Stevens, Sharon Kay; Mrs. Tony Petrik 270, 271
Stocker, Patricia Browning 152
Sullivan, Amanda J. Johnson; Mrs. Wm. 186-187
Sullivan, Dora; Mrs. J.H. Esslinger 77p, 186-189
Sullivan, Dora Mahala 228, 230p, 231p, 232
Sullivan, Nola Katron; Mrs. J.H. Esslinger 186, 189
Sullivan, William R. 186-187
Sunny, Louisa Chisholm; Mrs. Ben Haikey 19, 20
Talbot, Mary 228
Teller, Catherine; Mrs. Samuel Plummer 165-167
Tenny, Mrs. John 77p

Index

Terry, Gladys Walton; Mrs. Terry B. Bland 157p-160
Thomas, Charles H. 36
Thomas, Rev. J.S. 115
Thompson, I.M. 127
Tidwell, Mattie; Mrs. Stockton Fears 40
Tobias, Betty Jean Haikey 21
Tomlinson, Bill 159
Tomlinson, Gladys Walton 157p-160
Townsend, Warlene McCarty 251
Trusler, G.H. 58
Tucker, Bob 175, 177
Tucker, Carole Janette; Mrs. D.L. Kennedy 175, 177
Tucker, Eula Williams; Mrs. M.L. Tucker 175-177
Tucker, John 176p
Tucker, Marvin L. 175p-177
Tucker, Peggy; Mrs. Bob Tucker 177
Turley, Maude M.; Mrs. Walter Lester 218
Updike, David 250p
Valcon, Old 242p-243
Vann, Bessie; Mrs. Roley McIntosh III 25
Walker, G.S. 232
Walker, Willard "Willie" 214
Waller, L., "Waller Drugs" 58
Waller, R.A. 136
Waller, W.F. 129
Wallingford, R.A. 207
Walton, Gladys Terry Tomlinson 157p-160
Walton, Grace Elizabeth Ross 261
Walton, Hannah 263
Walton, John Wilber "Jack" 260p-263, 265
Walton, Luckey 157, 194p
Walton, Mary Carolyn Huckaby 157
Walton, J.W. 258
Walton, William Wesley 157, 158p-160
Walton, William Wilder 157
Walton, Z. Gladys; Mrs. Terry; Mrs. Tomlinson 157p-160

Index

Warterfield, Dorothy Barth; Mrs. Floyd E. W. 81
Warterfield, Floyd Edward 81
Wells, Fred 98, 161-162
Wells, Helen Gaddy 98, 161p-162
Wells, John 144
Wells, Lovina J.; Mrs. W.P. Fraker 97
Wertz, Mrs. J.H. 126-128
Whitely, Hazel; Mrs. H. Cecil Rhoades 57, 292
Whiteley, Larry 250p
Whitmer, F.A. 112
Wilborn, Florence H.; Mrs. T.M. Hunsecker 105
Willbanks, Minnie McKim 126
Williams, Cleo E. Lowry 58, 67-71, 69p, 228-229
Williams, Eula; Mrs. Marvin Tucker 175
Williams, Governor Robert Lee 203
Williams, Ida Knight 72, 75, 77p
Williams, James 47p
Williams, Martha 63
Williams, Merida Caleb, "Mac" 47p-49, 60-61p, 236
Williams, Cleo; Mrs. Mac C. 69p, 77p, 128, 155-156
Williams, Cleo; Mrs. Mac C. 159, 228-229p, 234
Williams, Ida Knight; Mrs. Newt 72p, 227-228; 234
Williams, Robert 63
Williams, Shorty 198
Williams, Wm. N. "Newt" 43, 44, 47p-48, 60-62p, 63
Williams, Wm. N. "Newt" 72p, 208-209, 258
Wilson, A.L. 58
Wilson, Bessie Mae; Mrs. Truman Smith 171p-174
Wilson, Bruce Lamont 182-183
Wilson, Cecil Mark 182-183
Wilson, David A. III 180-183
Wilson, David Albert "Deacon" 178, 179p-183, 200
Wilson, David Albert, Jr. "Dave" 179, 182, 200p, 202
Wilson, Harriet; Mrs. "Deacon" Wilson 178-183, 200
Wilson, Harry 178
Wilson, Joseph Samuel 171-172

Index

Wilson, Lula G. Burdette 178-182
Wilson, Madeline; Mrs. Schmidt 181
Wilson, President Woodrow 192
Wilson, Robert Lawrence "Bob" 180, 182
Wilson, Stella Claire Beardsley 179, 182
Wilson, William M. "Will" or "Bill" 179, 182
Wise, Donald A. 46, 74
Woodward, Donald E. "Woody" 81, 82
Woodward, Frankie Barth 81
Woodward, Mary Riseling 81
Wortman, Leo S. 133, 239p-240, 244p-248, 259
Wortman, Sterling, Leo Sterling, Jr. 248
Wortman, Mary B.; Mrs. James D. Spangler 248
WW I Veterans Memorial Blanket 199p-202
Yargee, "Sukie"; Mrs. David M. Hodge 22, 24
York, Isabel; Mrs. Lafayette Reed Brooks 50
Young, Freida; Mrs. Clarence W. Haikey 19
Zingre, Josie; Mrs. William C. Sprague 111, 127, 228

We hope you enjoyed this book. Read more informative and inspiring stories about our pioneers as the Broken Arrow Legacy Lives On in Part 2.

DON'T MISS IT!

This book will be available at The Museum Broken Arrow and select local retailers.

www.ingramcontent.com/pod-product-compliance
Lightning Source LLC
Chambersburg PA
CBHW050125170426
43197CB00011B/1716